ORGANIZATIONAL EFFECTIVENESS

A Comparison of Multiple Models

ORGANIZATIONAL AND OCCUPATIONAL PSYCHOLOGY

Series Editor: PETER WARR
MRC Social and Applied Psychology Unit, Department of Psychology,
The University, Sheffield, England

A complete list of titles in this series appears at the end of this volume.

ORGANIZATIONAL EFFECTIVENESS

A Comparison of Multiple Models

Edited by

KIM S. CAMERON

National Center for Higher Education Management Systems
Boulder, Colorado

DAVID A. WHETTEN

School of Commerce and Business Administration
University of Illinois
Urbana, Illinois

 ACADEMIC PRESS, INC.

(Harcourt Brace Jovanovich, Publishers)

Orlando   San Diego   New York   London
Toronto   Montreal   Sydney   Tokyo

ACADEMIC PRESS, INC.
Orlando, Florida 32887

United Kingdom Edition published by
ACADEMIC PRESS, INC. (LONDON) LTD.
24/28 Oval Road, London NW1 7DX

Library of Congress Cataloging in Publication Data
Main entry under title:

Organizational effectiveness.

    Includes indexes.
    1. Organizational effectiveness. I. Cameron, Kim S.
II. Whetten, David A. (David Alfred), Date   .
HD58.9.O733 1982   658.4'012   82-22611
ISBN 0-12-157180-7

PRINTED IN THE UNITED STATES OF AMERICA

85 86 87 88   9 8 7 6 5 4 3 2

Contents

3 STANLEY E. SEASHORE
A Framework for an Integrated Model of Organizational Effectiveness

4 KARL E. WEICK
RICHARD L. DAFT
The Effectiveness of Interpretation Systems

5 WALTER R. NORD
A Political–Economic Perspective on Organizational Effectiveness

6 WILLIAM H. STARBUCK
PAUL C. NYSTROM
Pursuing Organizational Effectivness That Is Ambiguously Specified

7 PAUL S. GOODMAN
ROBERT S. ATKIN
F. DAVID SCHOORMAN
On the Demise of Organizational Effectiveness Studies

II

COMPARISONS AND IMPLICATIONS OF MULTIPLE MODELS OF EFFECTIVENESS

8 L. L. CUMMINGS

Organizational Effectivness and Organizational Behavior: A Critical Perspective   187

9 GARRY D. BREWER

Assessing Outcomes and Effects   205

10 LAWRENCE B. MOHR

The Implications of Effectiveness Theory for Managerial Practice in the Public Sector   225

11 CAROL T. SCHREIBER
Organizational Effectiveness:
Implications for the Practice of Management   241

12 KIM S. CAMERON
DAVID A. WHETTEN
Some Conclusions about Organizational Effectiveness   261

Contributors

Numbers in parentheses indicate the pages on which the authors' contributions begin.

Robert S. Atkin (163), Graduate School of Industrial Administration, Carnegie-Mellon University, 5000 Forbes Avenue, Pittsburgh, Pennsylvania 15213

Garry D. Brewer (205), School of Organization and Management, Yale University, New Haven, Connecticut 06520

Kim S. Cameron (1, 261), National Center for Higher Education Management Systems, P.O. Drawer P, Boulder, Colorado 80302

L. L. Cummings (187), J. L. Kellogg Graduate School of Management, Northwestern University, 2001 Sheridan Road, Evanston, Illinois 60201

Richard L. Daft (71), Department of Management, Texas A&M University, College Station, Texas 77843

Paul S. Goodman (163), Graduate School of Industrial Administration, Carnegie-Mellon University, 5000 Forbes Avenue, Pittsburgh, Pennsylvania 15213

Lawrence B. Mohr (225), Department of Political Science and Institute of Public Policy Studies, The University of Michigan, Ann Arbor, Michigan 48109

Walter R. Nord (95), Graduate School of Business and Public Administration, Washington University, St. Louis, Missouri 63130

Paul C. Nystrom (135), School of Business Administration, The University of
   Wisconsin–Milwaukee, Milwaukee, Wisconsin 53201

Benjamin Schneider[1] (27), Departments of Management and Psychology, Michigan State University, East Lansing, Michigan 48824

F. David Schoorman (163), Department of Psychology, University of Maryland,
   College Park, Maryland 20742

Carol T. Schreiber[2] (241), Human Resources Program Development, General
   Electric Company, Fairfield, Connecticut 06431

Stanley E. Seashore (55), Survey Research Center, Institute for Social Research, The University of Michigan, Ann Arbor, Michigan 48106

William H. Starbuck (135), School of Business Administration, The University
   of Wisconsin–Milwaukee, Milwaukee, Wisconsin 53201

Karl E. Weick (71), Graduate School of Business and Public Administration,
   Cornell University, Ithaca, New York 14853

David A. Whetten (1, 261), School of Commerce and Business Administration,
   University of Illinois, Urbana, Illinois 61801

[1]Present address: Department of Psychology, University of Maryland, College Park, Maryland
20742.

[2]Present address: Human Resources Division, Department of Consulting and Research, Chemi-
cal Bank of New York, 52 Broadway, New York, New York 10004.

Preface

A common criticism of the literature on organizational effectiveness is that it is fragmented and noncumulative. Reviews of past books on effectiveness have been especially critical of the lack of integration and systematic comparison present in each of them (see, for example, Pennings, 1978, and Steers, 1978). The main purpose of this book is to address directly the issues of nonintegration and noncomparability.

Although we reject the idea that one universal model of effectiveness can be developed, presenting different perspectives on effectiveness independent of one another improves neither our understanding of effectiveness nor our ability to conduct good research. In this book, differing perspectives of organizational effectiveness are presented by the contributors, but they are not discussed in isolation. Each author's perspective is systematically compared with the others in order to highlight the basic assumptions of each approach, the trade-offs necessary in using one approach versus another, and the strengths and weaknesses of each approach.

Understanding organizational effectiveness requires an understanding of multiple models. Because none of the models are universally applicable, understanding the relative contributions of several different models, and how these models relate to one another, is the only way to appreciate the meaning of this construct. In this book, we attempt to clarify the meaning of organizational effectiveness by comparing multiple models using three main mechanisms.

First, we have asked contributing authors to ground their perspectives on effectiveness in a particular disciplinary framework. By identifying the theoretical and philosophical roots of a particular perspective, it can be more directly compared and contrasted with other perspectives whose roots also have been identified. Just as knowing about one's ancestral history helps illuminate personal and family characteristics and helps make differences with other individuals or families more understandable, so identifying the roots of different models of effectiveness is intended to provide a similar function.

Schneider's Chapter 2, "An Interactionist Perspective on Organizational Effectiveness," is grounded in the tradition of industrial–organizational psychology. Chapter 3 by Seashore, "A Framework for an Integrated Model of Organizational Effectiveness," is grounded in sociology and systems theory. Weick and Daft in Chapter 4, "The Effectiveness of Interpretation Systems," have written from the traditions of cognitive and social psychology. Nord grounds Chapter 5, "A Political–Economic Perspective on Organizational Effectiveness," in macroeconomic and critical theories. Starbuck and Nystrom's Chapter 6, "Pursuing Organizational Effectiveness That Is Ambiguously Specified," derives from an operations research/management science framework. And Goodman, Atkin, and Schoorman ground Chapter 7, "On the Demise of Organizational Effectiveness Studies," in postivistic philosophy and microeconomics. They specifically attempt to avoid associating strongly with any one social science discipline, but they are explicit about their philosophical underpinnings.

Even though each of these perspectives is grounded in a particular set of assumptions, no author has limited his view to only one discipline. Each addresses issues that are best labeled interdisciplinary. However, the conceptual boundaries of effectiveness are drawn by the parent discipline or philosophy from which each author writes.

The second mechanism for systematically comparing these various perspectives on effectiveness is a set of integrating questions. Each contributing author addresses the same nine questions at the conclusion of his chapter. These questions raise theoretical and conceptual issues, empirical and research issues, and practical and managerial issues. The questions addressed by each of the authors are as follows:

Theoretical Issues

1. What are the major theoretical predictions or hypotheses that derive from your perspective regarding relationships between effectiveness and other organizational variables (e.g., structure, technology, information processing, individual satisfaction)?

2. How does your perspective expand our understanding of the behavior of organizations?

3. Does the definition of organizational effectiveness change when considering different types of organizations (e.g., public–private, professional–industrial, large–small) or different stages of development (e.g., early stages, institutionalized stages, decline)?

Research Issues

1. What are the major indicators (criteria) of organizational effectiveness using your perspective?

2. How would one test the efficacy of your approach compared to other approaches to effectiveness?

3. What are the major methodological issues of operationalizing effectiveness using your perspective (e.g., those relating to levels of analysis, data collection, predictors, key variables)?

Practical Issues

1. What prescriptions or guidelines for improving success are suggested by your approach? Are there any counterintuitive recommendations?

2. What diagnostic tools could managers use to monitor success using your approach?

3. What trade-offs, dilemmas, or dysfunctional consequences might be experienced by managers using your approach?

This is the first time we know of that authors using different models attempt to address the same set of issues from their own unique perspectives. The purpose of this exercise is to compare directly these perspectives on theoretical, empirical, and practical grounds; to make explicit certain areas that may not otherwise have been addressed by the authors; and to provide another basis for judging the trade-offs inherent in the models.

The third mechanism for systematic comparison is the inclusion of review and critique chapters. We asked four individuals to serve as both critics and integrators for the different perspectives on effectiveness. We requested that they evaluate the different models by answering the general question: "What do these perspectives add to, and how are they integrated with, organizational behavior theory, organizational evaluation, or the management of public or private sector organizations?" Cummings (Chapter 8, "Organizational Effectiveness and Organizational Behavior: A Critical Perspective") accepted the task of reviewing the six models from the standpoint of organizational behavior theory. Brewer (Chapter 9, "Assessing Outcomes and Effects") was asked to write from the standpoint of the evaluation of organizations. Mohr (Chapter 10, "The Implications of Effectiveness Theory for Managerial Practice in the Public Sector") used the perspective of public management. And Schreiber (Chapter 11, "Organizational Effectiveness: Implications for the Practice of Management") wrote as a private sector manager. These chapters provide a stronger basis for comparison and integration than the typical commentary format used in most edited books and conference proceedings. Here we asked each integrating author to examine all of the initial chapters in terms of their individual and collective contributions to theory, research, and practice.

This book should prove most interesting to two main groups: scholars and researchers seeking to understand and measure organizational effectiveness, and practitioners who are faced with the problem of managing and improving their own organization's effectiveness. This book is a valuable tool for managers because the chapters not only provide well thought out approaches to effectiveness as a construct, but also practical suggestions for improving effectiveness in organizations.

Acknowledgments

One of the important features of this book is the quality of the contributing authors. The group includes some of the most distinguished names in the organizational sciences. Editing and commenting on their chapters was both humbling and enlightening. They took our suggestions for revision well and went the second mile in thoughtfully responding to our questions. The task of responding to the integrating issues was both time consuming and difficult for the authors of Chapter 2–7, as was attempting to compare and integrate the various models for the authors of Chapters 8–11. The high quality of their thinking and scholarship is clearly evidenced in their chapters. Our sincere thanks to them for their superb efforts.

Others who deserve both credit and thanks for contributing to the book are Judy Butler, Carrie Andree, and Rita Scherr for typing and retyping manuscripts, and our families, Melinda, Katrina, Tiara, Asher, Cheyenne, and Brittany Cameron, and Zina, Bryan, Shauna, Bradley, and Katie Whetten. They have provided both inspiration and support throughout this project.

KIM S. CAMERON
DAVID A. WHETTEN

1

Organizational Effectiveness: One Model or Several?

In the past two decades, at least seven books have been produced on the subject of organizational effectiveness (Ghorpade, 1970; Goodman & Pennings, 1977; Mott, 1972; Price, 1968; Spray, 1976; Steers, 1977; Zammuto, 1982). Without exception, each begins by pointing out the conceptual disarray and methodological ambiguity surrounding this construct. In addition, several hundred articles and book chapters have been written in that period (see Cameron, 1982a, for a review), and almost all acknowledge that little agreement exists regarding what organizational effectiveness means or how properly to assess it. Unfortunately, this plethora of writing and research has failed to produce a meaningful definition of organizational effectiveness, let alone a theory of effectiveness. The writing has been fragmented, noncumulative, and frequently downright confusing. Some writers have become so discouraged by the literature on effectiveness that they have advocated abandoning the construct altogether in scholarly activity (Hannan & Freeman, 1977). Goodman (1979a), for example, has asserted that "there should be a moratorium on all studies of organizational effectiveness, books on organizational effectiveness, and chapters on organizational effectiveness [p. 4]."

Despite its chaotic conceptual condition, however, organizational effectiveness is not likely to go away, and Goodman's advice will probably go unheeded. There are theoretical, empirical, and practical reasons why. Theoretically, the construct of organizational effectiveness lies at the very center of all organiza-

1

ORGANIZATIONAL EFFECTIVENESS
A Comparison of Multiple Models

tional models. That is, all conceptualizations of the nature of organizations have embedded in them notions of the nature of effective organizations, and the differences that exist between effective and ineffective organizations. For example, contingency theories emphasize the match between organizations and some aspect of their external environments (Child, 1974, 1975; Galbraith, 1977; Lawrence & Lorsch, 1969). An appropriate match is assumed to be effective while an inappropriate match represents ineffectiveness. Theories of organizations are grounded in notions of effective designs, strategies, reward systems, leadership styles, and so on, and these are among the factors that form the basis of criteria of organizational effectiveness.

Empirically, the construct of organizational effectiveness is not likely to go away because it is the ultimate dependent variable in organizational research. Evidence for effectiveness is required in most investigations of organizational phenomena. The need to demonstrate that one structure, reward system, leadership style, information system, or whatever, is *better* in some way than another makes the notion of effectiveness a central empirical issue. Often, terms are substituted for effectiveness such as performance, success, ability, efficiency, improvement, productivity, or accountability, but some measure of effectiveness is usually what is required. (Moreover, the terms being substituted for effectiveness are seldom any more precisely defined than is effectiveness.)

Practically, organizational effectiveness is not likely to go away because individuals are continually faced with the need to make judgments about the effectiveness of organizations. For example, which public school to close, which firm to award a contract to, which company's stock to purchase, or which college to attend are all decisions that depend at least partly on judgments of organizational effectiveness. Whereas the criteria upon which those decisions are made often are difficult to identify, and whereas considerations other than effectiveness are always relevant (e.g., political and social consequences), individuals nevertheless engage regularly in personal evaluations of organizational effectiveness.

This also points out one reason why organizational effectiveness is more problematic for organizational researchers than for the general public. Researchers have struggled to develop general models for consistently and systematically measuring and defining effectiveness, whereas members of the general public have less trouble making judgments about organizational success. When direct evidence for success is not available (e.g., productivity or output), almost any secondary, but visible, criteria are selected as a basis for judgments (e.g., furnishings of the buildings, or the appearance of organization members). Unfortunately, the public's judgments often are based on criteria that are unrelated to or inconsistent with organizational performance.

It is because of the important place organizational effectiveness holds in organizational theory, research, and practice that the concept should not, indeed cannot, be abandoned. It deserves even more systematic and fine-grained analysis than it has received heretofore. This book represents an attempt to analyze and compare various major perspectives on effectiveness systematically and to make explicit the theoretical, empirical, and practical value of each. It will become clear that trade-offs among different models of organizational effectiveness are required of theoreticians, researchers, and practitioners. No one approach to effectiveness is inherently superior to another. Rather, the usefulness of each approach depends on certain choice factors. Therefore, this book does not strive to develop a universal, or ideal, model of organizational effectiveness. Instead, it examines several models that may be ideal in particular circumstances. Our hope is that a clearer understanding of the concept of effectiveness will emerge from this book, and that further research on effectiveness will be stimulated by the comparisons made among the various models.

UNDERSTANDING
ORGANIZATIONAL EFFECTIVENESS

In introducing the first book written explicitly on the subject of organizational effectiveness, Price (1968) stated that "the purpose of this book is to present the core of what the behavioral sciences now know about the effectiveness of organizations: what we really know, what we nearly know, what we think we know, and what we claim to know [p. 1]." As it turned out, Price's assertion was somewhat exaggerated because many of the propositions that he claimed were known about effectiveness were not known then, and still are not known in the behavioral sciences. The causal associations between certain predictor variables and effectiveness that were claimed to exist simply never have been empirically demonstrated.

The purpose of this chapter is quite the opposite of Price's. Its purpose is to point out that universalistic propositions linking a set of variables to effectiveness can never be known because the meaning of the dependent variable continually changes. Depending on the model of organizational effectiveness being used, the relationships may disappear, become irrelevant, increase, or reverse themselves. What is needed, therefore, is not a set of propositions designed to set forth universal relationships, but a clarification of the various models of organizational effectiveness—their roots, strengths, and weaknesses—and how they relate to one another. Of particular value is to identify the trade-offs inherent in accepting one model versus another, and how relationships among variables change when different models are used.

Reasons for Multiple Models

The remainder of this chapter examines three reasons why multiple models of organizational effectiveness exist in the social sciences. Each of these statements points out a major obstacle to developing a single, coherent, consensual view of this construct. Though these three statements do not exhaust the list of obstacles that could be identified, they do lie at the heart of the problems organizational scientists have had with organizational effectiveness.

These statements suggest that organizational effectiveness is closely associated with conceptualizations of organizations. Variety in conceptualizations of organizations leads to variety in models of organizational effectiveness. From this variety, problems with specifying definitions of effectiveness and with assessing criteria of effectiveness arise. These problems are discussed in the following sections.

1. MULTIPLE MODELS OF ORGANIZATIONAL EFFECTIVENESS ARE PRODUCTS OF MULTIPLE, ARBITRARY MODELS OF ORGANIZATIONS

Authors have conceptualized organizations in a variety of ways. For example, organizations have been called networks of objects (Tichy & Fombrun, 1979), rational entities in pursuit of goals (Perrow, 1970), coalitions of powerful constituencies (Pfeffer & Salancik, 1978), individual need-meeting cooperatives (Cummings, 1977), meaning-producing systems (Pondy & Mitroff, 1979), information-processing units (Galbraith, 1977), open systems (Thompson, 1967), collegiums (Millett, 1962), garbage cans (March & Olsen, 1976), language games (Wittgenstein, 1968), psychic prisons (Morgan, 1980), machines (Taylor, 1911), social contracts (Keeley, 1980), and so on. Each of these conceptualizations highlights, even uncovers, organizational phenomena that were missed or ignored by the others. Research conducted under these different conceptualizations focuses on different phenomena, proposes different relationships among variables, and judges effectiveness differently. (Chapters 2–7 in this volume exemplify this point.)

Changes in conceptualizations of organizations, in fact, have been at the center of the development of organizational theory. From early machine analogies (Taylor, 1911) and classical bureaucracies (Weber, 1947) where organizational efficiency was the ultimate dependent variable, conceptualizations have changed toward more complexity and variety. The emphasis has changed from efficiency to effectiveness, but with each new conceptualization a new meaning of effectiveness has been introduced.

Nonconsensual Conceptions. Whereas some authors have vigorously championed their own conceptualization as the most appropriate one, there is no evidence to suggest that one way of looking at organizations is any better than another. Keeley (1980), for example, contrasted the open systems (organismic) perspective on organizations with the social contract perspective and argued that the social contract perspective is superior in understanding organizational behavior and performance. Katz and Kahn (1978), however, argued for the opposite view. Following von Bertalanffy (1956), Miller (1955), and others, they suggested that the biological notion of living systems captures the most accurate picture of organizations. McMullen (1976) suggested that

> If one looks at the best established theories of science, the kinetic theory of gases for instance, or the nuclear theory of the atom, one immediately realizes that the confidence we place in them results not merely from their successful predictions of novel facts, but at least as much from their behavior as lead-metaphors in the process of conceptual and model change over a considerable period [p. 567].

Confidence in one conceptualization as opposed to another, therefore, results from the superior predictions made possible, the clarity that can be achieved, and the improvement in organizations that results from viewing organizational phenomena from a particular framework. In the organizational sciences, however, there are no universally accepted conceptualizations of organizations. One reason is that the worth of conceptualizations is judged on the basis of their completeness, not on the basis of their accuracy. That is, conceptualizations are accepted if they highlight relevant organizational phenomena previously ignored in other models. No conceptualization so far has mapped all the relevant phenomena.

Some writers on organizational effectiveness have continued to debate the superiority of one model of effectiveness over other models (Bluedorn, 1980; Connolly, Conlon, & Deutsch, 1980; Price, 1972; Stasser & Denniston, 1979). These debates have not proven fruitful, however, because they are based on different conceptualizations of what an organization is. Because different models of organizational effectiveness follow directly from different organizational conceptualizations, their differences relate to disparate emphases, not to superiority of one over the other. An effective organization-as-social-contract, for example, is not the same as, and may even be contradictory to, an effective organization-as-rational-goal-pursuer. The first conceptualization emphasizes an absence of organizational goals and purposes where participant needs are supreme. The second emphasizes the presence of organizational goals and purposes where participant needs are subordinate to organizational accomplishment (see Keeley, 1980, for example). Multiple constituency models of effectiveness (Connolly *et al.,* 1980; Miles, 1980; Pfeffer & Salancik, 1978) are consistent with the first case, while the goal model (Bluedorn, 1980; Campbell, 1977; Price, 1972; Scott, 1977) follows from the second.

The Desirability of Variety. Other writers have argued that a clear conceptualization of organizations is not needed to understand effectiveness, and is even undesirable (Daft & Wiginton, 1979; Morgan, 1980; Weick, 1977). A variety of incomplete or ambiguous conceptualizations serves to expand understanding not detract from it, according to these writers, and conceptualizations are seen as wholly arbitrary. For example, Weick suggested that increased understanding of effectiveness results from pointing out contradictory examples of commonly held conceptions. Though organizations are smooth running, for example, they also are clumsy and wandering. (Also see Chapters 2, 6, and 11 in this volume.) Morgan (1980) pointed out that increased insight can be achieved by using a variety of metaphors to describe organizations, not just one.

> Viewing organizations systematically as cybernetic systems, loosely coupled systems, ecological systems, theaters, cultures, political systems, language games, texts, accomplishments, enactments, psychic prisons, instruments of domination, schismatic systems, catastrophes, etc., it is possible to add rich and creative dimensions to organization theory [p. 615].

Daft and Wiginton suggested that a single conceptualization of organizations is impossible because of the limitations of language, or of the symbols used to make sense of organizational phenomena. No single symbol, model, or metaphor can capture the complexity of organizations, so a variety of different ones are required.

Attempts to Develop Taxonomies. Despite these arguments, several attempts have been made by organizational scientists, both theoretically and empirically, to produce an overarching framework, or categorization scheme, that labels and distinguishes organizations one from another. The rationale for these attempts is that a fundamental element in the development of any scientific body of knowledge is the availability of a widely accepted and usable classification scheme (Hempel, 1965; McKelvey, 1975). Some of these attempts at taxonomy development have been motivated by the biological taxonomic structure, that is, by grouping phenomena together on the basis of similar characteristics. For example, Parsons (1960) advocated classifying organizations on the basis of similar functions in society; Etzioni (1961) suggested compliance and authority systems as a basis; Blau and Scott (1962) used prime beneficiary of the organization's actions; Perrow (1967) used technology; Katz and Kahn (1978) used contribution to society; and Boulding (1956) used system complexity. Each of these theoretical schemes has been criticized as being inadequate, however (Hall, Haas, & Johnson, 1967; McKelvey, 1975; Weldon, 1972), so empirical attempts have been made. The best known of these attempts were done at Ohio State by Haas, Hall, and Johnson (1966) and at the University of Aston by Pugh, Hickson, and Hinings (1969). At Ohio State, 210 organizational characteristics were used, and at Aston, 64 characteristics were included. Factor analysis was the primary method used in both studies to derive a taxonomy. Unfortunately, no workable classification scheme resulted from either of these studies, and no clear conception of organizations was produced. Subsequent research also has been unsuccessful, so organizational scientists continue to use a variety of arbitrary conceptualizations.

This condition, having no agreed upon conception of an organization, has contributed to the variety surrounding organizational effectiveness. Depending on which conceptualization is accepted, an entirely different set of criteria of effectiveness are given attention in the organization. It also serves as the basis for a second major reason why multiple models of effectiveness exist, the lack of definition of the construct space.

2. THE CONSTRUCT SPACE OF ORGANIZATIONAL EFFECTIVENESS IS UNKNOWN

Organizational effectiveness is a construct. Constructs are abstractions that exist in the heads of people, but they have no objective reality. They cannot be pinpointed, counted, or observed. They exist only because they are inferred from the results of observable phenomena. They are mental abstractions designed to give meaning to ideas or interpretations. One difference between *constructs* and *concepts* is that concepts can be defined and exactly specified by observing objective events. Constructs cannot be so specified. Their boundaries are not precisely drawn (Kaplan, 1964; Kerlinger, 1973). Examples of other constructs in the social sciences are leadership, needs, intelligence, motivation, and satisfaction.

As a construct, the total meaning of organizational effectiveness is unknown. Some authors, for example, have used variables such as productivity to stand as an indicator of organizational effectiveness (Goodman, 1979b; Pennings, 1975). But productivity is a *concept,* and its total meaning can be captured by measuring the amount of organizational output. The total meaning of effectiveness comprises more than the concept of productivity, however, and productivity represents only one aspect of the total construct space.

Models That Do Not Model Reality. This difference between concepts and constructs helps explain why the construct space of organizational effectiveness is unknown. A number of models have been proposed by authors and argued to encompass the total meaning of effectiveness. The most widely used models are the goal model (Bluedorn, 1980; Price, 1972), the system resource model (Seashore & Yuchtman, 1967), the internal processes or maintenance model (Bennis, 1966; Nadler & Tushman, 1980), the strategic constituencies model (Connolly *et al.,* 1980; Keeley, 1978; Pfeffer & Salancik, 1978), and the legitimacy model (Miles & Cameron, 1982; Zammuto, 1982).[1] No one of these models captures the total construct space or the total meaning of effectiveness. Whereas each is valuable in its own right because it includes distinctions

---

[1]Other models have been proposed (for example, see Cunningham, 1977; and Fosler, 1978), but the five listed here are by far the most widely used.

absent in the others, none has enough explanatory power to supercede other approaches (see Molnar and Rogers [1976] and Stasser and Deniston [1979] for some empirical comparisons).

For example, Cameron (1980, 1981) provides illustrations of when the goal model, which defines effectiveness as the extent to which an organization reaches its goals, is incomplete because not only are goals often difficult (or impossible) to identify (see Chapters 6 and 10 in this volume), but organizations are sometimes judged ineffective even when their goals are accomplished. On the other hand, organizations are sometimes judged to be effective even though they do not accomplish any of their goals. The system resource model defines effectiveness as the extent to which an organization acquires needed resources. Yet Cameron points out that some organizations are judged to be effective even though they fail to acquire needed resources, whereas others are deemed ineffective even when resources are acquired in abundance. Exceptions also are illustrated by the internal processes model, the strategic constituencies model, and the legitimacy model as well. Organizations can be effective when internal processes are operating poorly (internal processes model), when strategic constituencies are not satisfied (strategic constituencies model), or when the organization does not achieve legitimacy with its public (legitimacy model). Contrarily, judgments of ineffectiveness are shown to arise even when internal processes are good, strategic constituencies are satisfied, or the organization achieves legitimacy. The problem is that each of these models maps part of the construct space of effectiveness, but not all. And other relevant criteria of effectiveness are ignored by all of them (see Chapters 5 and 9 in this volume). Moreover, it has not been clear up to now just what part of the construct space of effectiveness each of these models refers to, or how they relate to one another.

This lack of mapping of the construct space of organizational effectiveness has led to a sense of confusion and chaos in the literature, as well as to multiple models of the construct. What criteria are legitimate indicators of effectiveness (and therefore inside the construct space) are unknown as are the criteria that are not legitimate indicators of effectiveness (and therefore outside the construct space). For example, "member satisfaction" has been used as a *predictor* of effectiveness (outside the construct space), as an *indicator* of effectiveness (inside the construct space), and as a *result* of effectiveness (outside the construct space) (see Campbell, 1977; Cummings, 1977; Lawler, Hall, & Oldham, 1974; Miles & Randolph, 1980). Furthermore, different criteria have served as indicators of effectiveness even though they are unrelated or contradictory. Both efficiency (an absence of slack) and adaptability (an availability of slack) may be indicators of effectiveness, for example. Not only are they contradictory criteria, but, as in the case of member satisfaction, it is not clear what their relationships are to the construct space. They may be included in the construct space of effectiveness as criteria, predictors of and therefore outside the construct space, or they may be produced by an organization's effectiveness.

Attempts to Discover Boundaries. Authors have attempted in at least two ways to identify the boundaries of the construct space of effectiveness, or to determine what is and what is not a criterion of effectiveness. One way is theoretical; the other way is empirical. As just pointed out, no theoretical model has succeeded in mapping the total meaning of effectiveness. Price (1968) was the first to attempt to develop a comprehensive theory by reviewing and integrating 50 studies. He derived 34 propositions linking certain predictor variables to effectiveness. Unfortunately, his inventory of propositions has stimulated no follow-up research and has largely been disregarded as a theory of effectiveness. This is because he ignored contingency relationships in his propositions; the attributions of causality were not supported; the studies he reviewed represent a potpourri of approaches, indicators, and organizational types, and many can be only loosely called effectiveness studies; and he ignored the problem of broad construct boundaries by limiting effectiveness to the attainment of operative goals. Subsequent critiques of effectiveness as goal attainment have pointed out the fallacy of that single oversimplified definition (Cameron, 1978; Kanter & Brinkerhoff, 1981).

Subsequent authors have been reticent to propose a general theory of organizational effectiveness. Most books on the subject of effectiveness have been collections of essays that elaborate various conceptual and methodological problems but offer no guidelines for solutions (Ghorpade, 1970; Goodman & Pennings, 1977; Spray, 1976).

The lack of success in delineating the boundaries of organizational effectiveness theoretically has led authors to attempt to do it empirically. For example, some authors have derived long lists of criteria of effectiveness that they claimed to be comprehensive. Seashore and Yuchtman (1967) generated criteria of performance for 75 insurance agencies by factor-analyzing 76 objectively recorded performance measures. The 10 resulting factors were integrated into the system resource model. The boundaries of the effectiveness construct were then drawn so that only criteria relating to the organization's bargaining position in acquiring scarce and valued resources were included.

Mahoney and his colleagues (Mahoney, 1967; Mahoney & Frost, 1974; Mahoney & Weitzel, 1969) factor analyzed 114 variables derived from the literature and developed 24 independent criteria dimensions. These dimensions were compared to manager ratings of overall, ultimate organizational effectiveness to determine their appropriateness as criteria in the construct space. A different construct space was identified for organizations using different types of technologies.

Quinn and Rohrbaugh (1981) used criteria of effectiveness claimed by

Campbell (1977) to be a comprehensive list of all criteria used in past research. Using a panel of experts to reduce and combine this list, Quinn and Rohrbaugh found that the clustered criteria closely match four major theoretical perspectives on organizations: rational goal models, open systems models, decision process models, and human relations models. Certain fundamental value dimensions were empirically identified that undergird those major theoretical perspectives, and that individuals use in judging organizational effectiveness. The construct space for effectiveness was defined by these three major values dimensions: organization concerns versus individual concerns, flexibility versus control, and means versus ends.

These examples illustrate some reasons why empirical approaches have failed to bound the construct of organizational effectiveness. Each set of authors approached the problem with a different methodology, and, predictably, each derived a different set of indicators. The boundaries and meaning of the construct are not the same for any of them. One reason is because in empirical approaches the results are based on limited *types* of organizations with unique characteristics. Molnar and Rogers (1976), for example, showed that effectiveness in public-sector organizations has a different meaning than effectiveness in private-sector organizations. Another reason for the differences in the examples is that the number of constituencies from whose point of view effectiveness was judged was limited. In general, easily obtainable data were used, and important constituencies holding different performance criteria for the organization were ignored. A third reason is that levels of analysis and focus of activity differed among the criteria selected. Subunit goal attainment was used in one study while organizational resource acquisition was used in another. Finally, the conceptualization of organizations accepted by the researchers may have restricted relevant criteria. Data reduction procedures may have eliminated important criteria of effectiveness from consideration, so that the construct space ended up being narrowly defined.

This lack of homogeneity among criteria in empirical studies is common. In comparing 21 empirical investigations of organizational effectiveness on the basis of the nature of the criteria used and the sources from which the criteria were obtained, Cameron (1978) found that 80% of the criteria selected in those studies did not overlap. Most authors relied on unique indicators of effectiveness. Campbell, Brownas, Peterson, and Dunnette (1974) attempted to overcome this problem of diversity by prescribing the boundaries of effectiveness as broadly as possible. They compiled what they called a listing of "all variables that have been proposed seriously as indices of organizational effectiveness." However, not only do those variables differ in level of specificity, level of analysis, and independence, but Campbell (1977) admitted that it is not clear which of these variables actually should be included as criteria of effectiveness. Their "closeness to the final payoff" (i.e., effectiveness) is unknown.

The Advantages of Unboundedness. It has become clear that with the divergence of models and criteria used in relation to organizational effectiveness, no single, unambiguous meaning of the construct is available. However, this lack of specificity of the construct space of effectiveness is not viewed universally as a negative. There are some writers who argue that defining the construct space of organizational effectiveness would be dysfunctional because it would restrict organizational possibilities. To understand this argument, consider the similarity between constructs and metaphors. Constructs, like metaphors, are most valuable when gaps exist between descriptive reality and the construct; that is, when the operationalization of the construct does not capture all the details present in the objective world. In arguing that all organizational theory is essentially metaphorical, Morgan (1980) pointed out that new insights and scientific progress occur not when constructs and metaphors closely match reality (such as pointing out that an organization is like a group of people), but when the construct or metaphor contains some falsehood (such as pointing out that an organization is like a psychic prison). When some falsehood is present, new imagery arises and previously unrecognized alternatives are considered. An unprescribed construct such as organizational effectiveness allows for a wide variety of organizations to be simultaneously judged as effective, even with contradictory characteristics. Similarly, it allows for criteria to be included that are not even recognized as important by the organization's major constituencies, but that may become crucial to the survival of the organization in the future. Defining the construct space of effectiveness may restrict these prerogatives. Complexity and ambiguity in effectiveness models are thus required to map the complexity and ambiguity of organizations.

The absence of a clearly mapped construct space for organizational effectiveness, then, has helped prohibit the development of a single, universal model, and it has contributed to a wide variety of approaches and criteria being used in attempts to assess the construct. On the other hand, it is not the divergence or lack of consensus that is disconcerting about the effectiveness literature. Rather, it is the lack of awareness of the relationships among the various approaches and models to one another—that is, their relative locations in the construct space—that has caused writing on effectiveness to be so noncumulative and disarranged. One purpose of this book is to help clarify the relationships of some of the major models of effectiveness to one another.

3. THE BEST CRITERIA FOR ASSESSING ORGANIZATIONAL EFFECTIVENESS ARE UNKNOWN

It is to be expected that when the construct space of effectiveness is unclear, its measurement also will be unclear. One reason that the best criteria for assessing effectiveness are unknown is that organizational effectiveness is inherently subjective, and it is based on the personal values and preferences of individuals. Writers such as Van de Ven and Ferry (1980), Bluedorn (1980), and others refer to organizational goals as being manifestations of individual preferences and values, so goals, for them, are the best criteria for measurement. Agreement on certain preferences or goals causes them to be advanced as the major criteria of effectiveness for the organization. Pfeffer and Salancik (1978) argued that the preferences of the most powerful constituency should be used as the criteria by which effectiveness is measured. This is because the most powerful constituency can impose its preferences on the organization over the objections of less powerful constituencies. For these writers, then, the measurement task is to develop a list of goals and priorities preferred by the relevant constituencies of the organization.

There are some inherent difficulties with attempting to assess individual preferences and values in research on effectiveness, however. Four problems, in particular, result in an obfuscation of preferences as the criteria of effectiveness. *First,* individuals frequently cannot identify their own preferences for an organization. *Second,* preferences change, sometimes dramatically, over time. *Third,* a variety of contradictory preferences are almost always pursued simultaneously in an organization. And *fourth,* the expressed preferences of strategic constituencies frequently are unrelated or negatively related to one another and to judgments of organizational effectiveness.

Problems in Identifying Preferences. Regarding the first problem, the inability to identify preferences, Nisbet and Wilson (1977) reviewed evidence from a large number of empirical studies and concluded that individuals have little or no ability to accurately report their cognitive preferences. They pointed out that what is reported is usually based on some a priori implicit theory or past behavior thought to be plausible, not on the preferences people actually hold. Slovic and Lichtenstein (1971) also reviewed a variety of studies and observed a weak correlation between reported self-insight (knowledge of implicit preferences or motivating factors) and objective choices (preferences or actions that were behaviorally selected as being important). Argyris and Schon (1978) made a distinction between "theories in action" and "theories in use." Theories in action, or the principles guiding the behaviors displayed by individuals, are seldom cognitively mapped. Therefore, the theories people hold in their heads frequently do not match the theories they act on.

There appears to be ample empirical evidence, therefore, to suggest that individuals frequently cannot report accurately the criteria of organizational effectiveness that they implicitly hold. Nor are they aware of the factors that motivate their judgments or evaluations of an organization. When researchers ask various constituency members to specify important criteria of effectiveness, there is no assurance that the criteria they enumerate will be consistent with the criteria they use implicitly to judge effectiveness.

Even when presented with lists of effectiveness criteria, individuals some-times have difficulty selecting those they hold as important and those they do not. Gross and Grambsch (1968), for example, asked administrators and senior faculty members in colleges and universities to identify which were the most important of 47 different goals in their institutions. The results revealed that all of the goals were rated as important. Respondents could not differentiate among the goals that were important for evaluating effectiveness and those that were not.

Techniques such as policy capturing (Hammond, McClelland, & Mum-power, 1980; Slovic & Lichtenstein, 1971) nominal group or delphi techniques (Delbecq, Van deVen, & Gustafson, 1975), and multiattribute utility theory (Huber, 1974) have been devised to help overcome this problem of criteria identification. However, each of those techniques simply serves to weight or to rank-order preferences. Preference curves are the desired outcomes. These techniques do not, however, ensure that the criteria of effectiveness identified by individuals a priori are the most important ones or the ones implicitly held. They rely on individuals' ability to specify accurate preference criteria, and it is this ability that is suspect.

Changing Preferences.   The second problem with the subjective nature of effectiveness is that preferences, and therefore criteria, may change dramat-ically over time. Miles and Cameron's (1982) study of the tobacco industry chronicles the changing preferences for cigarettes and smoking between 1950 and 1979. It illustrates how consumer ratings of tobacco-firm effectiveness have been altered dramatically. Regardless of how well the firm does, it may be rated as effective or ineffective because of the changing values of constituents. Research by Cameron and Whetten (1981) of 18 simulated production organi-zations found that the preferences of members of these organizations changed over organizational life-cycle states. In early stages of the organization's devel-opment, members preferred criteria of effectiveness that emphasized individual levels of performance (such as succeeding at personal tasks) and acquisition of inputs (for example, obtaining individual resources). In later stages of develop-ment, members' preferences changed toward organizational-level outputs (such as total organization productivity). Preferences for effectiveness in individual input acquisition and task accomplishment became unimportant. Thus, the bases for judging effectiveness changed over time in the minds of organizational members regardless of actual organizational performance.

A study of a state department of mental hygiene by Quinn and Cameron (1982) also illustrates how preferences change over time and thereby affect ratings of effectiveness. The department was considered highly effective by legislators and the public during its first 5 years of existence because of its innovative approach to treatment. However, after a series of critical newspaper exposes, preferences changed among those groups and the department was forced to reorganize to conform to a changed set of preferences.

Changing preferences also may be a result of changes in the relevant constituencies of an organization. For example, nonsmokers were not an important interest group for tobacco firms until they organized antismoking campaigns (Miles & Cameron, 1982). Environmentalists became a significant constituency for Boise Cascade and forced financial reorganization only after a period of remarkable firm growth where concern for negative environmental effects was perceived as low (McDonald, 1975). Third-party insurers took on critical importance to doctors, nurses, and hospitals as more and more people began to rely on medical insurance or federal medicaid to cover medical expenses (Zammuto, 1982).

These examples illustrate how changing preferences can complicate the assessment of organizational effectiveness. Depending on *when* the assessment is made, criteria of effectiveness and the relevant group of constituencies may differ markedly. The relationships among criteria at two different points in time often are not clear, so that effectiveness in the past may not be a good predictor of effectiveness in the present or the future.

Organizational Pursuit of Contradictory Preferences. The third problem with preferences as the basis for measuring organizational effectiveness—the simultaneous pursuit by organizations of contradictory preferences—has been referred to by a variety of writers. Weick (1976), for example, indicated that educational organizations are examples of "loosely coupled systems" where a defining characteristic is the presence of contradictory preferences in the organization. Later, he alluded to some of the contradictory preferences in other types of organizations by pointing out that not only do preferences exist for organizations to be efficient, controlled, and benevolent, but contradictory preferences also exist, which lead to organizational grouchiness, clumsiness, and galumphing (Weick, 1977).

In their study of U.S. tobacco firms, Miles and Cameron (1982) found that the public holds contradictory preferences toward the tobacco industry. On the one hand, some constituencies prefer to maintain and even increase tobacco and cigarette sales in order to acquire tax revenues and enhance the national balance of payments. Several states are highly dependent on the billions of dollars in tax revenues accruing from tobacco production and sales, and a substantial contribution is made to a favorable balance of payments by tobacco exports. On the other hand, some of these same constituents prefer to decrease tobacco production and cigarette manufacturing because of the personal health hazards associated with smoking. Preferences to expand production and manufacturing while at the same time to decrease production and manufacturing appear simultaneously among the strategic constituencies of these firms.

A study of different domains of effectiveness in colleges and universities indicates that organizations may pursue one set of criteria in one domain of activities and a different and possibly contradictory set of criteria in another domain of activities. For a college or university to be highly effective in the academic domain (e.g., activities relating to the scholarly development of students and faculty) for example, was found to be negatively related to being highly effective in the external adaptation domain (e.g., activities relating to the responsiveness to community needs). That is, organizations frequently pursued different domains of activities simultaneously, but doing better in one domain resulted in doing worse in another domain (Cameron, 1981). Contradictory preferences can exist at the same time because one domain of activities may be independent of another. When they are not independent, "incrementalism" is practiced (i.e., trading off one set of preferences against another; Lindblom, 1959), "satisficing" strategies are pursued (i.e., fulfilling all preferences to only a limited extent; Cyert & March, 1963), or "sequencing" occurs (i.e., alternating emphasis among preferences; Cyert & March, 1963).

When researchers attempt to assess organizational effectiveness, one cause for confusion is uncovering these contradictory preferences or criteria. Some writers have attempted to address contradictory criteria by distinguishing between doing *good* versus doing *well* (Miles & Cameron, 1982), where "good" refers to achieving legitimacy and "well" refers to achieving efficiency; by distinguishing between *desirable* results versus *desired* results (Zammuto, 1982), where "desirable" results are based on values, and "desired" results are based on goals; or by distinguishing between *doing things right* (efficiency) versus *doing the right things* (effectiveness) (Kanter & Brinkerhoff, 1981). The authors in each case suggest that focusing on "good," "desirable," or "right things" is a way to bring clarity to preferences. However, these distinctions are only partially helpful because the factors composing the performance defined as good, desirable, or focused on right things still may be contradictory within organizations (see Chapter 6 in this volume).

Lack of Agreement among Constituency Preferences. The fourth obstacle in identifying the best criteria of effectiveness is that the expressed preferences of an organization's strategic constituencies often are unrelated or negatively related to one another and to their actual judgments of organizational performance (see Chapter 3 in this volume). Strategic constituencies are individuals or groups who have a substantial stake in the organization. These include resource providers, users of the organization's products or services, producers of the organization's output, groups whose cooperation is essential to the organization's survival, or those whose lives are significantly affected by the organization. In general, strategic constituencies have some type of dependency relationship with the organization.

It is generally acknowledged that the viewpoints of strategic constituencies are critical in assessing effectiveness. But identifying the appropriate constituency is problematic. Sometimes writers have advocated using representatives from various constituencies as a dominant coalition (Cameron, 1978; Pennings & Goodman, 1977), some have tried to identify the single most important constituency such as managers (Mahoney, 1966; Osborn & Hunt, 1974), organization members (Cummings, 1977; Van de Ven & Ferry, 1980), or customers (Bass, 1952; Schneider, Parkington, & Buxton, 1980), and some have suggested using multiple constituency perspectives separately (Connolly et al., 1980; Keeley, 1978). But all possible constituencies can never be assessed for an organization (the importance of some constituencies is unrecognized, for example, or constituencies are not organized), so choices are always required that focus on certain constituencies' preferences and not others. Two problems arise as a result of these choices.

First, research has found that different constituencies hold different preferences for effectiveness for an organization. For example, comparing ratings of effectiveness for 97 small businesses among five strategic constituencies (government, customers, suppliers, creditors, and owners), Friedlander and Pickle (1968) found that 5 of 15 relationships compared were negatively correlated, and only 4 of the 15 relationships were positively correlated at the .05 level of significance. That is, these five groups had low levels of agreement on ratings of effectiveness, and there was more disagreement than agreement regarding organizational effectiveness.

Whetten's (1978) study of New York State manpower agencies asked agency staff and local community leaders to judge the effectiveness of a particular agency. These ratings were negatively correlated ($r = -.42 < .001$) with the major output of the agencies (i.e., the number of placements in employment). Furthermore, different sets of criteria were used by these two groups in making their judgments, and some of the criteria were almost polar opposites. Rohrbaugh's (1981) assessment of the effectiveness of employment service offices throughout the United States revealed a similar pattern. Constituencies inside the agencies had strong agreement on some criteria, but no agreement on others.

A study of the U.S. tobacco industry by Miles and Cameron (1982) also found that different constituencies held different preferences and expectations for the tobacco firms, and this resulted in widely different judgments of effectiveness. For example, the consuming public tends to hold the value of having the firms do *good* (e.g., not harming smokers' health), rather than to do *well* (e.g., producing cigarettes efficiently). Doing good enhances legitimacy; doing well enhances profitability. On the industry level, the tobacco firms were rated as ineffective by the public, but as highly effective by stockholders and owners (that is, they do well but not good).

This latter example illustrates the trade-off between internal constituency preferences (stockholders and owners) and external constituency preferences (consumers) that Dubin (1976) suggested is inherent in every organization. Internal and external constituency preferences are incompatible, according to Dubin, and both cannot be satisfied.

The incompatibility of constituency preferences has led some authors to suggest that it is the preferences of the most *powerful* constituency that should be identified (Pfeffer & Salancik, 1978). But this suggestion raises the second problem with constituency preferences. That is, the most powerful constituency can seldom be identified in organizations with multiple constituencies (and few organizations rely on only one major constituency). Like effectiveness criteria, the relative power of a constituency is partly based on subjective assessments, and the judgments change depending on who is doing the rating. In rating the relative power of the major constituencies of colleges, for example, faculty members, administrators, trustees, funders, and legislators all produced different rankings (Cameron, 1982b). It was impossible to determine objectively which constituency was most powerful because each group gave a different answer. Even if it is assumed that the most powerful constituency could be identified, no organization could survive by focusing only on one constituency's preferences while ignoring other constituencies.

Solving Multiple Preference Problems.   One potential solution to the problem of contradictory or unrelated constituency preferences is illustrated in Figure

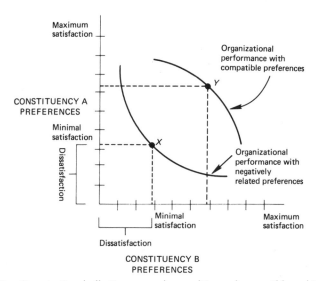

FIGURE 1.1.   Organizational effectiveness under conditions of compatible and incompatible constituency preferences.

1.1. Each axis in the figure represents the preferences of a different constituency. Members of constituency A prefer that the organization perform at the very top of the scale on the vertical axis. Members of constituency B prefer that the organization perform at the right-hand end of the horizontal axis. A point is identified for each constituency that represents minimal satisfaction of preferences, or a minimally satisfying level of performance for the organization. Below that point, the constituency is dissatisfied. If the preferences of constituencies A and B are largely unrelated (or negatively related) as Friedlander and Pickle (1968) and Whetten (1978) found, then a preference curve can be drawn to illustrate the organization's performance. The more the organization pursues constituency A's preferences, the less satisfied constituency B is and vice versa. However, a point can be identified (point X) where both constituencies are minimally satisfied. The organization's performance is not high on either set of preferences, but it is satisfactory. This multiple constituency perspective implies that *satisfactory* effectiveness is better for the organization than is maximum effectiveness on any one constituency's criteria. Organizational effectiveness is increased, according to this perspective, only as constituency preferences become more compatible. In that case, point Y on the second preference curve can be identified where both constituencies are satisfied while the organization performs at a higher overall level. One way for compatibility in constituency preferences to be produced is through the development of an "organizational saga" (Clark, 1970) or a special sense of mission and identity that is widely shared among constituencies and that leads to similar expectations for the organization. Classical organization development interventions provide one methodology for accomplishing this aim (Cameron & Quinn, 1982).

Unfortunately, points X and Y can seldom, if ever, be identified for an organization because of at least three problems in Figure 1.1. First, neither the axes nor the scales on the axes are precisely known. The criteria used by constituencies are difficult to determine, and the point of minimum satisfaction is unknown. Moreover, the axes are multidirectional because of the varying relationships among the criteria held by a single constituency. Second, the total number of relevant constituencies for the organization makes the figure N-dimensional instead of two-dimensional. Each constituency's set of criteria for effectiveness may have a unique relationship with every other constituency's set of criteria, so a performance curve would be difficult to draw. Third, the criteria of effectiveness held by each constituency changes in relation to other constituencies' criteria. Negotiations and trade-offs constantly occur based on the self-interest of each constituency as each is interested in having its preferences satisfied by the organization. Therefore, the shape of the performance curve is variable and a hypothetical point X would never exist in one place for long.

Are Preferences Relevant? Some authors have argued that the debates over which criteria or which constituency is best for assessing effectiveness are meaningless. They deny the necessity of identifying preferences and values at all, and instead argue for the population ecology perspective on organizations (e.g., Hannan & Freeman, 1977). This view holds that organizational effectiveness is relevant as a construct only as it relates to the survival or demise of organizations. Organizational survival in the population ecology perspective is a product of environmental selection, not a product of organizational action guided by preferences or values. So organizations are effective because their form and functions match the requirements demanded by an immutable external environment. Ineffectiveness is evidenced by the organization's not being "selected" by the environment (i.e., organizational demise). Values and preferences of constituencies have no place in this model.

This deterministic view of organizational effectiveness, which claims that the effectiveness of organizations is largely determined by uncontrolled factors, claims to eliminate individual preferences and managerial action as relevant components of effectiveness. Survival is the "best" criterion. However, rather than solving the confusion around criteria selection, this viewpoint perpetuates it. Identifying survival as the best criterion is itself a product of an individual value or a preference, and there are no more compelling reasons to accept survival than to accept any other criterion as best (e.g., flexibility). As Kaufman (1976) points out, it is sometimes better both for the organization and for its constituencies that it does not survive. The current controversies in many communities relating to the closing of elementary schools illustrates this point. Organizational demise is effective for some constituencies; others prefer survival.

In summary, another major reason for the impossibility of developing a single model of organizational effectiveness is that the best criteria for measuring the construct cannot be agreed upon. This is because the criteria are subjective and grounded in the preferences and values of individuals, and because it is often not clear who the best individuals (constituencies) are to ask.

CONCLUSION

These three problems—multiple conceptualizations of organizations, unbounded construct space, and an absence of consensual criteria—serve as the major factors that have led to the development of multiple models of organizational effectiveness. This construct, therefore, has become something of an enigma. On the one hand, it is a central construct in the organizational sciences for theoretical, empirical, and practical reasons. Almost all studies of and theories about organizations are based, at least implicitly, on the construct of effectiveness. On the other hand, no theories of organizational effectiveness per se are possible, the criteria for assessing the construct are both divergent and difficult to identify, and prescriptions for improving organizational effectiveness are not founded on systematic research.

The central thesis of this book is that advancement in this field is predicated not on achieving the ambition of developing the universal theory of effectiveness. Instead, the necessity of utilizing multiple models should be recognized. Our advocacy of multiple models, however, should not be interpreted to mean the uncritical or habitual adoption of a favorite perspective in all assessments of effectiveness. What we advocate, instead, is a better understanding of the assumptions, strengths, and weaknesses of the various approaches. This understanding will help us better evaluate when each of the models is best utilized.

As a construct, organizational effectiveness is similar to an unmapped terrain, where the responsibility lies with investigators to chart it. There are multiple landmarks, but no one overall viewpoint can be reached where the whole terrain is visible at once. The task is to determine the relationships of the more limited views of the terrain to one another as the observers move from one perspective to another. Randomly recording viewpoints without considering how they relate to one another serves little purpose in understanding the terrain. So does focusing on phenomena that are too narrow in scope. The viewpoint has to be sufficiently broad to capture meaningful parts of the landscape.

In organizational effectiveness studies, different attempts to map the terrain have mostly been recorded with no consideration given to how they relate to one another. Isolated assessments have been the norm, and theoretical treatises have generally attempted to replace rather than to add to one another. Some recordings have been too general to provide much insight into the characteristics of the terrain, and some have focused too narrowly on univariate ratings or limited viewpoints. Multiple perspectives (models) are required to understand organizational effectiveness, but the results of these multiple perspectives must be recorded in relationship to one another. In this manner, a cumulative literature mapping this contruct space can be developed.

REFERENCES

Argyris, C., & Schon, D. *Organizational learning: A theory of action perspective.* Reading, Mass.: Addison-Wesley, 1978.

Bass, B. M. Ultimate criteria of organizational worth. *Personnel Psychology,* 1952, 5, 157–173.

Bennis, W. G. The concept of organizational health. In W. G. Bennis (Ed.), *Changing organizations.* New York: McGraw-Hill, 1966.

Blau, P., & Scott, R. *Formal organizations*. San Francisco: Chandler, 1962.

Bluedorn, A. C. Cutting the gordian know: A critique of the effectiveness tradition in organization research. *Sociology and Social Research*, 1980, *64*, 477–496.

Boulding, K. General systems today—the skeleton of science. *Management Science*, 1956, *2*, 197–208.

Cameron, K. S. Measuring organizational effectiveness in institutions of higher education. *Administrative Science Quarterly*, 1978, *23*, 604–632.

Cameron, K. S. Critical questions in assessing organizational effectiveness. *Organizational Dynamics*, 1980, *9*, 66–80.

Cameron, K. S. Domains of organizational effectiveness in colleges and universities. *Academy of Management Journal*, 1981, *24*, 25–47.

Cameron, K. S. *A comprehensive bibliography of organizational effectiveness*. Boulder, Colo.: National Center for Higher Education Management Systems, 1982. (a)

Cameron, K. S. Multiple constituencies and organizational effectiveness in higher education. Working Paper Series, National Center for Higher Education Management Systems, Boulder, Colo.: 1982. (b)

Cameron, K. S. & Quinn, R. E. The field of organization development. In R. E. Quinn & K. S. Cameron (Eds.), *Classics of organization development*. Oak Park, Ill.: Moore Publishing, 1982.

Cameron, K. S., & Whetten, D. A. Perceptions of organization effectiveness across organizational life cycles. *Administrative Science Quarterly*, 1981, *26*, 525–544.

Campbell, J. P. On the nature of organizational effectiveness. In P. S. Goodman & J. M. Pennings (Eds.), *New perspectives on organizational effectiveness*. San Francisco: Jossey-Bass, 1977. Pp. 13–55.

Campbell, J. P., Brownas, E. A., Peterson, N. G., & Dunnette, M. D. The measurement of organizational effectiveness: A review of relevant research and opinion. Final Report, Navy Personnel Research and Development Center, Minneapolis: Personnel Decisions, 1974.

Child, J. Managerial and organizational factors associated with company performance. Part 1. *Journal of Management Studies*, 1974, *11*, 175, 189.

Child, J. Managerial and organizational factors associated with company performance. Part 2. *Journal of Management Studies*, 1975, *12*, pp. 12–27.

Clark, B. R. *The distinctive college: Antioch, Reed, and Swarthmore*. Chicago: Aldine Press, 1970.

Connolly, T., Conlon, E. M., & Deutsch, S. J. Organizational effectiveness: A multiple constituency approach. *Academy of Management Review*, 1980, *5*, 211–218.

Cummings, L. L. Emergence of the instrumental organization. In P. S. Goodman & J. M. Pennings (Eds.), *New perspectives on organizational effectiveness*. San Francisco: Jossey-Bass, 1977. Pp. 56–62.

Cunningham, J. B. Approaches to the evaluation of organizational effectiveness. *Academy of Management Review*, 1977, *2*, 463–474.

Cyert, R. M., & March, J. G. *A behavioral theory of the firm*. Englewood Cliffs, N.J.: Prentice-Hall, 1963.

Daft, R. & Wiginton, J. C. Language and organizations. *Academy of Management Review*, 1979, *4*, 179–192.

Delbecq, A. L., Van de Ven, A. H., & Gustafson, D. H. *Group techniques for program planning*. Glenview, Ill.: Scott Foresman, 1975.

Dubin, R. Organizational effectiveness: Same dilemmas of perspective. *Organization and Administrative Sciences*, 1976, *7*, 7–14.

Etzioni, A. *A comparative analysis of complex organizations*. New York: Free Press, 1961.

Fosler, R. S. State and local government productivity and the private sector. *Public Administration Review*, 1978, *38*, 22–28.

Friedlander, F., & Pickle H. Components of effectiveness in small organizations. *Administrative Science Quarterly*, 1968, *13*, 289–304.

Galbraith, J. *Organizational design: An information processing view*. Reading, Mass.: Addison-Wesley, 1977.

Ghorpade, J. *Assessment of organization effectiveness*. Santa Monica, Calif.: Goodyear, 1970.

Goodman, P. S. Organizational effectiveness as a decision making process. Paper presented at the 39th Annual meetings of the Academy of Management, Atlanta, 1979. (a)

Goodman, P. S. *Assessing organizational change*. New York: Wiley, 1979. (b)

Goodman, P. S., & Pennings, J. M. *New perspectives on organizational effectiveness*. San Francisco: Jossey-Bass, 1977.

Gross, E., & Grambsch, P. V. *University goals and academic power*. Washington, D.C.: American Council on Education, 1968.

Haas, J. E., Hall, R. H., & Johnson, N. J. Toward an empirically derived taxonomy of organizations. In R. V. Bowers (Ed.), *Studies on behavior in organizations*. Athens, Ga.: University of Georgia Press, 1966.

Hall, R. H., Haas, J. E., & Johnson, N. An examination of the Blau-Scott and Etzioni typologies. *Administrative Science Quarterly*, 1967, *12*, 118–139.

Hammond, K. R., McClelland, G. H., & Mumpower, J. *Human judgment and decision making: Theories, methods, and procedures*. New York: Praeger, 1980.

Hannan, M. T., & Freeman, J. The population ecology of organizations. *American Journal of Sociology*, 1977, *82*, 929–964.

Hempel, C. G. *Aspects of scientific explanation*, New York: Free Press, 1965.

Huber, G. P. Methods for quantifying subjective probabilities and multi-attribute utilities. *Decision Sciences*, 1974, *5*, 3–31.

Kanter, R. M., & Brinkerhoff, D. Organizational performance: Recent developments in measurement. *Annual Review of Sociology*, 1981, *7*, 321–349.

Kaplan, A. *The conduct of inquiry*. Scranton, Pa.: Chandler, 1964.

Katz, D., & Kahn, R. L. *The social psychology of organizations* (2nd ed.). New York: Wiley, 1978.

Kaufman, H. *Are government organizations immortal?* Washington, D.C.: Brookings, 1976.

Keeley, M. A social justice approach to organizational evaluation. *Administrative Science Quarterly*, 1978, *22*, 272–292.

Keeley, M. Organizational analysis: A comparison of organismic and social contract models. *Administrative Science Quarterly*, 1980, *25*, 337–362.

Kerlinger, F. N. *Foundations of behavioral research*. New York: Holt, Rinehart, and Winston, 1973.

Lawler, E. E., Hall, D. T., & Oldham, G. R. Organizational climate: Relationship to organizational structure, process, and performance. *Organizational Behavior and Human Performance*, 1974, *11*, 139–155.

Lawrence, P. R., and Lorsch, J. W. *Organization and environment*. Homewood, Ill.: Irwin, 1969.

Lindblom, C. E. The science of muddling through. *Public Administration Review*, 1959, *20*, 79–88.

Mahoney, T. A. Managerial perceptions of organizational effectiveness. *Administrative Science Quarterly*, 1967, *14*, 357–365.

Mahoney, T. A., & Frost, P. J. The role of technology in models of organizational effectiveness. *Organizational Behavior and Human Performance*, 1974, *11*, 122–138.

Mahoney, T. A., & Weitzel, W. Managerial models of organizational effectiveness. *Administrative Science Quarterly*, 1969, *14*, 357–365.

March, J. G., & Olsen, J. P. *Ambiguity and choice in organizations*. Oslo, Norway: Universitetsforlaget, 1976.

McDonald, J. *The game of business*. Garden City, N.Y.: Anchor Press, 1975.

McKelvey, W. Guidelines for the empirical classification of organizations. *Administrative Science Quarterly*, 1975, *20*, 509–525.

McMullen, E. History and philosophy of science: A marriage of convenience? In R. S. Cohen & M. W. Wartofsky (Eds.), *Boston studies in the philosophy of science,* 1976, *32,* 585–601.

Miles, R. H. *Macro organizational behavior.* Santa Monica, Ca.: Goodyear, 1980.

Miles, R. H., & Cameron, K. S. *Coffin nails and corporate strategies.* Englewood Cliffs, N.J.: Prentice-Hall, 1982.

Miles, R. H., & Randolph, W. A. Influence of organizational learning styles on early development. In J. R. Kimberly & R. H. Miles (Eds.), *The organizational life cycle.* San Francisco: Jossey-Bass, 1980.

Miller, J. G. Toward a general theory for the behavioral sciences. *American Psychologist,* 1955, *10,* 513–531.

Millett, J. *The academic community.* New York: McGraw-Hill, 1962.

Molnar, J. J., & Rogers, D. C. Organizational effectiveness: On empirical comparison of the goal and system resource approaches. *Sociological Quarterly,* 1976, *17,* 401–413.

Morgan, G. Paradigms, metaphors, and puzzle solving in organizational theory. *Administrative Science Quarterly,* 1980, *25,* 605–622.

Mott, P. E. *The characteristics of effective organizations.* New York: Harper and Row, 1972.

Nadler, D. A., & Tushman, M. L. A congruence model for organizational assessment. In E. E. Lawler, D. A. Nadler, & P. Cammann (Eds.), *Organizational assessment: Perspectives on the measurement of organizational behavior and the quality of working life.* New York: Wiley, 1980. Pp. 261–278.

Nisbet, R. E., & Wilson, T. Telling more than we can know: Verbal reports on mental processes. *Psychological Review,* 1977, *134,* 231–259.

Osborn, R. N., & Hunt, J. C. Environment and organizational effectiveness. *Administrative Science Quarterly,* 1974, *19,* 231–246.

Parsons, T. *Structure and process in modern societies.* New York: The Free Press, 1960.

Pennings, J. M. The relevance of the structure-contingency model for organizational effectiveness. *Administrative Science Quarterly,* 1975, *20,* 393–410.

Pennings, J. M., & Goodman, P. S. Toward a workable framework. In P. S. Goodman & J. M. Pennings (Eds.), *New perspectives on organizational effectiveness.* San Francisco: Jossey-Bass, 1977.

Perrow, C. A framework for the comparative analysis of organizations. *American Sociological Review,* 1967, *32,* 194–208.

Perrow, C. *Organizational analysis: A sociological view,* Belmont, Calif.: Wadsworth, 1970.

Pfeffer, J., & Salancik, G. R. *The external control of organizations.* New York: Harper and Row, 1978.

Pondy, L. R., & Mitroff, I. Beyond open systems models of organization. In B. Staw (Ed.), *Research in organizational behavior.* Greenwood, Conn.: JAI Press, 1979, pp. 13–40.

Price, J. L. *Organizational effectiveness: An inventory of propositions.* Homewood, Ill.: Irwin, 1968.

Price, J. L. The study of organizational effectiveness. *Sociological Quarterly,* 1972, *13,* 3–15.

Pugh, D. J., Hickson, D. J., & Hinings, C. R. An empirical taxonomy of work organizations. *Administrative Science Quarterly,* 1969, *14,* 115–126.

Quinn, R. E., & Cameron, K. S. Life cycles and shifting criteria of effectiveness: Some preliminary evidence. *Management Science,* 1982, 27.

Quinn, R. E., & Rohrbaugh, J. A competing values approach to organizational effectiveness. *Public Productivity Review,* 1981, *5,* 122–140.

Rohrbaugh, J. Operationalizing the competing values approach. *Public Productivity Review,* 1981, *5,* 141–159.

Schneider, B., Parkington, J., & Buxton, V. Employee and customer perceptions of service in banks. *Administrative Science Quarterly,* 1980, *25,* 252–267.

Seashore, S. E., & Yuchtman, E. Factorial analysis of organizational performance. *Administrative Science Quarterly*, 1967, *12*, 377–395.

Scott, W. R. Effectiveness of organizational effectiveness studies, In P. S. Goodman and J. M. Pennings (Eds.), *New perspectives on organizational effectiveness*. San Francisco: Jossey-Bass, 1977.

Slovic, P., & Lichtenstein, S. Comparison of Bayesian and regression approaches to the study of information processing in judgement. *Organizational Behavior and Human Performance*, 1971, *6*, 649–744.

Spray, S. L. *Organizational effectiveness: Theory, research, and application*. Kent, Ohio: Kent State University Press, 1976.

Stasser, S., & Deniston, L. O. A comparative analysis of goal and systems models designed to evaluate health organization effectiveness. *Proceedings of the Academy of Management*, 1979, 342–347.

Steers, R. M. *Organizational effectiveness: A behavioral view*. Santa Monica, Calif.: Goodyear, 1977.

Taylor, F. W. *Principles of scientific management*. New York: Harper and Row, 1911.

Thompson, J. D. *Organization in action*. McGraw-Hill, 1967.

Tichy, N., & Fombrun, C. Network analysis in social settings. *Human Relations*, 1979, *32*, 923–965.

Van de Ven, A. H., & Ferry, D. *Measuring and assessing organizations*. New York: Wiley, 1980.

von Bertalanffy, L. General systems theory. *General Systems* (Yearbook of the Society for General Systems Theory), 1956, *1*, 1–10.

Weber, M. *The theory of social and economic organization*. A. M. Henderson & T. Parsons, trans. New York: Free Press, 1947.

Weick, K. E. Educational organizations as loosely coupled systems. *Administrative Science Quarterly*, 1976, *21*, 1–19.

Weick, K. E. Re-punctuating the problem. In P. S. Goodman & J. M. Pennings (Eds.), *New perspectives on organizational effectiveness*. San Francisco: Jossey-Bass, 1977.

Weldon, P. D. An examination of the Blau-Scott and Etzioni typologies: A critique. *Administrative Science Quarterly*, 1972, *17*, 76–78.

Whetten, D. A. Coping with incompatible expectations: An integrated view of role conflict. *Administrative Science Quarterly*, 1978, *23*, 254–271.

Wittgenstein, L. *Philisophical investigations*, GEM Anscombe, trans. Oxford: Blackwell, 1968.

Zammuto, R. F. *Assessing organizational effectiveness: Systems change, adaptation, and strategy*. Albany, N.Y.: SUNY-Albany Press, 1982.

MULTIPLE MODELS OF ORGANIZATIONAL EFFECTIVENESS

BENJAMIN SCHNEIDER

An Interactionist Perspective on Organizational Effectiveness[1]

THE ATTRACTION–SELECTION–ATTRITION FRAMEWORK

This chapter builds on some ideas from interactional psychology and vocational and industrial psychology as a basis for a psychological perspective on organizational design and organizational effectiveness. The basic theses of this chapter are: (*a*) organizations are defined by the kinds of people who are attracted to them, selected by them, and who remain in them; (*b*) as a result of the attraction–selection–attrition cycle, organizations can become overly homogeneous resulting in a decreased capacity for adaptation and change; and (*c*) in the face of turbulent environments, organizations can remain viable by attracting, selecting, and retaining people in differentiated roles who are externally and future oriented.

Each of these theses emerges from a consideration of the nature of the relationship between persons and situations. This relationship is addressed from the perspective of contemporary personality theory, especially that group of theorists called interactionists.

[1]The writing of this chapter was supported by the Organizational Effectiveness Research Group, Psychological Sciences Division, Office of Naval Research under Contract No. N00014-79-C-0781, Contract Authority Identification Number NR 170-894, Benjamin Schneider, Principal Investigator.

27

ORGANIZATIONAL EFFECTIVENESS
A Comparison of Multiple Models

Interactionism

Interactionism is a burgeoning subfield in the psychology of personality. It posits that behavior follows from naturally occurring transactions between persons and settings. Interactionism is a reaction to extreme forms of personalism and situationism, each of which attributes observed behavior primarily to the attributes of persons, or the attributes of situations, respectively. The classic personologist would be any one of a number of trait theorists (e.g., R. B. Cattell) or psychodynamicists (e.g., Freud); the classic situationist would be Skinner. Mischel, Jeffrey, and Patterson (1974) present the differences between personologists and situationists as follows:

> Advocates of trait theory seek to discover underlying, generalized dispositions that characterize persons relatively stably over time and across many situations, and search for behaviors that may serve as "signs" of such dispositions. Behaviorally [situationally] oriented psychologists, on the other hand, focus on behavior directly, treating it as a sample from a wider repertoire rather than as a sign of generalized inner attributes. Unlike trait psychologists, behavioral psychologists see behavior as highly dependent on the situation in which it occurs and therefore do not assume broad generalization [of behavior] across diverse situations . . . [p. 231].

Though not new in concept, the current growth of interactionism in psychology is attributable primarily to Mischel's (1968) critique of personalism and Bowers's (1973) answering critique of situationism.

Mischel's (1968) review of the failure of traits to make valid transsituational predictions of behavior and his promotion of a conceptualization of personality based primarily on social learning theory (Mischel, 1973) served as stimulus to renewed interest in interactionism. Bowers's (1973) elegant retort to Mischel's early work suggested that Lewin's famous dictum, $B = f(P, E)$, had a basis in empirical fact. Perhaps Bowers's (1973) major contribution to the discussion of the causes of behavior was his explication of the cognitive (or, as he called it, biocognitive) view of personality, that is, the role of perception in integrating person and setting:

> An interactionist or biocognitive view denies the primacy of either traits or situations in the determination of behavior; instead, it fully recognizes that whatever main effects do emerge will depend entirely upon the particular sample of settings and individuals under consideration. . . . More specifically, interactionism argues that *situations are as much a function of the person as the person's behavior is a function of the situation* [p. 327; italics in original].

The spirited debate between these two scholars yielded new interest and insight into both personality and the etiology of situations. The former has emerged in some writings as social construction competencies (Mischel, 1973) and the latter as the outcome of naturally occurring personal interaction (Schneider, 1983).

Perhaps most importantly, organismic (i.e., dynamic) modes of thinking about behavior have emerged from the variety of subdisciplines making contributions to interactionism. McGuire (1973), an experimental social psychologist, captured the nonmechanistic characteristic of interactionism best when he noted: "Simple a-affects-b hypotheses fail to catch the complexities of parallel processing, bi-directional causality, and reverberating feedback that characterize cognitive and social organization [p. 448]." As Endler and Magnusson (1976, p. 13) noted, the most central theme emerging from the modern person/situation interaction conceptualization of behavior is its organismic perspective. This perspective, in contrast to a mechanistic one, views people and situations in continual and cyclical reciprocal interaction, causing and affecting each other. In brief, this perspective assumes that, as Bowers (1973) noted, person and situation are difficult if not impossible to separate.

What this means in practice is that researchers can no longer think about person–situation interaction as only an algebraic multiplicative term in an Analysis of Variance (ANOVA) table or moderated multiple regression formula; they must also consider the reality of natural interactions, the reality of ongoing person–person and person–environment transactions. Pervin and Lewis (1978a), for example, discuss five different ways of thinking about interaction (e.g., algebraic, additive, interdependent, descriptive, and reciprocal action–transaction). Terborg (1982) is similarly effective in explicating these various perspectives in his paper on alternative views of person × situation interaction.

Though interactionism has been concentrated in the psychology of personality (with at least three recent books of readings: Endler & Magnusson, 1976; Magnusson & Endler, 1977; Pervin & Lewis, 1978b), there appears to be growing interest on the part of other psychologists (e.g., Cronbach & Snow, 1977, on aptitude–treatment interactions in educational and training settings) and industrial–organizational psychologists (e.g., Terborg's 1977 and Schneider's 1978 work on ability–situation interactions in the work setting) to borrow concepts from the field. Of course, an original in terms of interactionist thinking in the study of leadership and work behavior is Fiedler (1967).

Vocational and Industrial Psychology

For the most part, the personality theorists doing research in, and writing about, interactional psychology have ignored the heavy concentration of interactionist ideas in vocational and industrial psychology. Of all contemporary theorizing about work, career theory has been most explicit about the nature of person–situation interaction. For example, Super's (1953) concept of a career as a person–occupation synthesis or merger, Holland's (1973) idea that career choice is a function of self-selecting a match between self and occupational environment, and Hall's (1971) view of career subidentity development as an individual behavior–organizational responsiveness–reward cycle, all make explicit the person–situation interaction idea. Indeed, Schein (1978) calls the second part of his book on careers "Career Dynamics: The Individual– Organization Interaction."

In addition, the industrial psychologists' traditional concern for employee selection and attrition are, at their basis, interactionist in perspective. Thus, the attempt in personnel selection studies to define job requirements, and to find people with the required abilities, and the work on understanding employee turnover as an outcome of person–situation incompatability are both interactionist in perspective and both at the core of industrial psychology. It is true that the better the fit of a person's ability to the requirements of a job the more likely the job will be done competently (Ghiselli, 1966, 1973; Pearlman, Schimdt, & Hunter, 1980) and the more satisfied workers are with their work situations the less likely they are to leave them (Mobley, 1977; Price, 1977; Porter & Steers, 1973).

In what follows, a framework for understanding organizational viability will emerge. This framework builds on the interactionist assumption that as a result of natural person–person interaction, person and situation are frequently integrated. How person and setting come to be relatively integrated is presented as the outcome of a cycle of attraction–selection–attrition. This cycle suggests some of the causes for person–situation integration but also suggests some potentially negative consequences for organizations if steps are not taken to prevent them. Basically the thesis is that organizations are viable when they attract, select, and retain diverse kinds of people who are able and willing to comprehend what an organization's goals should be and to behave in ways that push the organization toward the future.

Attraction and Attrition: The Human Side of Organizational Effectiveness

The attraction and attrition of employees are rarely addressed as elements in the study of organizational effectiveness. For example, Campbell, Bownas, Peterson, and Dunnette (1974) noted that:

> A neglected area of research [on organizational effectiveness] has been the effects on the organization of significant changes in the kinds of people that are entering it. The entire domain of organizational effectiveness research and organization change has a very environmentalistic point of view [p. 226].

ATTRACTION

The literature on occupational entry and organizational choice suggests that people are differentially attracted by the attributes and characteristics of particular kinds of career and work environments. Most notable of these theories is one proposed by Holland (1973).

Holland proposed that occupations can be clustered into types and that those types were useful in characterizing both people and work environments. As he put it (1976): "Vocational choice is assumed to be the result of a person's type, or patterning of types *and* the environment [p. 533]" and that "the character of an environment emanates from the types [of people] which dominate that environment [p. 534]." In essence, then, Holland proposed that career environments are characterized by the kind of people in them and that people choose to be in environments of a type similar to their own.

Hall (1976, p. 36) notes that not much research has been conducted on Holland's formulation as a model of organizational attraction. However, Schneider (1976) has noted that the apparent chasm separating occupational from organizational choice seems easy to bridge. Holland's view is that occupations can be clustered into six major categories: intellectual, artistic, social, enterprising, conventional, and realistic. It can be shown that these labels might also be used to categorize the goals of organizations. For example, YMCAs and mental hospitals have social goals; insurance companies and stock brokerages have enterprising goals; and orchestras and theaters have artistic goals. The point is not to use Holland's classification scheme as *the* means for clustering organizations but to suggest that Holland's views on career or vocational choice are applicable to organizational choice. He would suggest that the organizations people join are similar to the people who join them.

There is no research that tests this hypothesis using Holland's strategy for clustering organizations. However, similar views on person–organization fit have successfully been researched using organizational choice as the dependent variable of interest. For example, Tom (1971), building on Super's (1953) view of occupational choice as self-image implementation, showed that people's self-perceptions were more consonant with descriptions of their most-preferred organization than with their descriptions of any other organization. Vroom (1966), who based his work on an expectancy theory formulation, showed that a good fit between MBA's desired outcomes from work and their instrumentality perceptions for various organizations predicted actual organizational choice. These studies support the idea that people's own characteristics (self-image, desires) are predictive of the kinds of work settings to which they will be attracted.

Perhaps the strongest evidence for the idea that people tend to cluster into types with similar attitudes and similar behaviors is presented in the work of Owens (cf. Owens & Schoenfeldt, 1979). Owens and his colleagues have pursued the idea that, based on biodata, one can classify persons into clusters that will be useful for understanding differences in the behavior of members of different clusters. Owens and Schoenfeldt have been able to show that people in different biodata clusters differ in such ways as their responses to projective stimuli, academic achievement, major while in college, memory capacity, interests, attitudes, response to monetary incentives, leadership roles on campus, and so forth. Owens and Schoenfeldt consistently find that cluster membership is as useful in predicting individual behavior as is data about the specific individual; their data clearly suggest that people of like type behave in like ways.

The findings of Tom, Vroom, Holland, and Owens and Schoenfeldt are examples of how persons and work situations can become relatively inseparable through the operation of a similarity–attraction process not unlike the one proposed by Byrne (e.g., 1971) to explain diadic attraction. Certainly the interest inventory literature supports the idea that people with similar attributes tend to be attracted to similar occupations and careers (Crites, 1969). Indeed, the evidence from studies on employee attrition clearly indicate that when individuals are no longer attracted to organizations, they will leave them (Porter & Steers, 1973).

ATTRITION

The study of employee turnover has, in a real sense, been both the dependent variable in attraction (career and occupational choice) research and a practical problem for industrial psychologists. Operating under the assumption that high turnover is costly for organizations, industrial psychologists have studied both the causes and consequences of attrition.

The literature on turnover has been reviewed many times (e.g., Brayfield & Crockett, 1955; Mobley, 1977; Porter & Steers, 1973; Price, 1977; Vroom, 1964) and a consistent finding has been that, though there exist some complex mediators (availability of job alternatives, state of the economy [Mobley, 1977]), satisfaction and attrition are meaningfully negatively related. More specifically, Porter and Steers (1973) showed that dissatisfaction with various work and work-setting issues affect turnover:

> Sufficient evidence exists to conclude that important influences on turnover can be found in each of these categories [of concern]. That is, some of the more central variables related to turnover are organization-wide in their derivation (e.g., pay and promotion policies), while others are to be found in the immediate work group (e.g., unit size, supervision, and coworker relations). Still others are to be found in the content of the job (e.g., nature of job requirements. . . [p. 169].

These very issues, of course, are important elements in the identification of the nature of work settings vis-à-vis a career framework like Holland's (1973) or even the organizational choice model of Vroom (1966). This suggests that, from an interactionist perspective, the nature of jobs, interpersonal relationships, and reward systems that organizations display to workers must fit their needs or attrition will follow the predictable dissatisfaction that will arise (Wanous, 1980).

The interactionist perspective suggests that organizations that, on the surface, appear to be one thing yet are, in fact, different, will attract employees who have needs that do not "fit." Perhaps this is why researchers have been able to show that clarification of the nature of organizational practices and policies regarding such issues as job content and supervision practices (in what is called realistic recruitment) seems to yield decreased attrition levels (Wanous, 1980). Supporting this conclusion are the studies cited by Porter and Steers (p. 166) that reveal that people who take jobs that do not fit their tested vocational interests are more likely to quit (Boyd, 1961; Ferguson, 1958; Mayeske, 1964).

A result of the processes of career and organizational attraction and attrition might be to narrow the range of types of people in any one organization. That is, if the full range of needs and abilities is not attracted to each occupation, career, or organization, then there will be a restriction in the range of abilities and needs represented (Schneider, 1976). This restriction in range may yield "right types" (Alderfer, 1971; Argyris, 1957)—people who share common experiences and orientations. Thus, people with similar abilities and needs tend to be attracted to particular settings, and people with similar sets of positive reactions to their experiences tend to remain in those settings. Interactionist thinking would lead to the conclusion that this restriction in the range of people in particular organizations would yield organizations, occupations, and careers that were characterized by the kind of people who are attracted to them and remain in them. That is, over time, interpersonal interaction would result in people and situation becoming integrated. If this happened, it would produce relative homogeneity and a certain amount of routine in response to stimuli from the external world. It could be predicted, then, that if the larger environment was relatively turbulent then organizations would be generally unable to respond to events outside the restricted range of the people's abilities and experiences.

Fortunately this conclusion need not necessarily follow. On the one hand organizations can somewhat control their destinies by playing an active role in the selection decisions they make and, on the other hand, organizational goals can also play an important role in how narrow the range of employees becomes. In the sections that follow, the role goals play in the attraction–selection–attrition cycle is explicated and then the topic of selection is considered.

Goals

Though interactionism has a great deal to say about how person–person interaction in settings yields what those settings become, and attraction and attrition theory tells us that like types end up in similar places, none of these perspectives says anything special about what people are attracted to, interact with, and leave. That is, when the issue of interest is organizational effectiveness, it is organizations that are the focus of the discussion.

Organizations do not just exist; organizations have life cycles with beginnings—and, frequently, with endings. As Kimberly and Miles (1980) have shown, the life cycle of organizations has infrequently been addressed.

In the present chapter, organizations are conceptualized as systems that must continually evolve in order to remain viable. These systems are assumed to be activated and directed by goals. For the moment, what is important about goals is that (a) someone begins an organization with them, and (b) mostly by happenstance, as a result of natural interaction, some organizational structures and processes emerge for moving the organization to goal accomplishment. The first issue, goals and the beginnings of organizations, is important because it emphasizes the fact that all organizations have goals, clear or not. Consideration of the second topic, the relationship between goals and organizational structures and processes, will be presented as an outcome of the attraction–selection–attrition cycle.

An organization's initial goals come from the people or person in power—people who, by their decisions, can affect the levels of activity and directionality of the organization. Of course, the people in power may change, and it is sometimes thought the organization's goals will change when the people in powerful positions (president, chief executive officer) change. However, after the initial phase(s) of organizational growth it is all those defining behavioral characteristics of organizations—organizational structure, technology, management philosophy, reward systems, staffing processes—that constitute the operational definition of organizational goals; where an organization is going is not where someone *says* it is going but where its internal behavioral processes actually take it! Thus, while early in an organization's life, goal statements can energize and direct activity, over time it is the structures and processes that emerge out of the interactions of people for accomplishing the initial goal statements that sustain activity and maintain directionality. It is, then, the processes that emerge for accomplishing historical goals, not current goals, that give organizations stability and, in the face of changing environments, that may result in decay (witness the lag in time between the auto industry's goal to downsize cars and processes for actually producing smaller vehicles).

The importance of goals for the present thesis is that, as shown in Figure 2.1, they form a hub from which all organizational processes emerge. Thus, people are attracted to organizations because of organizational goals, organizations select people who appear to be able to help the organization achieve its goals, and people who achieve their own goals there will tend to remain in the organization. The role of goals in attraction, selection, and attrition is important because "the choices made at time of creation . . . powerfully shape the direction and character of organizational development [Miles, 1980, p. 431]."

The reason why early goals shape the future is because they determine the kinds of people in the organization, and it is from those people and their interaction that the form of the organization will emerge. Thus, out of the natural interactions of people making choices about the procedures required for goal accomplishment will come the early form of the organization. That early form, of course, will play an important role in who is attracted to an organization and who will remain in it.

The study of organizational effectiveness (or the more general study of organizational design), then, must pay careful attention to the attraction, selection, interactional patterns, and withdrawal processes of people. Organizational structures and processes such as technology, structure, communication, leadership, etc. (cf. Steers, 1977) are of consequence to the study of organizational

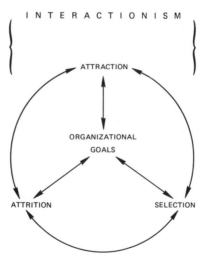

FIGURE 2.1. Cyclical relationships between organizational goals, attraction, selection, and attrition.

effectiveness because they emerge out of the interaction patterns of people (Weick, 1969) who pursue their view of organizational imperatives. In other words, organizational processes like those just named are, in a real sense, to be viewed as *dependent* variables, as well as independent variables, in the study of organizations.

Campbell *et al.* (1974) noted that the study of organizational effectiveness has proceeded from a very environmentalist point of view: The turbulent environment, size, levels of hierarchy, technology, etc., are the foci of research. The present view of organizations is radical in that it places these situational variables in their appropriate place—they are cyclically both independent and dependent variables interacting with (i.e., causing and being caused by) the types of people who are attracted to and retained by organizations. The present view of organizations, then, is based on the assumption that because people's behavior determines organizational behavior, the important questions of interest in studying organizational effectiveness have to do with understanding the cycles of *goal definition* → *organizational design* → *attraction* → *selection* → *attrition* → *comprehension* → *goal definition* that characterize a particular organization. It can be predicted that the clearer an organization is about the importance of monitoring organizational imperatives and setting in motion processes for appropriate goal definition and coping with change, the more viable the organization will be. The way organizations can make this happen is by ensuring that they attract, select, and retain people who will actually engage in these future-oriented kinds of behaviors. Consideration of the role of personnel selection as a determinant of the kinds of people in organizations will reveal the importance of these issues for organizational viability.

Selection

Beginning with their relatively dramatic success during World War I, industrial psychologists have evolved a technology for predicting individual effectiveness at work. This technology builds on two major suppositions:

1. The best predictor of future performance is past performance.
2. Ability to learn and/or do a job is predictable based on pre-job assessments of task-relevant personal attributes.

Personnel selection is the embodiment of the functionalist tradition in psychology: concern for the purpose, or function, of behavior, and belief in individual differences. In a real sense, Darwin's theory of adaptation and effectiveness is the philosophical basis for modern personnel selection, especially through the influence of Galton and Spearman in England and James McKeen Cattell in the United States (Boring, 1950). These men believed in individuals as the locus of behavior and that some individuals were more fit than others for survival and adaptation.

Without getting into the issue of heredity versus environment (both Galton and Spearman did), it seems clear that the personnel selection approach to the prediction of individual behavior at work or school has been useful. Biographical information blanks and interviews have been used very successfully to make predictions for job incumbents as different as clerks and managers (Schneider, 1976), and aptitude testing has been shown effective for jobs like accounting, insurance sales, and bank tellers (Ghiselli, 1966).

A major question concerning personnel selection has always been the generalizability of predictors from setting to setting for the "same" job. Thus, although Ghiselli (1966, 1973) was able to show reliable predictions of job performance for the same jobs in different settings (and using different measures of similar job-related aptitudes), sufficiently discrepant results in the literature and Equal Employment Opportunity Commission regulations led to the admonition to "revalidate in each new setting."

Recently Schmidt and his colleagues (cf. Pearlman et al., 1980; Schmidt & Hunter, 1977; Schmidt, Hunter, & Pearlman, 1982) have developed an algorithm for estimating the generalizability of validity of predictors across settings. The algorithm takes into account differences in validity coefficients from setting to setting, attributing those differences to a number of sources of nonrandom error. For example, in a recent effort, they (Pearlman et al., 1980) showed that for 32 distributions of correlations resulting from validity studies of 10 types of aptitude tests for the prediction of clerical performance, about 75% of the variance in validity coefficients in each of the 32 distributions was accountable for by test and criterion unreliability effects, range restrictions effects, and sampling error. These findings suggest that there is relatively little situational specificity to the validity of tests—that *measurement* effects, not situational differences, account for differences in validity coefficients. In the words of the authors (Pearlman et al., 1980, p. 399):

> The results of this study . . . cast serious doubt on the traditional belief that employment test validities are situationally specific. In our judgment, these combined findings justify the conclusion that situational specificity is largely an illusion created by statistical artifacts.

In other words, clerical aptitude tests are accurate predictors of clerical performance regardless of the situation in which the tests are used. What are the implications of these findings for organizational effectiveness?

One interpretation of these data is that one organization will be more effective than another if it used appropriate aptitude tests as a basis for selecting new employees. This conclusion *may* be true but it is not necessarily true.

What can be concluded is that an organization that uses appropriate tests will probably be more effective than it was when it used no tests (Taylor & Russell, 1939).

A more sophisticated question about the role of selection in organizational effectiveness would ask how well a particular selection system meets the goals set for it and whether those goals, in turn, move the organization to organizational level goal accomplishment and continued viability.

Professionally developed selection systems do assess the extent to which particular predictors are valid for job performance. Indeed an organization that uses professionally developed selection systems will have a large number of predictors, a few for each of the differentiable jobs on which performance is thought to be important for the organization as a whole. It is important to know, however, that predictors are thought to be useful when they are accurate for predicting job performance according to current standards of performance effectiveness. That is, the aim of all personnel selection programs is the prediction of who will be able to perform on jobs as they currently exist (Schneider, 1976). At the level of everyday operatives (clerical personnel, bank tellers, machinists, and so on) this might be slightly risky but at the managerial level this may be very dangerous. This may be dangerous because of the *changing* nature of the world with which many managers are forced to deal and because of the attraction–attrition issues discussed earlier.

The latter is meant to indicate that the processes in organizations for goal accomplishment emerge from the naturally occurring interactions of people. Sometimes, however, early decisions about goal accomplishment are incorrect and sometimes decisions that were correct at one point in time fail to fit newer realities. A major issue for organizations, then, is the comprehension of newer realities and selecting appropriate strategies for dealing with them.

If organizations do not have people who can comprehend new realities and make appropriate strategic decisions for redirecting organizational energies, they will experience what Argyris (1976) calls "dry rot." Dry rot, according to Argyris, refers to the tendency of organizations over time to become increasingly unresponsive to signals from the larger environment that change is necessary. Organizations, he notes, tend to attract and retain managerial people who are "right-types," that is, people who have similar comprehensions, similar experiences, and similar reactions. This very similarity yields stability but also, perhaps decay.

Little is known in industrial psychology about the individual attributes associated with the motivation to attend to the organization's larger environments or the ability to accurately comprehend them. Certainly it is too easy to fall back on either March and Simon's (1958) "bounded rationality" view of decision makers or the more contemporary deterministic conceptualizations suggesting that chief executive officers (and other decision-makers) have essentially no discretion over the direction their organizations take nor their level of activation (Aldrich, 1979; Pfeffer & Salancik, 1978). These views make it sound like organizations, not people, make decisions or that environments, not the *people* in those environments, structure options for organizational decision-makers. At its core, however, the viable organization will always have people who can comprehend the nature of the relationship between their organization and the larger environment and carry out the process of goal redefinition so essential to the continued viability of the organization.

This suggests the necessity for organizations to have managers who are boundary spanners (Adams, 1976; Thompson, 1967), people who are the focus of organization–environment interaction. It is people who occupy these roles who are in the best position to comprehend new realities and the necessity for the organization to redirect its energies. It is people who have comprehension competency, the ability to make sense out of the larger environment, that organizations must attract, select, and retain. These are the kinds of individuals who should be willing and able to provide information to continually lead others to question their comprehension of the imperatives of the organization and to avoid groupthink (Janis, 1972).

An analogy to Janis's (1972) groupthink construct will serve to clarify the current conceptualization. Janis showed that decision-making groups reveal six major defects that contribute to their failure to solve problems adequately (Janis, 1972, p. 10):

1. The group's discussions tend to be limited to only a few possibilities.
2. The group fails to examine the nonobvious risks and drawbacks associated with an early decision preferred by a majority of the members.
3. The members avoid decisions that are initially evaluated as unsatisfactory by the majority of the group.
4. Members make little or no attempt to obtain expert information about the costs and benefits to be expected from alternative courses of action.
5. The group reacts to factual information and input from experts, the mass media, and outside critics by selectively perceiving what they want to.
6. The members spend too little time discussing all the ways the chosen action may be hindered or sabotaged.

Janis assumed that these six defects result from groupthink but that they "can arise from other forms of human stupidity as well—erroneous intelligence, information overload, fatigue, blinding prejudice, and ignorance [p. 11]."

The ideas presented in this chapter suggest that these defects will have a tendency to emerge in organizations as a result of the naturally occurring interaction patterns of similar people. That is, through a natural cycle of attraction, selection, and attrition, groupthink and inertia is more likely;

groupthink and inertia, then, are interpretable as outcomes of the process of the emergence of organizations. It can be predicted that unless organizations consciously adopt strategies for avoiding inertia, they may suffer from the kinds of deficient decision making that resulted in the Bay of Pigs fiasco. Janis suggests some potential case studies of organizational decisions that might help illustrate the phenomenon: Grunenthal Chemie, the German manufacturer of Thalidomide, which ignored reports regarding birth defects arising from use of the drug by pregnant women; Ford Motor Company and the Edsel; and so forth.

Janis's prescriptions for avoiding groupthink fit well with the ideas presented earlier on comprehension of the larger environment by boundary-spanners and they are noted in the following (Janis, 1972, pp. 209–211):

1. Each member of a decision-making group must be required to play the role of critic, and the leader must be accepting of criticism so that she or he serves as a role model.
2. Leaders should delegate responsibility to policymaking groups without stating preferences for particular outcomes. An atmosphere of open inquiry and impartiality is more likely, then, to prevail.
3. Organizations should have a policy of establishing several independent policy-planning groups to work on the same policy question, each carrying out its deliberations under a different leader.

The dilemma for organizations, of course, is how to accomplish these prescriptions in the context of the push to "like-types." That is, though Janis' prescriptions appear difficult enough to implement when only the group phenomenon exists, they become more problematic when one considers the additional inertia resulting from the attraction–selection–attrition cycle. One questions the possibility of finding people who can meet these kinds of demands, people who are psychologically healthy and mature enough to withstand pressures to conformity. Fortunately, as will be noted in more detail later, the picture is not totally bleak. It is not totally bleak for three important reasons: (a) personnel selection systems in most organizations ensure the selection of somewhat different kinds of people because most organizations contain many different kinds of jobs with different kinds of requirements; (b) managers as a group tend to be not quite so narrow-minded and blind to the future as the preceding suggests; and (c) the natural tendency for organizations to be differentiated by function results in at least some confrontation when decisions affecting everyone need to be made.

In what follows, the preceding three issues and others will be addressed in detail as a series of conclusions about the theoretical, methodological, and practical implications of the attraction–selection–attrition view of organizations are presented.

THEORETICAL, METHODOLOGICAL, AND PRACTICAL IMPLICATIONS

Theoretical Issues

MAJOR THEORETICAL OUTCOMES

The perspective presented here, grounded as it is in natural interaction at work, leads to thoughts on three major theoretical issues in the study of organizations: (1) the "people" element in organizational design and effectiveness; (2) organizational change; and (3) relationships to other organizational variables (e.g., structure, technology).

1. Because goals only *initially* activate and give direction to organizations, it is critical for organizations to attract, select, and retain people who, through interaction with each other and the larger environment, continually monitor that environment and use their perceptions as stimuli to direct and redirect the organization's activities. Only through constant sensing will the structures and processes that emerge in organizations be appropriate vehicles for the solution of the tasks at hand and those which may emerge in the future.

Many organizations depend on a kind of natural selection to ensure the acquisition and retention of these special kinds of people, concentrating instead on the prediction of the behavior of everyday operatives. Though such concentration provides organizations with a certain amount of diversity, most people are probably not adept at the kind of comprehension required for sensing the multiple constituencies existing in an organization's environment that require attention. Organizations can undergo potentially shattering cycles of recruitment and turnover because of misguided thinking on matching CEOs (chief executive officers) to an organization's current goal-oriented practices and procedures (or, worse, to an organization's goal *statements*) when it is the future ("future-perfect thinking," Weick, 1979) that usually receives the least attention.

Thus, emerging from the four streams of thought presented earlier (interactionism, attraction, selection, and attrition), it is clear that organizations, unless they are pushed, will tend toward stability or slow decay. Indeed, following Aldrich's (1979) concept of organizational niche, we can hypothesize that, in the absence of people who serve as sensors and goal redefiners to direct and redirect them, organizations will occupy increasingly narrow niches, constricting and constraining choices and options resulting in stability or slow decay.

A major benefit to be accomplished by attracting, selecting, and retaining "nonright-types" is the maintenance or expansion of the organization's environmental niche. Conventional marketing, lobbying, and other attempts at controlling the environment based on past successes (Child, 1972), will not be as effective as those which are relevant to the organization's future.

Fortunately, the situation for the selection of nonright-types may not be as bleak as portrayed here. For example, Campbell, Dunnette, Lawler, and Weick (1970) show that the

> construct of effective executiveship . . . includes such factors as high intelligence, good verbal skills, effective judgment in handling managerial situations, . . . and organizational skill; dispositions toward interpersonal relationships, hard work, being active, and taking risks; and temperamental qualities such as dominance, confidence, straightforwardness, low anxiety, and autonomy. Moreover, men rating high in overall success report backgrounds suggesting a kind of "life-style" of success—excellent health, scholastic and extracurricular leadership in high school and college, assumption of important responsibilities rather early in life, high ambition, and active participation in religious, charitable, or civic groups [pp. 195–196].

Though this description makes one feel less depressed about the leadership of organizations, the variables on which the executives were assessed (intelligence, dominance, high ambition, etc.) and the criteria of success (salary and/ or climbing the corporate ladder) should be viewed with some skepticism. Variables like boundary-spanning capabilities, capacity for balancing conflicting multiple constituencies, political sophistication, ability to transform perceptions into action, ability to make decisions under ambiguity, and so on were not assessed as predictors nor were the criteria of effectiveness necessarily relevant to organizational viability.

This is not meant to suggest that such issues *could not* be assessed, just that they *have not* been assessed. Clearly it is possible to design, for example, an assessment center process (e.g., Moses & Byham, 1977) for evaluating these kinds of competencies. Indeed, it might even be feasible to gather data on people that suggest the extent to which they are likely to serve as the kinds of hatchet men or other anomolies that Rickards and Freedman (1978) suggest are important for organizations.

Another possibility in the selection mode is the further development of what Latham, Saari, Pursell, and Campion (1980) call the situation interview. This interview procedure presents people with likely–critical decision situations and asks them to report their most likely behaviors. It should be noted that this kind of procedure, and the assessment center method, are clearly in keeping with the comprehension competencies idea mentioned earlier; all that is needed is the design of situations that require sense-making, boundary-spanning, and outward- and future-oriented behaviors.

At the organizational level itself, perhaps of greatest hope for avoiding sameness–stability and decay is the fact that organizations tend toward differentiation (Lawrence & Lorsch, 1967). Differentiation, or functional specialization, should yield organizations that attract, select, and retain many different kinds of people with different vantage points on the required directionality of the organization. The interactionist perspective presented here clearly suggests that the "departmental identification of executives" (Dearborn & Simon, 1958) is a sign of organizational health and not something necessarily to be changed. Parenthetically, it is also clear why loosely coupled systems (Weick, 1976) may be more effective than traditional, hierarchically controlled systems: Whenever "the system" needs to make a decision there will be (a) many critics and (b) many policymaking groups, each composed of like types but between them almost guaranteeing a complete exploration of the issues.

2. On the topic of organizational change, the present framework suggests that change will be difficult. More specifically, it can be hypothesized that the older an organization is and the more undifferentiated it has been, the more time consuming will be the change. This hypothesis follows from an "internal" view of organizations, one that emphasizes that, over time, organizations build up inertia that keeps them moving in predetermined ways down predetermined paths. Young organizations should be relatively easy to change because of the relative lack of inertia but, as they age and keep attracting, selecting and retaining like types, change should be increasingly difficult. Another way of saying this is that as organizations work themselves into increasingly tight niches, they lose degrees of freedom with respect to change. This will be especially true when an organization strives for and achieves homogenization because the entire system will tend to be composed of people of a similar sort.

We may also deduce from this developmental view of organizations that newer organizations will have higher turnover rates than older ones. This hypothesis follows from the idea that the operating processes of an organization emerge from the interacting behaviors of organizational members rather than in a fully formed version. As the systems emerge, they become more definitive, yielding on the one hand, turnover of those who do not fit but, at the same time, clearer information for potential new members to use as a basis for choice.

Note here that this principle assumes that the processes that evolve are sufficiently operational in form that they yield relatively clear specification of the organization's directionality. Without such specification, goal attainment is unknown because feedback is not possible. We can deduce, in turn, that poor goal definition yields chaos because people have a difficult time making appropriate participation choices (entry and withdrawal) (Wanous, 1980). When people make poor participation choices because of ambiguity in goal specification the result is different individuals in the same setting attaching personological meaning to organizational imperatives.

Paradoxically, it follows that organizations that have been functioning under conditions of poor or diverse goal definition and loosely coupled (Weick, 1976) or underbounded (Alderfer, 1979) organizations will be easier to change; that is, they will be easier to activate and direct. Typically, but obviously not always, these will be younger organizations. Older organizations, then, will generally have operating processes with more definition and stability. As organizational process definition is merely a reflection of people, it is the people who need to be changed if one desires a changed system.

Though early writings on organizational change, especially those coming out of the T-group movement (e.g., Bennis, Benne, & Chin, 1961), addressed change at the individual level, more recent essays conceptualize change primarily in terms of organizational subsystems (incentives, management philosophy, job design). These writings (see Alderfer, 1977, for a review) typically fail to entertain change through either attraction and attrition or individual counseling as viable alternatives (see Beer, 1980, for an exception). However, the present framework indicates that it is primarily through these kinds of people changes that organizational change will occur.

Anecdotal and some research evidence suggest that organizations can overreact to the necessity for organizational redirection by arranging for an immediate transfusion of "new blood." For example, mergers, takeovers, or the suggestions of consultants can result in the hiring of extreme nonright-types, that is, people who do not fit at all. Like mismatched blood, the host organism reacts to reject the foreign body. As Alderfer (1971) showed, antagonism, mistrust, conflict, etc. can be the result. Without legitimizing and institutionalizing the necessity for change, and having mechanisms for handling change, it can be predicted that what Alderfer found would be the norm.

These findings suggest a final thought on change: Different organizations, because they are most likely composed of different types of people, will require different change strategies. Precisely what the different types of change strategies need to be cannot now be specified, but the present framework suggests a contingency theory of change is probably a necessary feature of the change arsenal. For example, returning to Holland's (1973) categorization of careers, change efforts in enterprising occupations (e.g., stock brokerage houses) might need to be conducted differently than in more social industries (e.g., YMCAs).

3. With respect to the relationship between the present perspective and other organizational variables, the major deduction is that goals, structure, and technology, the characteristics of organizations most often thought of as providing organizational definition, are mediating or dependent variables in the present view. Thus, centralization, functional specialization, formalization, span of control, etc. are states that follow from the kinds of people who were the founders of organizations and the choices those people made about the niches they attempted to occupy and exploit as they pursued their goals. In turn, the decisions about niche (i.e., market), in large measure, determine technology

(Child, 1972). I say "in large measure" because people, through innovation, can themselves dictate the technology.

Perhaps the most interesting facet of the present framework vis-à-vis structure and technology is that the concentration on people may help explain why structure and technology have so successfully resisted efforts at conceptualization and empirical verification. Even when the larger environment of the organization is taken into account as a moderating variable, these two central issues resist clarification and the relationship between the two assumes various forms (Hickson, Pugh, & Pheysey, 1969; Mahoney & Frost, 1974). The latter authors, in particular, come closest to the present conceptualization when they show that different technologies may require different forms of activity in order to be effective. Although they concentrated on different technologies, it may be that the true issue that was underlying their findings was the type of people, that is, different kinds of *people* need to be dealt with in different ways for their units to be effective.

In summary, the present framework has resulted in a number of deductions regarding attraction to organizations, attrition from organizations, the kinds of people organizations need to select, organizational change, and the source of structure and technology.

EXPANSION OF UNDERSTANDING OF
ORGANIZATIONAL BEHAVIOR

The field of organizational behavior (OB) has emerged out of various older disciplines, primarily psychology and sociology. Pugh (1966), in an important but somewhat overlooked paper, reviewed the underpinnings of OB coming from the "individual theorists" (primarily selection researchers) and concluded that such efforts had not yielded much in the way of an understanding of organizational functioning.

This chapter attempts to fill this void by describing a framework for understanding the behavior of organizations that rests almost completely on the nature of the people in the setting. Thus, at the most fundamental level, the present framework posits that organizational behavior is understandable as the aggregate of the behavior of naturally interacting people pursuing some shared goal. The goal they share is organizational viability (that is, the maintenance of a superstructure in which their behavior is rewarded and supported). Though this is an egocentric view of the reason for organizational viability it is consistent with the person-centered focus of the chapter.

This position is important because it focuses attention on the humanness of organizations (i.e., the physiology of organizations) rather than on the structure of organizations (i.e., the anatomy of organizations) arguing that the former dictates the latter. This is true because of the developmental perspective presented earlier that suggests that the first chores of organizations are niche selection, activation, and direction that are followed by the adoption of structures and technologies for goal accomplishment. Organizational decay comes from failure to repeat this cycle continually, from a rigidity emerging out of inertia created by an attraction–selection–attrition cycle grounded in past successes rather than the demands of the future.

In essence, then, the present thoughts on effectiveness direct scholars' views to the input side of organizational design rather than to throughput as the important causative element. This should not be taken to suggest that early post-entry experiences are unimportant. It is through early, organizationally imposed and controlled, encounters with the norms of behavior in a place that newcomers diagnose their "fit" to the setting and make the kinds of judgments that predispose them to stay or leave (Wanous, 1980). These early encounters with the organization and subsequent judgments by employees about "fit" are the reasons why most turnover in organizations occurs early in the tenure of employees. The style of the organization is easily diagnosed by newcomers because of the many media through which they "get the message": formal skill training, informal education about the context by other employees, apprenticeship–mentorship, debasement experiences, and seduction (Van Maanen & Schein, 1979; Wanous, 1980).

In summary, then, the present view of behavior places great emphasis on understanding the nature of people in a setting as a first step in organizational diagnosis because all of the observed practices and procedures flow from the kind of people there.

DEFINITION OF ORGANIZATIONAL EFFECTIVENESS

Continued viability is the way effectiveness has been conceptualized throughout. The present definition of organizational effectiveness is particularly appropriate to the private sector because public sector organizations almost never "fail" in the sense of dying. The framework, however, does suggest that public sector organizations may tend to be stable as the result of inertia due to a lack of a mix of person types and the relative independence of units from one another. Thus, both the lack of the necessity for confrontation between units and the lack of across-unit career pathing can lead to homogenization within units. In brief, the less a unit's directionality is confronted the more likely it is to tend to stability.

In the present conceptualization, size and stage of development have been addressed as important issues although no actual numbers or stages have been explicated. Thus, smaller and newer organizations were thought to be less homogeneous, more easily changed, and so forth whereas larger and older organizations were viewed as stable, difficult to change, and experiencing lower turnover rates.

Research Issues

MAJOR INDICATORS (CRITERIA) OF
ORGANIZATIONAL EFFECTIVENESS

The ultimate criterion for the present concept is continued organizational viability. However, I agree with Campbell (1977) that *"the* meaning of organizational effectiveness is not a truth that is buried somewhere waiting to be discovered if only our concepts and data collection methods were good enough [p. 15]."

Rather, the present perspective is a variant of the systems view of effectiveness (i.e., it specifies the attributes of an effective organization, a priori). These attributes are the attraction, selection, and retention of people who continuously question, probe, sense, and otherwise concentrate on their organization of the future. Assessment of organizational effectiveness, then, demands data on the relative expenditure of effort–money–energy–manpower directed at attracting and retaining people whose major contribution to the organization is the push toward adaptation and change by constantly sensing and questioning the long-term viability of the organization's environmental niche. Subordinate to these data, but also necessary, are data concerning the attraction, selection, and attrition of operatives, those who are necessary to the maintenance and direction of the organization.

COMPARATIVE RESEARCH IMPLICATIONS

The major implication of accepting a systems, compared to a goal-oriented, view of organizational effectiveness is that the accomplishment of specific goals is important; activation, maintenance, and directionality toward continued viability are the processes that require assessment. Thus, though organizations can achieve specific goals, the range of potential goals is so great as to make comparative research unfeasible. Indeed, Hannan and Freeman (1977) argue forcefully that comparative research is at best problematic and at worst not possible, especially with goal-accomplishment perspectives on effectiveness.

The present perspective, being a systems view, provides for a relativistic vantage point regarding commitment of organizational resources to self-assessment and possible redirection and change. As such, the position avoids some of the problems mentioned by Hannan and Freeman (1977). For example, Hannan and Freeman conceptualize the organizational survival approach only in terms of the continued ability of a system to extract resources from the larger environment whereas the present view proposes that it is the relative resources *spent* on the environment (i.e., on assessing the nature of the environment), not the resources acquired from the environment, that is important for long-term survival.

One issue touched on by Hannan and Freeman, but not thoroughly explored, concerns the question of time. In the present framework, time is an important variable both from a developmental perspective and an assessment perspective. As the former issue has already been addressed in some detail, additional discussion is not required here.

However, the latter issue is important because one form of comparative research, ipsative research, requires time. Here I refer to that class of designs generically called time series (Cook & Campbell, 1979) in which "subjects" serve as their own controls. Thus, an index of continued viability that follows from the ideas presented here is that effective organizations will continuously invest resources in generating data about what the future requires. When, over time, an organization is found to decrease investments in studying the utility and possibility of change, this should signal impending stability at best, and possibly decay. It would seem essential for organizations to self-monitor their relative investments in assessing the need for change or the relative (although not absolute) amounts may decrease over time, indexing future problems.

MAJOR METHODOLOGICAL ISSUES

The really interesting methodological issues to be grappled with concern organizational development questions. What kinds of people interacting with each other yield which forms of organization? What kinds of entrepreneurs select which kinds of niches? What kinds of organizations attract and/or lose which kinds of people? How does the choice of a particular market niche eventually impact technology and structure? Can "comprehenders" and "sense-makers" (Weick, 1969, 1979) impact organizational direction? Though human developmental research has been a major focus in the study of individuals, a similar emphasis has not been noticeable in the field of organization design (Kimberly & Miles, 1980). Yet it is clear that organizations do grow and develop and that this occurs as a consequence of variables similar to those in individual development: parentage, location, handicaps, etc. And, as with individuals, change does not cease, be it described as decline or growth.

A second important issue, this one raised when discussing the work of Holland (1973) and Schmidt (e.g., Pearlman et al., 1980), concerns the relative contribution of selection (both self and organizational) to organizational effectiveness. Especially with respect to selection by organizations, this kind of research has been ipsative in nature, that is, it has been known for 40 years that an organization can improve itself by making wiser selection decisions (Taylor & Russell, 1939). What we still do not know, however, is whether traditional selection procedures make one organization better than another. It was hypothesized earlier that the selection and retention of people with comprehension competency who will push for change should be reflected in long-term organizational viability but no research seems to exist on this issue.

It was shown earlier that a concentration on the past, that is, on selecting the kinds of managers who have achieved standard criteria of success in the past, may not be a useful focus for selection. One alternative, of course, is to concentrate on the kinds of people who have been successful in the past *at redirecting the organization so that it remains viable in the future.* This slight change in the criterion of interest in selecting managerial personnel would be a way of integrating the more personnel-oriented traditional Industrial–Organizational Psychology (I/O) ideas with contemporary thinking on organizational design and effectiveness.

Methodologically, a more difficult approach would incorporate ideas from content and synthetic validation studies (e.g., Guion, 1978). This approach, used effectively by human factors design people, predicts to the future by making judgments about the kinds of attributes people will need, for example, to operate a piece of machinery *prior to the time the machine is built.* Based on these estimates, selection procedures are designed that are *judged* to be predictive; Schneider (1976) has, indeed, called the process "judgmental validity." It was suggested earlier that assessment centers or situation interviews (Latham *et al.,* 1980) may be employed as vehicles for making these kinds of predictions about the kinds of people the managers of the future will need to be.

Finally, the issue of person–situation interaction as a methodological issue was addressed. Specifically it was noted that people interact with each other in more ways than $A \times B$ algebraic interactions. Indeed, the idea of reciprocal interaction as the fundamental building block in the design of organizations was a major theoretical thrust.

Practical Issues

PRESCRIPTIONS OR GUIDELINES

The framework has been quite prescriptive or normative in nature, indicating in a straightforward way that decay may follow inertia that follows from an *attraction → selection → attrition* cycle that naturally emerges in organizations and that naturally results in stability due to like types interacting with each other. These like-types will cease to be effective unless strong measures (a la Janis) are taken to combat what was called "dry rot."

A counterintuitive outcome of this approach was to suggest that the three forces of attraction, selection, and attrition are not necessarily of value to organizations at the managerial level because they depend, in one way or another, on evaluating the correlates of past effectiveness; what organizations require for continued viability is assessment of what the future manager may require. In this vein it was suggested that organizational effectiveness might be indexed by the investment an organization makes in constantly assessing its future requirements for viability.

It should be noted that this line of thinking could lead to the erroneous conclusion that the best predictor of future behavior is *not* past behavior. I would argue that we can indeed predict future behavior based on past behavior but the kind of future behavior that needs to be predicted may be different than any past behaviors that have been displayed. The challenge will be to isolate those *combinations* of past behavior that are predictive of future, new behaviors. The problem of selecting astronauts comes to mind.

DIAGNOSTIC TOOLS

It follows from the preceding that organizations must monitor their relative investments in attracting, selecting, and retaining people whose primary responsibility is to question, probe, sense, investigate, translate, and otherwise assess the need for and the procedures for change.

One not-so-obvious diagnostic technique of use to organizations would be to monitor newcomers' perceptions of the organization, its goals and its future orientation. Though ontogeny may not recapitulate phylogeny at work, newcomers, who need and seek cues and clues about organizational norms and values (Van Maanen, 1976), may be an excellent source of feedback on the current state of a setting. In a real sense, the socialization of newcomers in an organization may be an accurate mirror of the organization's goals and direction; newcomers will be sensitive to where current practices and procedures suggest the organization is going because they need this kind of information as a basis for their own adjustment process. In brief, if one desires information about an organization's activation, maintenance, and directionality, ask a newcomer!

This also suggests that the practice of asking current employees, regardless of how long they have been in the organization, to report on organizational practices and procedures may not be as useful as previously thought. Thus, rarely is tenure considered when evaluating survey responses even though Katz (1980) has clearly shown the effects of tenure on such responses:

> When employees continue to work at their same job positions for extended periods of time and begin to adapt to such long-term tenure, their principal concerns may gradually shift toward the consolidation and maintenance of their work environments. . . . One often hears the almost rote response of "leave us alone; we're doing just fine [p. 117]."

It is this orientation toward the familiar, the usual, the typical among established employees that must be monitored *and* compared to new employees.

TRADE-OFFS, DILEMMAS, AND DYSFUNCTIONAL CONSEQUENCES

The major issue fitting this broad label is the nonright-type. In the present framework, nonright-types assume a central role in organizational effectiveness, yet that very role will create suspicion, conflict, strain, ambiguity, and an obvious power struggle between the forces of stability and the forces of change (Alderfer, 1971).

Purposefully creating conflict in organizations may depart from the usual models of organizational effectiveness, but those models fail to recognize that management is a continual juggling act and that it is only when conflict over the directionality of organizational efforts ceases to exist that organizational decay will occur. Both the forces for stability and the forces for change must exist in uneasy balance for organizations to remain viable.

The stabilizing influence of long-tenured employees maintains directionality as does the keel of a sailboat. However, in the face of severe storms or, better, in the anticipation of storms, some changes in direction are required. Navigating organizational waters, then, requires people with both kinds of orientations.

It is when the uneasy balance of these forces is addressed that more contemporary theories and methods of organizational development become useful. It is not that implementation of organization development activities by themselves will make organizations effective, but such activities can yield strategies for listening, that is, for changers and maintainers to "hear" each other so that their continued behavior is guided by potentially disconforming ideas and evidence (Beer, 1980).

Naturally, organizations will pay the sensors and forces for change more money because they are rare, and thus valuable, people. Differentials in pay between people like CEOs and operatives, however, are rarely a source of friction in organizations as long as the organization remains viable; operatives typically acknowledge the utility and requirements for such people.

Of more concern will be the next level in the organization, say vice president. At this level of specialization, there may be conflict over having the chief executive officer's "ear," and it is particularly important for him or her to facilitate interchange among those at this level and between each of them and him or herself.

Great emphasis has been placed on the managerial role, especially those who are externally oriented comprehenders of the environment for, as noted, I believe that investing in such people is the true mark of the effective organization. I believe that people, not organizations, make decisions; that people *are* organizations; that organizations are differentially activated, directed, and maintained as a function of the nature of the people they attract, select, and retain; and, that over time organizations have a tendency to become internally homogenous and externally inflexible unless steps are taken to create the kind of tension necessary for appropriate decision making.

ACKNOWLEDGMENTS

I greatly benefitted from discussions with, and comments from, my colleagues Joel Aronoff, Larry Foster, Gareth Jones, Arnon Reichers, Neal Schmitt, John Wanous, and the editors of this volume, Kim Cameron and Dave Whetten. All errors of interpretation and logic are mine as I did not always listen to their good advice.

REFERENCES

Adams, J. S. The structure and dynamics of behavior in organizational boundary roles. In M. D. Dunnette (Ed.), *Handbook of industrial and organizational psychology*. Chicago: Rand McNally, 1976.

Alderfer, C. P. Effect of individual, group, and intergroup relations on attitudes towards a management development program. *Journal of Applied Psychology*, 1971, 55, 302–311.

Alderfer, C. P. Organization development. In *Annual review of psychology*. Palo Alto, Calif.: Annual Reviews, 1977.

Alderfer, C. P. Consulting to underbounded systems. In C. P. Alderfer & C. L. Cooper (Eds.), *Advances in experiential social processes* (Vol. 2). New York: Wiley, 1979.

Aldrich, H. E. *Organizations and environments*. Englewood Cliffs, N.J.: Prentice-Hall, 1979.

Argyris, C. Some problems in conceptualizing organizational climate: A case study of a bank. *Administrative Science Quarterly*, 1957, 2, 501–520.

Argyris, C. Problems and new directions for industrial psychology. In M. D. Dunnette (Ed.), *Handbook of industrial and organizational psychology*. Chicago: Rand McNally, 1976.

Beer, M. *Organization change and development: A systems view*. Santa Monica, Calif.: Goodyear, 1980.

Bennis, W. G., Benne, K. D., & Chin, R. (Eds.). *The planning of change: Readings in the applied behavioral sciences*. New York: Holt, Rinehart and Winston, 1961.

Boring, E. G. *History of experimental psychology* (2nd ed.). New York: Appleton-Century, 1950.

Bowers, K. S. Situationism in psychology: An analysis and critique. *Psychological Review*, 1973, 80, 307–336.

Boyd, J. B. Interests of engineers related to turnover, selection and management. *Journal of Applied Psychology*, 1961, 45, 143–149.

Brayfield, A. H., & Crockett, W. H. Employee attitudes and employee performance. *Psychological Bulletin*, 1955, 52, 596–424.

Byrne, D. *The attraction paradigm*. New York: Academic Press, 1971.

Campbell, J. P. On the nature of organizational effectiveness. In P. S. Goodman & J. M. Pennings (Eds.), *New perspectives on organizational effectiveness*. San Francisco: Jossey-Bass, 1977.

Campbell, J. P., Bownas, D. A., Peterson, N. G., & Dunnette, M. D. *The measurement of organizational effectiveness*. San Diego, Calif.: Navy Personnel Research and Development Center, 1974.

Campbell, J. P., Dunnette, M. D., Lawler, E. E., III, & Weick, K. E., Jr. *Managerial behavior, performance, and effectiveness*. New York: McGraw-Hill, 1970.

Child, J. Organization structure, environment and performance: The role of strategic choice. *Sociology*, 1972, 6, 1–22.

Cook, T. D., & Campbell, D. T. *Quasi-experimentation: Design and analysis issues for field settings*. Chicago: Rand McNally, 1979.

Crites, J. O. *Vocational psychology*. New York: McGraw-Hill, 1969.

Cronbach, L. J., & Snow, R. E. *Aptitudes and instructional methods: A handbook for research on interactions*. New York: Irvington, 1977.

Dearborn, D. C., & Simon, H. A. Selective perception: A note on the departmental identification of executives. *Sociometry*, 1958, 21, 140–144.

Endler, N. S., & Magnusson, D. (Eds.), *Interactional psychology and personality*. New York: Hemisphere, 1976.

Ferguson, L. W. Life insurance interests, ability and termination of employment. *Personnel Psychology*, 1958, 11, 189–193.

Fiedler, F. E. *A theory of leadership effectiveness*. New York: McGraw-Hill, 1967.

Ghiselli, E. E. *The validity of occupational aptitude tests*. New York: Wiley, 1966.

Ghiselli, E. E. The validity of aptitude tests in personnel selection. *Personnel Psychology*, 1973, *26*, 461–478.

Guion, R. M. Content validity in moderation: Cautions concerning fairness. *Personnel Psychology*, 1978, *31*, 205–213.

Hall, D. T. A theoretical model of career subidentity development in organizational settings. *Organizational Behavior and Human Performance*, 1971, *6*, 50–76.

Hall, D. T. *Careers in organizations*. Pacific Palisades, Calif.: Goodyear, 1976.

Hannan, M. T. and Freeman, J. Obstacles to comparative organizational studies. In P. S. Goodman & J. M. Pennings (Eds.), *New perspectives on organizational effectiveness*. San Francisco: Jossey-Bass, 1977.

Hickson, D. J., Pugh, D. S., & Pheysey, D. C. Operations technology and organizational structure: An empirical reappraisal. *Administrative Science Quarterly*, 1969, *14*, 378–397.

Holland, J. L. *The psychology of vocational choice* (rev. ed.). Waltham, Mass.: Blaisdell, 1973.

Holland, J. L. Vocational preferences. In M. D. Dunnette (Ed.), *Handbook of industrial and organizational psychology*. Chicago: Rand McNally, 1976.

Janis, I. L. *Victims of groupthink*. Boston: Houghton-Mifflin, 1972.

Katz, R. Time and work: Toward an integrative perspective. In B. Staw & L. L. Cummings (Eds.), *Research in organizational behavior* (Vol. 2). Greenwich, Conn.: JAI Press, 1980.

Kimberly, J. R. and Miles, R. H. (Eds.). *The organizational life cycle*. San Francisco: Jossey-Bass, 1980.

Latham, G. P., Saari, L. M., Pursell, E. D., & Campion, M. A. The situational interview. *Journal of Applied Psychology*, 1980, *65*, 422–427.

Lawrence, P. R., & Lorsch, J. W. *Organizations and environments*. Boston, Mass.: Division of Research, Harvard Business School, 1967.

McGuire, W. J. The Yin and Yang of progress in social psychology: Seven Koan. *Journal of Personality and Social Psychology*, 1973, *26*, 446–456.

Magnusson, D., & Endler, N. S. (Eds.). *Personality at the crossroads: Current issues in interactional psychology*. Hillsdale, N.J.: Erlbaum, 1977.

Mahoney, T., & Frost, P. The role of technology in models of organizational effectiveness. *Organizational Behavior and Human Performance*, 1974, *11*, 122–138.

March, J. G., & Simon, H. A. *Organizations*. New York: Wiley, 1958.

Mayeske, G. W. The validity of Kuder Preference Record scores in predicting forester turnover and advancement. *Personnel Psychology* 1964, *17*, 207–210.

Miles, R. H. Findings and implications of organizational life cycle: A commencement. In J. R. Kimberly & R. H. Miles (Eds.), *The organizational life cycle*. San Francisco: Jossey-Bass, 1980.

Mischel, W. *Personality and assessment*. New York: Wiley, 1968.

Mischel, W. Toward a cognitive social learning reconceptualization of personality. *Psychological Review*, 1973, *80*, 252–283.

Mischel, W., Jeffery, K. M., & Patterson, C. J. The layman's use of trait and behavioral information to predict behavior. *Journal of Research in Personality*, 1974, *8*, 231–242.

Mobley, W. H. Intermediate linkages in the relationships between job satisfaction and employee turnover. *Journal of Applied Psychology*, 1977, *62*, 237–240.

Moses, J. L., & Byham, W. C. (Eds.). *Applying the assessment center method*. New York: Pergamon, 1977.

Owens, W. A., & Schoenfeldt, L. F. Toward a classification of persons. *Journal of Applied Psychology Monograph*, 1979, *65*, 569–607.

Pearlman, K., Schmidt, F. L., & Hunter, J. E. Validity generalization results for tests used to predict job proficiency and training success in clerical occupations. *Journal of Applied Psychology*, 1980, *65*, 373–406.

Pervin, L. A., & Lewis, M. (Eds.). *Perspectives in interactional psychology.* New York: Plenum, 1978. (a)

Pervin, L. A., & Lewis, M. Overview of the internal–external issue. In L. A. Pervin & M. Lewis (Eds.), *Perspectives in interactional psychology.* New York: Plenum, 1978. (b)

Pfeffer, J., & Salancik, G. *The external control of organizations: A resource dependence perspective.* New York: Harper & Row, 1978.

Porter, L. W., & Steers, R. M. Organizational, work and personal factors in employee turnover and absenteeism. *Psychological Bulletin,* 1973, *80,* 151–176.

Price, J. L. *The study of turnover.* Ames: Iowa State University Press, 1977.

Pugh, D. Modern organizational theory: A psychological and sociological study. *Psychological Bulletin,* 1966, *66,* 235–251.

Rickards, T., & Freedman, B. L. Procedures for managers in idea-deficient situations: Examination of brainstorming approaches. *Journal of Management Studies,* 1978, *15,* 43–55.

Schein, E. H. *Career dynamics: Matching individual and organizational needs.* Reading, Mass.: Addison-Wesley, 1978.

Schmidt, F. L., & Hunter, J. E. Development of a general solution to the problem of validity generalization. *Journal of Applied Psychology,* 1977, *62,* 529–540.

Schmidt, F. L., Hunter, J. E., & Pearlman, K. Task differences as moderators of aptitude test validity in selection: A red herring. *Journal of Applied Psychology,* 1981, *66,* 166–185.

Schneider, B. *Staffing organizations.* Pacific Palisade, Calif.: Goodyear, 1976.

Schneider, B. Person–situation selection: A review of some ability-situation interaction research. *Personnel Psychology,* 1978, *31,* 281–297.

Schneider, B. Work climates: An interactionist perspective. In N. W. Feimer & E. S. Geller (Eds.), *Environmental psychology: Directions and perspectives.* New York: Praeger, 1983.

Steers, R. M. *Organizational effectiveness: A behavioral view.* Santa Monica, Calif.: Goodyear, 1977.

Super, D. E. A theory of vocational development. *American Psychologist,* 1953, *8,* 185–190.

Taylor, H. C., & Russell, J. T. The relationship of validity coefficients to the practical effectiveness of tests in selection: Discussion of tables. *Journal of Applied Psychology,* 1939, *23,* 565–578.

Terborg, J. R. Validation and extension of an individual differences model of work performance. *Organizational Behavior and Human Performance,* 1977, *18,* 188–216.

Terborg, J. R. Interactional psychology and research on human behavior in organizations. *Academy of Management Review,* 1981, *6,* 569–576.

Thompson, J. D. *Organizations in action.* New York: McGraw-Hill, 1967.

Tom, V. R. The role of personality and organizational images in the recruiting process. *Organizational Behavior and Human Performance,* 1971, *6,* 573–592.

Van Maanen, J. Breaking in: Socialization at work. In R. Dubin (Ed.), *Handbook of work, organization, and society.* Chicago: Rand McNally, 1976.

Van Maanen, J., & Schein, E. H. Toward a theory of organizational socialization. In B. Staw (Ed.), *Research in organizational behavior* (Vol. 1). Greenwich, Conn.: JAI Press, 1979.

Vroom, V. H. *Work and motivation.* New York: Wiley, 1964.

Vroom, V. H. Organizational choice: A study of pre- and post-decision processes. *Organizational Behavior and Human Performance,* 1966, *1,* 212–226.

Wanous, J. P. *Organizational entry: Recruitment, selection, and socialization of newcomers.* Reading, Mass.: Addison-Wesley, 1980.

Weick, K. E. *The social psychology of organizing.* Reading, Mass.: Addison-Wesley, 1969.

Weick, K. E. Educational organizations as loosely coupled systems. *Administrative Science Quarterly,* 1976, *21,* 1–19.

Weick, K. E. *The social psychology of organizing* (2nd ed.). Reading, Mass.: Addison-Wesley, 1979.

STANLEY E. SEASHORE

A Framework for an Integrated Model of Organizational Effectiveness[1]

This chapter will display a rather comprehensive schema designed to show the several classes of criteria that may be taken into account in assessing organizational effectiveness. To avoid producing another incoherent laundry list of effectiveness indicators, the schema will attempt to acknowledge the contributions of three distinctive theoretical approaches, and will leave the door open to accommodate the extensions and variations that will certainly arise. The aim is not to produce a neat, unified theory about, or a new definition of, the elusive concept of effectiveness, but rather to produce a framework that will aid coherent thought and judicious action by those who are compelled by their leadership roles or their research tasks to choose a definition of effectiveness that suits their unique purposes.

The orientation taken is, in part, sociological. That is, it will treat the symbiotic relationships between an organization and its environment of organized and unorganized constituencies. *Constituents* are persons acting in their own interest or as representatives of others and having some form of interdependency with the focal organization of study. In this inclusive sense, they are "members" of the organization with needs—their own and of others—to be fulfilled.

[1]The preparation of this chapter has been aided by fiscal support from the U.S. Army Research Institute under grant number MDA 903-78-G-03.

ORGANIZATIONAL EFFECTIVENESS
A Comparison of Multiple Models

The orientation taken is, in part, that derived from general systems theory as applied to human organizations. It will be assumed that human organizations share certain universal characteristics of behaving entities, with internally determined capacities and priorities that control their responsiveness to environmental factors.

The orientation is, in part, individualistic and psychological. That is, organizations come into being and are maintained by the activities of persons who are not only members of the organization but simultaneously are persons with attributes and self-identifications that are not derived from nor wholly integrated with their organization. This notion of "partial inclusion" is crucial, for it locates and defines a boundary region of organizations that must be taken into account.

The orientation is, in part, *cybernetic,* by which we mean the analysis of systems for selective use of information in the choice and decision-making activities of organizations to the ends of internal direction and control and of external accommodations.

The orientation is unmistakably practical. For persons in constituency roles to choose behaviors that approximate an optimization of those roles, they must continually evaluate the effectiveness of the focal organization and assess its likely future effectiveness. Such evaluations require the selection of effectiveness criteria that are pertinent to the immediate and longer-run interests of the constituency.

This chapter will have three parts. The first will outline a way to merge considerations of effectiveness from three perspectives (i.e., from the perspectives of systemic integrity, goal attainment, and decision-making competence). The second part will comment on the concept of "integration." The final pages will discuss some properties of advantages and limitations in this approach to the assessment of organizational effectiveness.

MERGING CONTEMPORARY THEORIES

Many people distinguish three main approaches to the understanding of organizational effectiveness. One views an organization as a natural system having its own survival and growth requirements and its own dynamics of activity and change. Another views the organization as a contrived instrument for attainment of specified short-run goals. A third approach treats the organization as an information-processing and decision-making entity, with a focus on factors of organizational control and direction. These are loosely labeled the *natural system model,* and *goal model,* and the *decision-process model.* We will argue that they are not incompatible and can be treated jointly within a common linking framework.

The approaches are seemingly conflicting in a number of ways. They take different views about the nature and origin of organizational purposes or goals. They take different views of the nature of the relationships between an organization and its environment. They require, for application, measurement of unlike aspects of organizational performances and unlike models for their interpretations.

The Natural System Model

The core image of an organization in the natural system approach is that of an intact behaving entity, autonomous except for interdependence with an environment in the form of information and energy exchanges. A source of this concept is a general systems theory, which seeks equivalencies across an array of behaving systems ranging from the single biological cell to the whole of complex societies. The derivation relevant to formal human work organizations has the name *open systems theory*. The central propositions of this theory are concerned with system boundaries, differentiation and integration of the subsystems that are "parts" of the focal system, input–transformation–output processes, boundary transactions, and system maintenance processes. There exist several good statements and elaborations of this theory, notably those of Baker (1973), Georgopoulos and Cooke (1979), and of Katz and Kahn (1978).

There are a number of variants on these central themes, and illustrative examples are warranted. Georgopoulos has worked out a scheme for assessment and description of work organizations based on the idea that all organizations share a small number of "basic problems" that must be "continuously solved" (i.e., managed) for the organization to be effective; though these problems relate to work efficiency and output, all of them, such as coordination, and strain control, plainly derive from an image of the organization as a self-maintaining system in dynamic equilibrium within an environment. J. G. Miller (1978) regards formal organizations to be fundamentally goalless in the sense that the systemic properties and processes are to be assessed, not narrowly with reference to outputs or end states, but more generally with reference to system equilibrium and maintenance.

There is some empirical support for such a view; for example, a factorial analysis of a roster of effectiveness indicators (chosen largely by top managers of the multiunit firm) gave factors that were, in the main, interpretable as system maintenance and adaptivity factors rather than goal achievement factors (Seashore & Yuchtman, 1967). Other variants on the natural system model incorporate the goal model in the sense that the focus is on optimizing system–environment relationships: "effectiveness" implies the output of goods or services to the environment of kinds and amounts that assure continuing and adequate inputs to the system.

The natural system model forces attention to certain aspects of organizational effectiveness that, until recently, were largely overlooked or undervalued:

1. The model suggests that effectiveness should be described and evaluated with reference to all attributes of the system that have some significant function in its adaptation, maintenance, and transformation processes.
2. There is a strong implication that effectiveness indicators must be treated as *intact sets*, not as indicators to be inherently and independently valued.
3. The model allows the idea that the meaning of a given indicator may be contingent in the sense that it may have different, or even opposite, value implications in different contexts.
4. Finally, the model moderates the distinction between "outcome" variables, on the one hand, and "causal" variables, on the other (except as a matter of analytic strategy), for there is operating a network of linkages that may be causal in both directions.

These features of the natural system model are suggestive rather than definitive as to the practical measurement of organizational effectiveness. It is not feasible to measure *all* attributes of an organization; selection of relevant aspects is an empirical matter to be guided by general systems theory and prior organizational research. *Intact sets* of indicators are needed to accommodate the contingencies and interactions that are known to operate with force; the "intact set" can, at best, be a simplified representation of the complex reality. The "outcomes" of interest are not defined by a linear model, but are themselves system characteristics such as stability, growth, decline, and change.

The Goal Model

The goal model employs the clear assumption that there are definable purposes or goals, such that the effectiveness of an organization can be represented by the attainment of, or progress toward, these goals. Additional criteria may be invoked when there are instrumental goals or states necessary for attainment of main goals. An example of such a hierarchical model of organization goals has been formulated by Seashore (1956).

As in the case of the natural system model, several variants exist. The most prominent of these variants is that specifying economic goals (e.g., work output, profit, growth) defined by the owner. Other variants emphasize emergent institutionalized goals sustained by the values of diverse constituencies and somewhat insulated from the purposes of the current leaders. Still others emphasize fluid change in goals as a consequence of continuous implicit negotiation among diverse influential individuals and coalitions (e.g., as in the March & Olsen [1976] "garbage can" theory of decision making).

The goal approach views an organization as an entity contrived and controlled to serve the purposes of the key influentials, including owners, managers, and others, whether "inside" or "outside" the organization, who have some controlling power in defining the operative purposes of the organization. The purposes, of course, need not be selfishly individualistic, but may be altruistic, public spirited, expressive of societal norms, or goals chosen by consensus or compromise among members and other constituencies.

The goal model has utility. It directs attention to the seeming purposefulness of some organizations. It forces attention to the value perspectives and assumptions that lead to the dominance of some goals over others. It makes explicit the linkage of the organization to its value-laden environment. It provides a convenient analytic tool for mapping the causal relationships between antecedent conditions, instrumental goals and means, and the ultimate or highest priority goals—a property of high importance in the context of policy formation, decision making, and action.

It is currently fashionable to be critical of the goal model, on grounds that it does not fit well some observed characteristics of organizations. Goals appear to change in priority rather too easily; goal sets are often (always?) internally incompatible; organizational behavior often contradicts espoused goals; organizations often survive indefinitely or grow without ever realizing any of their espoused goals; it is often difficult or impossible to get responsible spokesmen to agree on the nature of an organization's goals; organizations often are observed to act first and then discover later a "goal" to justify what has happened.

These problems are put in perspective if one assumes, as we propose to do, that the goal model refers not to some goals that are inherent in the organizational system itself, but instead to goals of persons related in some way to the organization. Purposiveness and goal formation are thus to be regarded as *psychological* phenomena, external to the organization but forming a crucial aspect of its environment. When managers, owners, or other influential groups or categories of people form their goals *for* an organization, these goals can become operative to the extent that they impinge on the organization's processes for environmental exchange, accommodation, and self-maintenance. The goal model makes eminently good sense when viewed as a model for describing the purposive forces exerted on the organizational system; it makes little or no sense when viewed as a model for self-generated purposiveness within organizational systems.

In short, we propose to put "goals" on the other side of the organization versus environment dichotomy.

Some will think that the foregoing ideas are not consequential for understanding organizational effectiveness. For some applications in analysis or evaluation that is true, for the distinction becomes trivial when there is consensus among all influential goal sources—a condition likely to be found only in very small or very autonomous organizations where the person of an influential is indistinguishable from his or her organizational role and function.

The Decision-Process Model

The core image underlying the decision-process model arises from the notion that organizations develop distinctive ways for employing information resources in the service of systemic integrity and goal attainment. These ways of dealing with information can be observed and measured; they can be assessed against criteria of intrinsic merit established by the logic of information usage; they can be assessed against "external" criteria of organizational outcomes or states in the domains of systemic integrity and goal attainment. In this context, an effective organization is one that optimizes the processes for getting, storing, retrieving, allocating, manipulating, interpreting, and discarding information. The effective organization is capable of accommodating a wide range of kinds of information. The effective organization has physical and human facilities capable of monitoring the quality of information and capable of the selective employment of information in problem-solving and behavior-controlling activity.

A number of people concerned about organizational effectiveness have focused on information-management and decision-making processes, and have done so from widely disparate disciplinary orientations. We will not attempt a census of contributions, but will give a few examples to illustrate the variety.

Jerald Hage (1974) is one of several who have offered cybernetic theories of organizational effectiveness. His book treats communication channels and networks, feedback loops, selective mobilization of information for specific uses, and the like; his treatment is highly evaluative, with reference to goal priorities, conflict resolution, forward planning, and system maintenance. His references to systemic integrity and goal attainment are explicit.

Others representing a behavioral approach to organizational decision processes include March and Simon (1958) on search behavior, limited rationality; Pettigrew (1973) on the political and power aspects of strategic decisions; Likert (1961) on participative, group-based decision processes. Argyris and Schon (1978) put the matter into a framework of organizational learning, in which they link individual-level choice processes to organizational norms and processes for information management. Weick (1969) suggests that certain "norms of disorganization" may facilitate problem solving within organizations. Vroom and Yetton (1973) prescribe optimizing decision rules for deciding how best to make decisions. Many others could be named. What they have in common is the view that organizations are, among other things, information-processing and decision-making entities that can be, and commonly are, evaluated against (a) rational standards of intrinsic goodness of decisions made; (b) appropriateness of decision process; or (c) impact on systemic integrity or goal attainment.

Collateral to the behavioral approaches to the effectiveness of organizational decision processes are those approaches focusing primarily on the "behavior" of data, not the behavior of persons (i.e., on automatized decision systems). It is fair for the assessor of organizational effectiveness to note the extent and appropriateness of the use of mechanical, electronic, and statistical–mathematical decision aids. More, however, is not necessarily better.

Certain features of the decision process models of organizational effectiveness deserve note. They tend to emphasize dynamic processes over time. They tend to be oriented to future effectiveness (tomorrow, or next year, or the next decade) rather than to the recent past, compared with the goal attainment indicators that tend to be historical, and the systemic integrity process models that tend to emphasize change, adaptivity, and response to environmental intrusions. These complementary dimensions of the three models are highly significant, for their inclusion in an integrated model allows estimation of organizational effectiveness over a future span of time under changing external conditions.

The issue of fit of decision processes to the organization's situation is crucial and difficult, requiring differentiation among organizations as to their youth or maturity, whether in information-rich or information-poor environments, whether possessing a relatively stable or instable goal structure, whether embedded in a simple or a complex array of influential constituencies.

It is evident that the decision-process model confronts the assessor of organizational effectiveness with a very large and diverse array of concepts and specific variables for measurement and evaluation. However, this is likewise true for the natural system and goal models. All three are amenable to simplifying hierarchical organization of concepts and to the devising of feasible operations for their measurement.

AN INTEGRATION OF MODELS

There is no need to choose one among the goal, natural system, and decision-process models, rejecting the others, for they are not competitive as explanatory devices; instead, they are nicely complementary, referring to different but interdependent facets of organizational behavior. As aids in understanding organizational effectiveness they differ in scope and utility. The natural system model appears, from a researcher's perspective, the more comprehensive as it offers strong advantages as to ultimate covergence with related theories growing out of other disciplines. Indeed, some theorists would attempt to force goal attainment and decision making into the mold of the natural system model, even though such a merging (compared with joint usage) would raise difficult and perhaps unsolvable problems as to organizational identity and boundary. The suggested central role of the natural system model does not preclude the use and testing of propositions arising from the other models. The "integration" of the three is to be facilitated by restricting the goal model to treatments of the goals imposed on the organization by persons (or constituencies) acting in roles that are not integral to the focal organization; by restricting the decision-process model to its own limited domain.

One may well ask what sort of an "integration" is proposed. It may seem to consist only of accepting all popular ideas and fitting them together in a patch-work design. When Pennings and Goodman (1977) took this route, colleagues scolded them gently for doing so, but it may well be that the design need not be merely a patchwork. The "integration" may take at least two forms of interest and utility.

Triangulation

Drawing on a little optimism, and some confidence in the orderliness of Mother Nature, one can assert that for most organizations, most of the time, there must be a state of compatibility among the three domains of effectiveness that have been described. Systemic integrity must exist in sufficient degree of balance among the component factors; goals must be attained to some sufficient degree—particularly those describable as system outputs of kinds that sustain resource input transactions; decision and control processes must be sufficiently appropriate and workable to deal with the problems relating to goal structures, systemic maintenance, and the maintenance of a sufficiently efficient goal-oriented input–throughput–output system. Insufficiency in any one of these areas, or even a single subpart of any one, puts the organization at risk. Sufficiency, in each case, is to be defined with reference to the impact of each domain of effectiveness on the other two. Assessment in all three domains, with cross references, should provide some relief from the prevailing criticisms of both theorists and practitioners—that the natural system model does not say enough about goal attainment, that the goal model ignores significant organiza-tional properties of predictive, diagnostic, and corrective importance, and that the decision-process model has rather little topical content of a generalizable sort useful for assessing trends and making comparisons among organizations.

Multiple Integrations

The term *effectiveness* is evaluative by definition and implies that some co-herent set of interests and value preferences is brought to bear. An important contribution of open system theory has been the growing awareness of a need to take into account different value perspectives. These are of at least four general classes:

1. Perspectives arising from the interests of subordinate and superordinate organizational units, in large hierarchical organizations
2. Perspectives arising from interests of members of the organization who import personal values and purposes that can, at best, be only partially reflected within the focal organization
3. Perspectives arising from interests of "outside" persons or organizations of interdependence
4. Perspectives representing the general societal or public interest.

This is a formal way of saying that organizational effectiveness can, and indeed must, be evaluated from the perspectives of different interested parties such as people in higher echelons in the case of hierarchically linked organizations (e.q., the commanding officer), members of the organization (e.g., managers, workers, labor union officers), exchange partners (e.g., suppliers, customers), and the general public (e.g., consumerism groups, EPA administrators, and the neighbors).

Organizations, as such, have no value perspective of "their own" even though they may take on properties compatible with some distinctive value priorities. The multiple value perspectives all arise outside of the organization, even though they may, in the case of members, be modified by the individual's experiences as a member. They are legitimated as factors in the assessment of organizational effectiveness to the extent that they are linked with persons or sets of co-acting persons having some power to establish or modify constraints on what the focal organization may do or try to do. The concept of "constituencies" thus takes on prime importance. The treatment of constituencies by Pennings and Goodman (1977) is illuminating in this context.

Constituents, then, as actors on the scene, are the principle "integrators." They integrate in unique ways, according to their respective value orientations and transaction relationships to the focal organization, and within the limits of their information and analytic resources. The act of integration consists merely of attending simultaneously to those interests, and forming judgments as a basis for actions. Constituents are persons, although they may act and react as representatives of unorganized but likeminded constituents. Some constituencies—say dispersed product customers—may attend only to product availability, utility, and cost; others, such as employees, managers, or owners, will work with a richer array of effectiveness indicators, different sets of values, and with greater potential for imposing their goal preferences on the organization. This is, of course, a rather untidy conception of how organizational effectiveness is assessed by the pertinent actors, but if that is the way the world operates we must accept it.

There are two significant observations to be derived from the foregoing assertions. First, we must abandon the notion that there exists some "true" or "objective" degree of organizational effectiveness for a given focal organization; the effectiveness estimates are always plural—potentially different and equally valid estimates for each constituent or constituency population. Second, there are powerful social dynamics operating that have the effect of inducing some degree of compatibility in value perspectives among key constituencies; for example, constituencies holding value perspectives distinctively unlike those of key constituencies, and lacking means for imposing their own values, tend to change their values or cease to be a significant constituency; that is, they die or quit or take their trade elsewhere. Third, it is important for the observer or researcher to identify the constituency or constituencies for whom effectiveness is being evaluated.

The researcher or theoretician is in a privileged position, as the value perspective applied may be one's own or someone else's. If one's own, the integration involves equal consideration of all three of the effectiveness domains I have described.

Members as Constituents

The schema that has been outlined clearly places members of an organization in roles as constituents, not as integral components of the organization itself. As constituents, members are differentiated from other constituents only by the comparative immediacy of their power to influence the organization and by their direct and value-laden concern with all three domains of organizational effectiveness. Like other constituents, they integrate evaluative information with reference to their own value perspectives, but commonly do so as members of organized constituency sets, or as representatives of unorganized but like-minded constituency sets. From the research perspective, the member–constituents are of unparalled importance and utility, as they are readily observable in their behavior as constituents while acting in their organizational roles and settings and, in addition, are qualified informants about other constituencies.

RESPONSES TO INTEGRATIVE QUESTIONS

Conceptual Issues

1. What are the major theoretical predictions or hypotheses that derive from your perspective regarding relationships between effectiveness and other

organizational variables (e.g., structure, technology, information processing, individual satisfaction)?
2. How does your perspective expand our understanding of the behavior of organizations?
3. Does the definition of organizational effectiveness change when considering different types of organizations (e.g., public–private, professional–industrial, large–small) or different stage of development (e.g., early stages, institutionalized stages, decline)?

In the offered framework, *organizational effectiveness* is treated as a name for a class of variables defined by their use in some descriptive or analytical context rather than by their autonomous definitional properties. Thus, *effectiveness* in a particular case is whatever some constituent or some researcher making attributions to a constituency says it is. This ambiguity of reference does not make the concept any less interesting, or any less theoretically useful, but it does require that any given measure of effectiveness (or set of indicators) be regarded as a partial representation of the concept and, in any case, a representation of transient phenomena. One may, and indeed must, make choices about which aspects of effectiveness are to be valued or examined; one must be explicit about the bases for choice and the risks of omission.

The model is not a "theory" in the hypothetico-deductive mode and thus does not contain fixed definitions and assumptions such that rules of logic require certain predictions or hypotheses and deny others. Theory must be imposed on the framework. However, only those theories can be employed that are compatible with the conceptual framework. For example, the hypothesis "individual member job satisfaction leads to (causes) organizational effectiveness" is not admissable because individual job satisfaction is itself defined by the model as a component of effectiveness. A modified hypothesis that "individual job satisfaction causes high organizational productivity" is an acceptable (although dubious and uninteresting) proposition because it does conform to the internal structure and dynamics of the framework, "productivity" and "satisfaction" being conceptually independent within the model. The model does admit numerous predictions and hypotheses of a more general sort that, in principle, are testable. These pertain, for the most part, to changes in relationships over time as between component indicators from different domains, or to the consequences of different degrees of structure and differentiation among powerful constituencies.

Two features of the model deserve special comment because they can have an impact on future theoretical developments. One pertains to the location of the value systems that allow valuing of organizations. The other pertains to the sources of initiative for organizational changes.

The model specifies that organizational effectiveness is not an objective state inherent in "the organization itself," but is instead a relational construct (i.e.,

fit to needs and interests of constituencies). The relevant values are, or originate from, "outside" of the organization, and these multiple value systems are
not assumed to be mutually compatible. Any assertions about the effectiveness
of an organization need to specify the indicators employed, the value system(s)
that prescribed their choice, and an identification or characterization of the
constituency (empirical or imagined) in which the value system is resident.
The notion of partial inclusions of persons as members of an organization
precludes the identification of "boundary" with "membership."

The model implies that judgments of absolute or relative effectiveness will
thus be made by influential constituents and that action implications will
follow. The notion of locating goal formation and change initiation "outside" of
the organization will be troublesome for some theorists and a relief to others.
Those of sociological bent will be glad to get rid of the people by calling them
environment and classifying them by type. Those of psychological persuasion
will welcome the invitation to treat individuals in exchange relationships with
organizations, and fulfilling roles in organizations, but not themselves defined
as constituting the organization. The model assigns to constituents the initia-
tives for goal modification, growth, and adaptation. Organizations may be lazy
(Weick, 1977), conservative (Miller, 1978), and repetitive (Katz & Kahn,
1978), but, in their changing mix and in their competition for advantage,
constituents may be active, radical, and innovative.

Research Issues

1. What are the major indicators (criteria) of organizational effectiveness
   using your perspective?
2. How would one test the efficacy of your approach compared to other
   approaches to effectiveness?
3. What are the major methodological issues of operationalizing effectiveness using your perspective (e.g., those relating to levels of analysis, data
   collection, predictors, key variables)?

The framework described does not specify a roster of major, or critical
criteria of organizational effectiveness. Their identification in a particular case
or class of cases becomes itself a research issue. The model does suggest some
criteria to be used in assigning relative importance among different indicators.
These criteria are of several different kinds. For example, the value priorities
of powerful constituencies for some purposes would take precedence over those
of weak constituencies in predicting future states. Further, consensus among
constituencies about a given indicator, or the prevalence of concern about a
given indicator, adds weight to that indicator (but not necessarily to effectiveness as viewed by others). The requirements of balance among the three do-

mains imposes the criterion that not all indicators can be from the same domain.

However, the notion that some indicators are inherently or generally more critical than others is at odds with the nature of the model that asserts, instead, the importance of simultaneous consideration for a diverse and numerous array of indicators, and their treatment as an intact set. Thus, the model has no particular implications with respect to the validity of contemporary folklore about key variables indicative of effectiveness. The central message of the model is that all such bits of wisdom, experience, or theory are constrained by assumptions (often unimagined as well as unstated) concerning the rest of the organizational characteristics. The model emphasizes the frailty of propositions that start with *"Ceteris paribus . . ."* Any manager who concentrates for long on a single, or a small number, of effectiveness criteria is probably headed for trouble.

The efficacy of this integrated model of organizational effectiveness should be subject to test in comparison with each of the three component models used alone, and in comparison with other models of different kinds. There is a difficulty, however, because the component and alternative approaches have different aims and different constraints in their use, and are therefore in substantial degree incomparable except under specified conditions. For example, the integrated approach described here would surely fare badly in comparisons based on parsimony, or on short-term goal attainment predictions derived from simple linear predictive models. It might fare much better in comparisons based on long-term outcome predictions, or on utility for early detection and correction of conditions that threaten organizational survival. This speculation rests on the emphasis given in the integrated model to factors of systemic integrity and decision-making competence, which have primarily a reference to future states and to potentiality for sustained or improved performance.

The application of this approach in research will require significant departures from prevailing practices. A recent review of published empirical research studies employing measures intended to represent organizational effectiveness shows that, with very few exceptions, the indicators used were few in number, exclusively drawn from the goal attainment domain, bound to a very short time span of reference, and value oriented solely to management interests. The approach here described demands multiple and diverse indicators, measurement at the levels of persons and subunits as well as for the organization as a total system, sampling of indicators from three domains, longitudinal or periodic measurement over a span of time, identification and characterization of significant constituencies, and the employment of nonlinear predictive and analytical systems. There is a formidable array of developmental tasks yet to be done. There exist a few examples of efforts of the prescribed diversity and scale (e.g., Goodman, 1979; Van deVen & Ferry, 1980).

Practical Issues

1. What prescriptions or guidelines for improving success are suggested by your approach? Are there any counterintuitive recommendations?
2. What diagnostic tools could managers use to monitor success using your approach?
3. What trade-offs, dilemmas, or dysfunctional consequences might be experienced by managers using your approach?

The concept of organizational effectiveness is plainly alive and well outside of the scholarly conference halls and seminar rooms. People who must act in relation to organizations will make such judgments. Even if all such judgments by constituents were "wrong" or inexact, we would still be compelled as scientists to try to understand the formation of evaluative judgments and their implications for buying, selling, quitting, getting sick, compromising, organizing, and all the other things that organizations do and that people do in organizational contexts. We need to do something better than dismiss the concept as a pathological fantasy or to claim it as a prerogative of some particular class of participants in organizational activity. There may be no single "correct" assessment of organizational effectiveness, but we still need to understand the bases for such assessments and to form ideas about how assessments can be made that better fit the action choice requirements of the several classes of constituents.

The approach described in this chapter is essentially descriptive, but it allows and guides the testing of causal and relational propositions of the kinds that key actors, such as managers, must use in their practical decisions. As it stands, the model is prescriptive only at a broad level of generality and abstraction. For example, the decision processes of an organization "should fit the case"; a manager should not rely exclusively on indicators of goal attainment; a manager should monitor with care and dependable information the systemic integrity of his or her organization. These are valid prescriptions, but they are also platitudes of little concrete help to a worried manager.

To move from platitudes to the specificity of diagnoses and predictions requires the use of a battery of measurement procedures and instruments selected to represent the three domains, and to employ in each domain a nested set of variables such that gross measures would serve to "locate" possible problems and finer-grained measures would help to explicate the problems.

This approach is already standard procedure in many organizations with respect to the domain of goal attainment. A manager of a factory, for example, is likely to have an information system that routinely delivers current and trend data for a small roster of variables that he or she considers to be of most importance. He or she is likely to have back-up data that can be employed for finer-grained diagnoses—perhaps to find out the causes for inventory build-up, or the sources of rising customer complaints. In this domain he or she is equipped with an array of causal propositions (theories?) and empirical analytic strategies that he or she uses with some confidence in taking corrective or preventive actions.

Few organizations, on the other hand, have similarly effective means for monitoring their effectiveness in the domains of systemic integrity and decision processes. Few track their key constituencies as well as they could and should. There exist means for doing so, although the technologies are still rudimentary and the associated empirical generalizations and theories need further development.

The approach described imposes some excruciating dilemmas upon managers, as well as other constituencies. These are implicit in such terms as *balance* along domains, *sufficient* to sustain an organizational system, and the like. Such terms correctly assert that the maintenance of organizational effectiveness over a span of time involves actions to "improve" one or another aspect of organizational functioning, but always at some cost and risk in other aspects. An exception would be an instance in which the point of action concerns some variable that is below that level necessary to sustain the others; in such a case, the negative side effects or foregone alternative actions count for little. The benefits from an approach to assessing organizational effectiveness in the manner described, because of its future orientations, lie in the potential for early warning of trouble and, therefore, the possibility for low-cost incremental accommodations to the condition of risk.

REFERENCES

Argyris, C., & Schon, D. A. *Organizational learning: A theory of action perspective.* Reading, Mass.: Addison-Wesley, 1978.

Baker, F. Introduction: Organizations as open systems. In F. Baker (Ed.), *Organization systems: General systems approaches to complex organizations.* Homewood, Ill.: Irwin, 1973.

Georgopoulos, B. S., & Cooke, R. A. Conceptual-theoretical framework for the organizational study of hospital emergency services. *ISR Working Paper Series* (unnumbered). Ann Arbor: Institute for Social Research, 1979.

Goodman, P. S. *Assessing organizational change.* New York: Wiley, 1979.

Hage, J. *Communication and organizational control.* New York: Wiley, 1974.

Katz, D., & Kahn, R. L. *The social psychology of organizations* (2nd ed.). New York: Wiley, 1978.

Likert, R. *New patterns of management.* New York: McGraw-Hill, 1961.

March, J. G., & Olsen, J. P. *Ambiguity and choice in organizations.* Olso, Norway: Universitetsforlaget, 1976.

March, J. G., & Simon, H. A. *Organizations.* New York: Wiley, 1958.

Miller, J. G. *Living systems.* New York: McGraw-Hill, 1978.

Pennings, J. M., & Goodman, P. S. Toward a framework of organizational effectiveness. In P. S. Goodman & J. M. Pennings (Eds.), *New perspectives on organizational effectiveness.* San Francisco: Jossey-Bass, 1977.

Pettigrew, A. M. *The politics of organizational decision making.* London: Tavistock, 1973.

Seashore, S. E. Criteria of organizational effectiveness. *Michigan Business Review,* 1956, *17,* 26–30.

Seashore, S. E., & Yuchtman, E. Factorial analysis of organizational performance. *Administrative Science Quarterly,* 1967, *10,* 377–395.

Van deVen, A. H., & Ferry, D. L. *Measuring and assessing organizations.* New York: Wiley, 1980.

Vroom, V., & Yetton, P. W. *Leadership and decision-making.* Pittsburgh: University of Pittsburgh Press, 1973.

Weick, K. E. *The social psychology of organizing.* Reading, Mass.: Addison-Wesley, 1969.

Weick, K. E. Repunctuating the problem. In P. S. Goodman & J. M. Pennings (Eds.), *New perspectives on organizational effectiveness.* San Francisco: Jossey-Bass, 1977.

KARL E. WEICK
RICHARD L. DAFT

The Effectiveness of Interpretation Systems

Consider the game of "twenty questions." Normally in this game one person leaves the room, the remaining people select a word that the person is to guess when he or she returns, and the only clue given about the word is whether it signifies an animal, vegetable, or mineral. The person trying to guess the word asks up to 20 questions that can be answered yes or no in an effort to guess what the word is.

Effectiveness in the game of "twenty questions" could be defined by several measures: whether the correct word is identified; number of guesses to get the word; speed with which the person gets close to the answer; quality of the questioning as determined by raters; time to complete the questioning; the ease with which others could step in, continue the line of questioning, and profit from the previous questions asked; the extent to which observers could see what the questioner was driving at; the extent to which each subsequent question yielded new information; etc. These measures all assess some feature of the process by which an interpretation is built up by the person who is "it."

Organizations play "twenty questions." They have limited time and questions, and they strive for the answer. The answer is discovering what consumers want that other organizations do not provide. The answer is finding that there is a market for pet rocks, roller skates, the idea that funerals are for the living, encounter groups, erasable ball point pens, or zero population growth. Many organizations presume that there is an answer to the puzzle of

71

ORGANIZATIONAL EFFECTIVENESS
A Comparison of Multiple Models

"twenty questions." They query the environment with samples, market surveys, test markets, and try to find an acceptable answer before their resources run out, before competitors corner the market, before people's interests change, or before more compelling opportunities in other product lines dominate the search.

All of these activities, whether in organizations or in "twenty questions," represent one form of interpretation. People are trying to interpret what they have done, define what they have learned, solve the problem of what they should do next. The success of their interpretations might be judged against the criteria just suggested—number of guesses, identifying the answer, quality of questioning—or by more traditional criteria of material outcomes and goal achievement. There are also economies implicit in the interpretation itself, economies that might be indexed by the elaborateness, length, plausibility, transparency, communicability, cumulativeness, or memorability of the line of questioning. Given human limits on information processing (Bruner, Goodnow, & Austin, 1956; March & Simon, 1958), interpretations might be graded crudely in terms of the degree to which they accommodate these limitations rather than ignore them. A vast computer retrieval system, for all its speed and volume, will not provide the synthesis and condensation available from solitary human activity. To accommodate human limitations in information processing thus can be more effective than to dismiss, ignore, or try to override those limitations.

INTERPRETATION SYSTEMS AND ORGANIZATIONAL EFFECTIVENESS

The notion of organizational effectiveness is complex, elusive, and multidimensional (Goodman & Pennings, 1977; Steers, 1975). Definitions of effectiveness seldom overlap, nor is there overlap among measurement criteria, levels of analysis, or causal variables (Cameron, 1978). The reason is that organizations themselves are vast, complex, fragmented, elusive, and multidimensional. Investigators must make assumptions about organizations and adopt a limited perspective, however faulty, to understand them. The view of organizations held by the researcher is typically reflected in the reported theory and measurement. A study of effectiveness may reflect assumptions that characterize organizations as input–output systems, resource allocation systems, collections of human beings with needs to be met, growth and survival systems, tools in the hands of goal-setting owners, coalitions of interest groups, transformation systems, etc.

The purpose of this chapter is to add even more assumptions, but in an orderly way. This chapter proposes an additional conceptualization of effectiveness, an additional set of variables, an additional set of measurement criteria. But it is a necessary addition, as reflected in Table 4.1. Table 4.1 organizes effectiveness models along Boulding's (1956) scale of system complexity. The strength of Boulding's scale is that it describes substantive changes in system complexity. Each increment on the scale represents a substantive change in the viewpoint about organizations. Simply adding more variables to an organizational effectiveness study would make it more complex in number of relationships, but that would not influence position on the scale. The basic view of organizations is what counts. A detailed description of the correspondence between scale levels and organizational phenomena is reported in Daft (1980) and Pondy and Mitroff (1978).

The arrangement in Table 4.1 suggests that the diversity and seeming confusion in the effectiveness literature are not pathological. The diversity simply represents different perspectives on organizations, and these perspectives can be ordered on the basis of assumptions underlying the organizational models. No single model can embrace all perspectives, nor should it try. The implication that a small administrative ratio is associated with greater effectiveness

TABLE 4.1
Effectiveness Models and Criterion Measures

Model	Effectiveness issues	Measurement
1. Framework	Arrangement of elements, resource deployment	Administrative ratio, direct–indirect labor
2. Clockwork	Stability, movement toward equilibrium	Retention, absenteeism, accidents, stability, turnover
3. Control system	Reaction to controller, feedback loops, organization as "tool."	Satisfaction, motivation, productivity, efficiency, compliance, reward structure
4. Open system	Acquire and transform resources, survival, seek goals	Resource acquisition, survival, profit, goal achievement
5. Growth system	Growth and adaptation, interplay among subunits	Growth, innovation, adaptability, integration
6. Differentiated system	Specialized information reception, nervous system, choice processes, multiple and ambiguous goals	Interpretation of environment, decision processes, information management, goal consensus
7. Symbol processing system	High-order human characteristics: self-awareness, symbolism, meaning	Organizational self-awareness, language processes, affective dimensions, cause maps

(Hall, 1977) represents the logic of a "framework." Productivity and efficiency measurements reflect "control systems" perspectives. Both the system resource (Yuchtman & Seashore, 1967) and goal approach (Price, 1968) make "open system" assumptions about organizations. Flexibility–adaptability, the most frequently used measure of effectiveness (Steers, 1975), is consistent with "growth system" logic. Most effectiveness models and measurements are at system levels 2–5. These models make assumptions about organizations that range from simple, mechanical devices to growing, changing systems requiring coordination and integration.

The notion of an interpretation system represents Level 6, "differentiated systems." Interpretation is the effectiveness issue for systems that are differentiated into highly specialized information receptors that interact with the environment. Information about the external world must be filtered and processed into a central nervous system of sorts, where choices are made. Interpretation is required in human organizations. The notion of interpretation systems thus represents a viewpoint of organizations omitted in other frameworks, and it represents a set of assumptions at the next higher level of system complexity. Organizations possess characteristics that typify all seven system levels in Table 4.1. But as Pondy and Mitroff (1978) pointed out, most research into organizations has made low-level system assumptions and does not capture dimensions congruent with the complex human dimensions of organizations. The notion of an interpretation system is one step in the other direction.

CHARACTERISTICS OF INTERPRETATION SYSTEMS

Organizations must make interpretations. Managers literally must wade into the swarm of events that constitute and surround the organization and actively try to impose some order on them. Organization participants physically act on the environment, attending to some of it, ignoring most of it, and talking to other people to see what they are doing (Braybrooke, 1964). Structure must be imposed on the apparent randomness in order for interpretation to occur. Interpretation is the process of translating these events, of developing models for understanding, of bringing out meaning, and of assembling conceptual schemes. The interpretation process is neither simple nor well understood, and a simple definition is unlikely to communicate an accurate image. The following ideas suggest what we mean by an interpretation system.

1. To do an interpretation is like trying to construct a reading of a manuscript that is "foreign, faded, full of ellipses, incoherencies, suspicious emendations, and tendentious commentaries, but written not in conventionalized graphs of sound but in transient examples of shaped behavior [Geertz, 1973, p. 10]."

2. Interpretations inform and modify that which they are intended to explain. Interpretations interpret interpretations rather than events.

3. Interpretations utilize special knowledge, sympathy, or imagination. The necessity for interpretations increases as data present something other than purely intellectual difficulties. The puzzles faced by organizational members resemble those puzzles found in puns, poems, dreams, abstractions, and foreign languages. In many cases, when a person examines a display, two or more causes could have produced the result, which means that the outcome is equivocal. Thus it is plausible to portray organizations as embedded in an environment of puns (Weick, 1979, pp. 171–175). This means that part of what separates better from poorer interpretations may be the degree to which the interpreter has knowledge or imagination to provide a plausible rendering of events that might have generated the present display.

4. Interpretation is like an act of translation from one language to another. Organizations take environmental events that have meaning, labels, fringes of understanding, claims and taken-for-granted qualities in the world of everyday life and impose their own labels, categories, and relationships on them in an effort to understand these events on their own terms. Past experience and language determine what we see, but to do an interpretation requires that we understand the other language as well. Only by testing our interpretations back on "the" environment can we know whether they are reasonable.

5. Interpretations are made a posteriori. Interpretations focus on elapsed action and what has occurred. They are the prototypic case in which action precedes cognition. The retrospective character of interpretations means that they are often dated, tied to particulars, situation-specific, self-justifying, complete, self-evident, and produce different versions of the "same" event over time.

6. Interpretations are quasi-historical. Much organizational sense-making consists of writing histories. A history is a kind of cause–effect map that depicts events in sequence. Retained histories can clarify either a tangible present outcome or a future outcome that has to be imagined. Research indicates that thinking about an event as completed and finished, even if it has yet to occur, makes it easier to construct an elaborate cause map. The human cognitive apparatus is more comfortable with past realities than with future possibilities (Weick, 1979).

History in hand, people who select interpretations for present enactments usually see in the present what they have seen before. In the strategy formulation process in organizations, hindsight is a primary determinant of current planning. Outcomes from previous decisions, especially the mistakes, are disproportionately salient in current thinking. Musings such as "We should have gone into home computers 5 years ago," and "Digital watches were a loser," have greater bearing on current interpretations than the current events being interpreted.

7. Interpretations construct environments rather than discover them. When interpretations are constructed, a biased search takes place for stimuli that could have produced that interpretation. The twist introduced by this feature for organizational theorists is that the environment then becomes an output of organizing processes, not an input to those processes. On the basis of enactments and interpretations, people construct a belated picture of some environment that could have produced those actions. The environment that is chosen did not necessarily determine directly the actions and the sense-making. Rather, it is erected after the fact as a plausible explanation for why those actions, labels, and interpretations could have occurred.

8. Interpretations are forms of punctuation. Interpretations consist of discrete labels that are superimposed on continuous flows of people and experience. All interpretations are arbitrary in the sense that they exclude portions of the flow. Interpretations introduce spacings within continuous flows that make induction possible. As the spacings are introduced at different positions, different inductions become more and less plausible. However, the relative ease with which spacings can be shifted while the display still makes sense is at the base of some of the problems people have trying to describe an effective interpretation system.

John Steinbeck (1941), talking about the artificiality of species categories in animals, alludes both to the arbitrariness of many interpretations and to the conditions that make this arbitrariness inevitable:

> Indeed, as one watches the little animals, definite words describing them are likely to grow hazy and less definite, and as species merge into species, the whole idea of definite independent species begins to waiver, and a scale-like concept of animal variations comes to take its place. The whole taxonomic method in biology is clumsy and unwieldy, shot through with jokes of naturalists and the egos of men who wished to have animals named after them [p. 207].

9. Interpretations are reasonable rather than right. Reasonable explanations accommodate more data than they exclude, are sufficient in the eyes of more than one person, are no worse than other explanations that can be generated, and handle some new instances that were not used to generate the original interpretation. These soft criteria are not especially demanding of either the data or of one's fellow perceivers. But the criteria are adequate for practical purposes and that is enough. The criteria permit sufficient elasticity in organizations that diverse interpretations can be held without this diversity endangering coordinated action (Fernandez, 1965).

A MODEL OF
ORGANIZATIONAL INTERPRETATIONS

The organizational activity of interpreting the environment is an awesomely complex, fuzzy process. Understanding it in detail may be beyond scientific reach. Nevertheless, in this section we identify what we believe are two key dimensions of the interpretation process, and we propose a model of organizational interpretations. This model provides a simple way to describe and understand different strategies that organizations may use to obtain their interpretations.

Enacted "Twenty Questions"

Many organizations undoubtedly play the interpretation game with the goal of finding the correct answer, just as in "twenty questions." The game of "twenty questions," however, is of limited value as a metaphor because there is one way in which it mocks many organizational worlds. Many such worlds have nothing that corresponds to "the answer." In everyday life the act of questioning may be much more influential in determining the correct answer than is the case with the clear-cut roles of asking and answering and the fixed answer present in the conventional version of "twenty questions."

"Twenty questions" becomes much more interesting if we introduce a variation suggested by the physicist John Wheeler. Once the player leaves the room so that those remaining can choose the word, the game unfolds in a different fashion. "While he is gone the other players decide to alter the rules. They will select no word at all; instead each of them will answer 'yes' or 'no' as he pleases—provided he has a word in mind that fits both his own reply and all the previous replies. The outsider returns and, unsuspecting, begins asking questions. At last he makes a guess: "Is the word 'clouds'?" Yes, comes the answer, and the players explain the game [Newsweek, March 12, 1979, p. 62]." When the questioner began, he or she assumed the answer already existed. Yet the answer came into being through the questions raised. If the player asked different questions, a different answer would emerge.

If some organizations play "twenty questions" in the traditional way, seeking the correct answer already in the environment, and if others play "twenty questions" John Wheeler's way, constructing an answer, then we have an interesting difference in interpretation behavior. This difference reflects the organization's assumption about the objectivity of its environment, and it provides a concept for thinking about what it means to have an effective interpretation system.

If an organization assumes that the external environment is objective, that events and processes are hard, measurable, and determinant, then it will play the traditional game to discover the appropriate or correct interpretation. The key for this organization is discovery through intelligence, rational analysis, vigilence, and accurate measurement. This organization will utilize linear thinking and logic, and will seek clear-cut solutions. This type of organization might assess its own effectiveness in terms of the number of questions needed to get the answer, or whether the answer is discovered at all.

If an organization assumes that the external environment is subjective, an entirely different strategy applies. The key is to construct, coerce, or enact a reasonable answer that makes previous action sensible and suggests some next steps. The interpretation shapes the environment more than the environment shapes the interpretation. In John Wheeler's brand of "twenty questions," better lines of questioning could ironically lead respondents to change their choice of words to fit the ideas implied by the questioner. If the questioner guesses the answer frequently and mentions several objects that resemble one another, there is a good chance that a conceptual set can be imposed on the respondents so that they consider a more restricted set of alternatives and become more predictable. Bizarre, loosely coupled questions could put enormous pressure on an audience to think of a single object that would fit all the diverse criteria implied in the line of questioning. The questions: "Does it taste less sour than a grapefruit?" "Could it float 24 hours on water?" "Will the demand for it increase in the next 5 years?" "Is there a synthetic version of it?" "Could I show it to my mother?" are sufficiently disarming as a set of questions that they would influence the answer.

In an interpretation system guided by subjective assumptions, effectiveness might not be assessed in terms of logic, intelligence, or discovery. These criteria are insensitive to the fact that the interpretation process is more interpersonal, less linear, more reciprocal, more flexible, more multivalued, more improvisational, and more subject to multifinality than organization scholars may realize. Effectiveness in a differentiated system may include the ability to deal with equivocality, the ability to coerce an answer useful to the organization, the ability to invent an environment and be a part of the invention.

Organizational Intrusiveness

Interpretation systems try to make sense of the flowing, changing, equivocal chaos that constitutes the sum total of the external environment. People in organizations try to sort this chaos into items, events, and parts that are then connected, threaded into sequence, serially ordered, and related to one another. In the course of interpretation, individuals, and perhaps the organization as a collective, develop cause maps (Bougon, Weick, & Binkhorst, 1977).

The strategy for developing cause maps may differ widely by organization. Some organizations may actively test the environment. These organizations leap before they look, perform trials in order to find what an error is, and discover what is feasible by testing presumed constraints. An example was reported by Garfinkel (1967) who asked students to offer a small fraction of the list price for items in a department store. Students were apprehensive, as they perceived a rule in most American stores that things must be purchased for the list price. After breaching the constraints, the students discovered they were able to get rather substantial reductions in price. The price rule seems to have force only because everyone expects it to be followed and no one challenges it. Breaching traditional, presumed constraints may lead to significant information inputs for the breacher. Organizations that are willing to test supposed boundaries can be called test makers, and they will develop interpretations quite different from organizations that behave within perceived boundaries and constraints.

Organizations that interpret without testing boundaries can be called "test avoiders" (Weick, 1979). These organizations may be relatively passive and may set up receptors to sense whatever inputs flow by the organization. These organizations would perceive that they must act and interpret within limits. However, knowledge of these limitations is not based on direct tests, but rather on avoidance of testing. On the basis of avoided tests, organizations presume that constraints exist in the environment that limit what they can do. Inaction is justified by perceived constraints and barriers that, in turn, make future action impossible. These constraints and barriers become predominant "things" in the environment that act as restrictions on the options managers invoke when confronted by problems.

One explanation for differential intrusion into the environment when making interpretations, is organizational age. Organizations may begin their existence as test makers and gradually develop an interpretation system that accepts rather than tests presumed boundaries. New organizations are disbelievers, are undoctrinated, and as newcomers they are less influenced by elaborate maps of limitations. They are more likely to wade in and develop a niche that test avoiders presume is uninhabitable. New organizations may discover that many fears of older organizations are unfounded, but that other fears are more valid. As time passes and more tests are employed, new boundaries may be drawn within which the developing organization restricts future behaviors.

For test-making organizations, accurate interpretations within the tested domain can normally be expected. Interpretation failure would normally involve a confounded test (Huck & Sandler, 1979) or the act of testing itself. Experimenting with a new product, for example, may violate expectations, but may be extremely successful. If the new product fails, the organization would still have accurate information, but at the cost of material losses. For the test-avoiding organization, vigilance within the rules might be considered successful interpretation activity. Interpretation failure is likely to be the accumulation of spurious knowledge based on untested errors of attribution.

An Interpretation Model

Based on the idea that interpretation systems may vary in their assumptions about the environment and in their intrusiveness into the environment, organizations can be categorized according to interpretation modes or styles. The two dimensions just described are organized into a model in Figure 4.1, which describes four general categories of interpretation behavior.

The enacting style reflects a test-making strategy under the assumption that the environment is subjective. These organizations construct their own environments. They gather information by trying new behaviors and seeing what happens. They experiment, test, and stimulate, and they ignore precedent, rules, and traditional expectations. This type of organization would tend to develop and market a product, such as Polaroid cameras, based on what it thought it could sell. The organization will construct a market rather than waiting for demand to tell it what to produce.

	Subjective	*Glancing* Nonlinear, constrained interpretations Rumor, hunch, other people, opportunistic actions.	*Enacting* Nonlinear, intrusive interpretations Experimentation, stimulation, coercion, testing, invent environment
ASSUMPTIONS ABOUT NATURE OF ENVIRONMENT			
	Objective	*Staring* Logical, constrained interpretations Routine documents, reports, publica- tions, information storage and re- trieval, passive detection	*Discovering* Logical, intrusive interpretations Data collection, questioning, sur- veys, active detection

Test-avoiding   Test-making

ORGANIZATIONAL INTRUSIVENESS

FIGURE 4.1 Model of Organizational Interpretation Styles.

The discovering style also represents an active organization, but the emphasis here would be on detecting the correct answer already in the environment rather than on shaping the answer. Carefully devised measurement probes would be developed and sent into the environment to relay information back to the organization. These data would determine organizational interpretations of perceived environmental requirements.

The other two styles represent a more passive approach to interpretation. Organizations characterized as *staring* tend to rely on formal data collecting, and the organizations would tend to develop interpretations within traditional boundaries. *Glancing* reflects a similar passive approach, but with less reliance on hard, objective data from the environment. Organizational participants act on limited information because hunch and opportunity to influence the environment will also influence their response. Examples of these two styles are illustrated by two clothing plants in England (Clark, 1978). The plants developed different interpretation systems for understanding the environment. The staring plant developed a data collection system to record routinely such things as economic conditions, past sales, and weather forecasts, and used a statistical model to predict sales and schedule production. The other plant gathered limited information from personal contacts with a few store buyers and visited a few stores to see what was selling. This plant used the glancing style, and based on hunch and expectations, managers would schedule styles and quantities that would both fit with and influence market demand.

Another example of interpretation styles is illustrated by the relationship between corporations and their shareholders. A few corporations actively influence and shape shareholder attitudes. The enacting organization may try to manipulate shareholder perceptions toward itself, environmental issues, or political candidates by sending information to shareholders through various media. Discovery oriented corporations actively stay in touch with shareholders to learn what they are thinking, and conduct surveys or use other devices to discover attitudes. A few corporations handle the shareholder relationships through routine data transactions (mailing out dividend checks, stockholder voting), which is typical of staring. Finally, the other corporations rely on informal, personal contact with shareholders. Managers use these opportunities (annual meetings, telephone contact about complaints and questions), both to learn shareholder's opinions and to shape and influence those opinions.

The model in Figure 4.1 thus represents different ways organizations interpret their external environment. The success or effectiveness of each style might be evaluated on different criteria by each organization, because they have different expectations. But for initial research purposes, general criteria of interpretation system effectiveness may have to be developed that apply across a range of organizational settings. These criteria should enable comparison of organizations along the lines of knowledge about the environment and extent of success in their interpretation of it. To these criteria we now turn.

INTERPRETATION SYSTEM EFFECTIVENESS

A divergent set of interpretation ideas have been explored in this chapter. We have argued that interpretation processes are ambiguous, complex, difficult to define, and are representative of Level 6 systems in Boulding's (1956) framework. We have also proposed that interpretations can be achieved with different strategies, including enacting, discovering, staring, and glancing. In this section we turn to the issue of assessing interpretation system effectiveness. Several ideas alluding to performance and effectiveness have appeared throughout the chapter, and in this section we discuss themes that we propose are common to interpretation effectiveness across a variety of human organization settings.

Under Level 6 assumptions, effectiveness is a function of the interpretation of cues about the environment. Organizational effectiveness is similar to interpretation accuracy. Other bases for assessing effectiveness, such as internal efficiency or resource acquisition, assume organizational dimensions at lower system levels. Thus if one organization imposes two different interpretations on a set of data or if two groups of people in an organization impose different interpretations on similar data, one interpretation will be said to be more effective than the other to the degree that it is (a) grounded in more detailed knowledge of the data; (b) informed by a taxonomy with a greater number of levels; (c) tied together with a greater number of perceived strong, causal linkages; (d) capable of reconstructing with more accuracy the initial data that the interpretation was built to explain; (e) selective in its claims for generality, simplicity, and accuracy; and (f) coercive of agreement on a smaller number of more general themes. These criteria come from a variety of sources but share two assumptions: (a) that people have bounded rationality; and (b) that efforts to achieve uniform cognitive agreements represent threats to social cohesion. People can agree to work together and coexist socially for apparently common ends that each of them, in fact, interpret somewhat differently. If people are forced to agree on detailed interpretations of these ends, then differences become more evident, similarities decrease, social ties weaken, and co-existence dissolves. This tension between the social and the cultural is chronic in interpretation systems and is managed anew in each situation. The six effectiveness criteria are a beginning point for the empirical assessment of interpretation systems.

Detailed Knowledge of Particulars

The key text from which this criterion emerges is found in Levi-Strauss's (1966) discussion of the incredible amount of knowledge so-called primitive people have about the plants and animals around them. He gives numerous illustrations of natural products that are used for medicinal purposes, products that reflect an astounding refinement and precision of detail. Siberian people, for example, use powder made of crushed feet of the *tilegous* bird to cure the bite of a mad dog and use water from an icicle hanging on the nest of the *remiz* bird for eye complaints. Given this incredible attention to detail, one might presume that because the natives find these natural products to be so useful, they know them in fine-grained detail. Levi-Strauss argues that the causal arrow goes the other way. "Animals and plants are not known as a result of their usefulness; they are deemed to be useful or interesting because they are first of all known [p. 9]."

When organizations act as if the environment is nothing but detail, each item is studied carefully. After an item is known fully, then it may be paired with a problem or another item and the pairing may be a solution of some kind. Usefulness comes quite late in the sequence and is a consequence of detailed knowledge.

There is a further way in which detailed description is effective. When people in organizations are confused by equivocal information, they are usually advised to deal with the information by putting it into a context (e.g., Heider, 1958). If the history and the surroundings of a puzzling item are known, then the item often becomes less puzzling. The relevance of this is that if any event–person–product is known more fully, then its surroundings will be registered more fully and this richer understanding of the surroundings supplies the context that keeps the isolated item from becoming a puzzle.

Thus, organizations with detailed knowledge of particulars have two advantages. First, they are provided with enriched contexts within which isolated items can be made more sensible. Second, they have increased chance to find uses for any pairings among the refined characteristics that have been discovered during their close observations. For these reasons, more is better in interpretation systems, more knowledge being indicative of contexts that facilitate sense-making and more chances of finding useful combinations for whatever problems may appear.

Multilevel Taxonomy

A classification scheme of any kind, no matter how crude, is better than no scheme at all. And a system that permits more gradations generates more accurate predictions than does one with fewer gradations. People can live with uncertainty but not with chaos and disorder. The demand for an order of some sort supercedes demands for clarity regarding links between means and ends. If a person does not know his/her place, cannot find a center to which other things can be related, and if there is no sense of what goes where, this is a much more harrowing experience than is confusion about which explicit means achieves which explicit end.

The crucial point is that taxonomies satisfy a demand for order (McKelvey, 1978). Furthermore, arrangements are typically overdetermined, which means that arrangements made on one basis generally lend themselves to similar arrangements on the basis of different criteria. For example, there is a logic of sensations in which laypeople group items on the basis of similar tastes and smells. It has often been the case that these arrangements are later accounted for by chemists, who retain the groupings but make them on the basis of different factors. Thus when people in organizations mumble about situations that seem to go together and situations that seem to differ, these mumblings show the operation both of interpretation systems and of efforts to introduce systematic qualities into those interpretations. The more fully this is done, the more effective the interpretation system.

Density of Causal Linkages

Information that is partitioned into labeled categories frequently is of most value for prediction and understanding when causal linkages are imposed among the categories. It is of some interest to know that the world consists of objects that are big, small, smokey, sour, heavy, noisy, and soft. It is of more interest to know that an increase in bigness is associated with an increase in heaviness, that increased sourness is associated with decreased softness, or that as things get smaller nothing happens. Each of these rational statements sets the stage for intervention, for melioration, for forecasting, for managing outcomes, for anticipating.

The power of causal statements is at the base of this criterion of effectiveness. In other research (Bougon et al., 1977), the argument has been made that interpretations are often stored in the form of cause maps. A *cause map* is the condensation of detailed events into a limited number of causally related variables. These maps represent a version of how the world is tied together. The power of these summaries is demonstated when they do two things:

1. When they can regenerate the details of an original event that has been summarized in summary form
2. When they are imposed on new puzzles and allow previous relevant interpretations to clarify current puzzles

Given the central role played by cause maps, effectiveness can be indexed by whether such maps exist, the density of ties, number of shared variables and shared linkages among people, and perhaps similarity among people in the speed with which similar maps unfold.

Capability of Reconstructing the Input

An interpretation, by definition, has less detail than the original data. It can be thought of as an abstract, a synopsis, a summary, or a typification. Although each of those terms has a slightly different connotation, all share the nuance that the original display has been edited. A substantial portion of organizational literature demonstrates that organizations are instruments that simplify. Whether that simplification is termed uncertainty absorption, equivocality removal, uncertainty avoidance, risk aversion, encoding, or whatever, the point is the same, that nuance and detail die.

Interpretations vary in the degree to which they allow the interpreter to reconstruct and recapture inputs that provoke the interpretation in the first place. For example, police dispatchers control the expectancies of officers on the beat by the codes they attach to cryptic phone calls that contain ill-formed requests for assistance of some unspecified kind (Manning, 1979). Officers able to reconstruct accurately the precipitating event encoded by the dispatcher are in a much better position to offer a graded response when they arrive than are officers who have been burned by previous interpretations that reconstructed the "wrong" reality.

The ability to reconstruct an input is not just a matter of safety. It involves the more general issue of information loss and the ease with which people can reverse unproductive lines of action and unproductive interpretations. Accurate reconstruction of original details makes it possible to build a second interpretation that may handle the original problem just as well, and perhaps be capable of handling newer problems that have arisen. The capability to reinterpret earlier situations in light of what has happened subsequently is being rational retrospectively. If original definitions cannot be undone and redone, organizations risk losing distinctive competence to newer competitors who are less saddled by dated interpretations of what the environment is like and how to cope with it.

Sensitivity to Commensurate Complexity

Warren Thorngate (1976) has proposed that it is impossible for any explanation to be simultaneously (*a*) general, (*b*) simple, and (*c*) accurate. A theory or explanation about a phenomenon can possess only two of these characteristics. If an explanation is general and simple, then it cannot be very accurate. If it is accurate and simple, it cannot be general. And if accurate and general, the explanation will not be simple. Explanations can not achieve all three dimensions simultaneously.

Effective interpretations accommodate to rather than deny the tradeoffs implicit in this principle. Claims are more modest and involve at most only two of the three criteria. Incompleteness of interpretations is acknowledged and expected.

Most organizations readily admit that their interpretations are incomplete and that there are other ways to make sense of the data. What is less common is an accurate diagnosis of the ways in which the interpretation is incomplete with steps then taken to develop additional interpretations that shore up the original view where it is weakest. Diagnoses and remedies based on tradeoffs among generality, accuracy, and simplicity are clues to the existence of self-limiting and self-correcting interpretation systems.

Pressures for Minimal Consensus

Common symbols are necessary to integrate people of differing interests, but identical interpretations of these symbols are not required for these people to continue their association. Patterned avoidance of interpretational agreement, in fact, tends to be associated with maintenance of social ties. This theme shows up repeatedly in the anthropological literature (e.g., Fernandez, 1965; Keesing, 1974; Wallace, 1961), and it is the basis on which we assert that consensus on interpretations is *not* a simple indicator of effective interpretation systems.

Too great a concern with cultural consensus seems to interfere with social consensus and the readiness to orient actions to one another. Fernandez (1965) proposes this interpretation of the phenomenon:

> The more rigorously regularized social interaction becomes, the more high-ly trained the participants in carrying out an increasingly alternative free interaction, the greater the possibility there is that the symbolic dimension of this interaction should have variable interpretation. This may be for two reasons. The participants are assured of solidarity in the forms of social interaction and need no longer seek it in cultural forms. If, in other words, coexistence is guaranteed socially, coherence need not be sought cultur-ally. Participants may reflect this state of affairs by either manifesting a disinterest in cultural meanings or by prohibiting the gratuitous interpreta-tion of these meanings [p. 912].

Notice some implications of this line of analysis. The greater the cohesive-ness of the group the *less* influence it should have over member's interpreta-tions, a prediction that seems directly opposite to our understanding of cohesion based on laboratory studies. If concern with symbolic meaning decreases when there is an increase in the coordination of social interaction, then a decrease in coordination should be associated with an increase in concern with symbols. People achieve coordination at the expense of deeply shared understandings of what that coordination is all about and what it operates in the service of. If we institutionalize ignorance, this may be because we value social consensus and uninterrupted interaction.

In thinking about interpretation it is easy to invoke words like consensus and sharing and to argue that the more homogeneous the interpretation among persons, the more effective the interpretation system. Modest overlap in interpretations may accompany successful coordination. But, as apparent similarity in meanings becomes more and more evident the student of effectiveness should suspect a more strained sociability among members and a greater likelihood that they will fail at any action that requires coordination. Interpretation systems that achieve perfect agreement are a cause for concern rather than relief.

CONCLUSION

It is not obvious that organizational effectiveness, which is itself a somewhat arbitrary interpretation imposed on organized activity, is especially relevant as a way to understand interpretation systems. The connotations of effectiveness include discrete events, single-valued outcomes, plausible junctures at which assessment can and should occur in a meaningful manner, prescience as to what constitutes better combinations of action and circumstance at some future time, and emphasis on outcomes rather than on process. To supply these connotations to interpretation systems may be to lose the phenomenon of interest. Interpretation is a process through which information is given meaning and actions are chosen. People in organizations are extraordinarily talented at normalizing deviant events, at reconciling outliers to a central tendency, at producing typifications, at making do with scraps of information, and at treating as sufficient whatever is at hand. The result of these tendencies is that workable interpretations can be built from scraps and can consolidate and inform still other bits and pieces of data. The process and the outcomes are a good deal less tidy than many of us have come to associate with effectiveness viewed in terms of other assumptions about organizations. The ideas proposed in this chapter suggest a viewpoint—perhaps a starting point of sorts—from which to interpret the richness and complexity of organizational activity.

Integrative Themes

THEORETICAL ISSUES

1. *What are the major theoretical predictions about the relationship between effectiveness and other organization variables (e.g., technology and structure)?* At this stage in the development of our ideas about interpretation systems, the notion of effectiveness does not relate to other organization variables in the

normal way. For one thing, elements such as technology and structure are to be interpreted. These variables provide pretexts for interpretation, are themselves to be examined as interpretations, are subject to varying interpretations, and can be examined for the extent to which they intrude into the attention of influential people in an organization.

Effectiveness in our framework is not measured in terms of output or efficiency. Effectiveness is more on the order of the "quality" of interpretations. So the question becomes how would something like organization structure or technology tend to influence interpretations, especially of the external environment. If subunits are the organization's sensors, then structural arrangements could influence interpretation. In a functional structure, units would be highly specialized and information interpretation would reflect the perspectives and goals of the functional activities. In a product form of organization (functions grouped together), the divergence of information may be reduced. Thus we can predict that organizational arrangements influence the types of interpretation fed into decision makers. The allocation of resources to boundary spanning activities may also influence interpretation as well as enactment of those interpretations. Creating a market research department may enable the organization to discover new characteristics in the environment. Creating a public affairs department may enable the organization to impose its viewpoint on the external environment. If structure is defined as the allocation of resources to various sensing and enacting functions, then this allocation will influence subsequent interpretation.

The relationship between traditional organizational variables and interpretation is so new that definite predictions are hard to make. Traditional variables may have less impact on such things as interpretation than they do on other facets of organizational behavior.

2. *How does the interpretation system perspective expand our understanding of the behavior of organizations?* The interpretation system perspective provides an effectiveness model that incorporates higher level processes in organizations (Pondy & Mitroff, 1978). The model represents the movement away from mechanical schemes of organization. Organizations are much more than input–output, resource consuming, goal-seeking systems. Organizations also have mechanisms to interpret ambiguous events and to provide meaning for participants. Organizations are as much a meaning system as they are an input–output system. They transform the equivocality and randomness outside the organization into specificity and direction within the organization. Perhaps this transformation of meaning is so widespread that we take it for granted, but it may turn out to be one of the most important functions that organizations perform. If organizations encounter increasing turbulence in their environments, the ability to provide stable frameworks within which participants can function may turn out to be a critical activity for survival.

3. *Does the definition of organizational effectiveness change when considering different types of organizations or different stages of development?* Yes and no. Because interpretation is essential in all organizing and because people organize around interpretations, similar processes should be seen in all kinds of organizations. The quality of interpretation may be an identifiable phenomenon regardless of organization type or stage of development. As a practical matter, however, organizations do vary from one another in ways that may influence interpretation processes. Young organizations have more to learn and fewer guidelines for interpretation than older organizations. Hence they are more likely to engage in "enacting" or "discovering" behavior to acquire their interpretations. They will tend to be test makers rather than test avoiders. Public organizations often seem to generate and manage less equivocality than private organizations, so an effective interpretation in state government might be in the "staring" mood. Public organizations often are storehouses for systematic, objective information.

To the extent that variables such as public–private and new–old represent differences in the environmental context, then the criteria set forth in this chapter should differentiate among degrees of interpretation effectiveness. Criteria such as degree of consensus or density of causal linkages vary across organizations and over the lifetime of organizations. These criteria would tend to capture differences in information processing in different organizational settings.

RESEARCH ISSUES

1. *What are the major indicators of organizational effectiveness?* At one level, the indicator of effectiveness is the correspondence between interpretation and the reality. We identified six major criteria: detailed knowledge, an elaborate taxonomy, causal linkages, capability of reconstructing the input, sensitivity to complexity, and able to keep disagreements tacit. At an operational level, a researcher might compare environment to interpretation, or measure internal information with regard to selectivity, exaggeration, omission, or condensation. These comparisons may reflect the ability of the interpretation to respond to external realities.

When the assumption is made that the organization functions in a subjective environment—reality is not fixed—then the measurement of effectiveness becomes more difficult. The organization enacts what it chooses to enact. It defines its environment based on what it wants to achieve. Of course if this definition does not correspond to activities in the environment or to the organization's ability to enforce its enactment, then the interpretation would be considered ineffective. Thus the interpretation is formed more by enactment than by gathering information, but some of the same dimensions would still apply to the interpretation. Probably the best bet for initial research into interpretation system effectiveness would be the six effectiveness criteria listed in the chapter.

2. *How would one test the efficiency of the interpretation system approach compared to other approaches to effectiveness?* Our approach is not directly comparable to other approaches. The point of Table 4.1 is that investigators make limiting assumptions about organizations. An organization may be viewed as a framework, control system, open system, or differentiated system. Assumptions about the purpose and function of the organization determines the criteria of effectiveness. The interpretation system view is concerned with specialized information reception, choice processes, and equivocality in the external environment. The ability of the organization to deal with equivocality, for example, is simply not comparable to the arrangement of physical elements in the organization under "framework" assumptions. Organizations are different depending on what we want to study. Effectiveness by one approach is not consistent or comparable to effectiveness by another approach.

3. *What are the major methodological issues in operationalizing effectiveness?* At this point, the methodological problems seem enormous. The interpretation system model is basically descriptive and provides a way to categorize and understand various forms of interpretation. Trying to make prescriptive statements, such as which mode of interpretation is superior, is risky. Concerning levels of analysis, the model in Figure 4.1 should be studied at the organizational level. Figure 4.1 reflects organizational strategies. The measurement of specific interpretations, however, should probably be conducted at the group level of analysis. Groups are formed around interpretations, and the form and quality of the interpretation could be assessed at that level.

Data collection poses many problems. The important data pertain to "meaning." In this sense, there will be no simple, tangible indicators, such as numbers of letters or telephone calls, that indicate interpretation system effectiveness. Investigators must be prepared to wade into the organization and attempt to understand at a deeper level how interpretations work. In some cases, the interpretation system may not be determinant. We may not be able to measure interpretation in any clear and objective way. It is an individual process, incorporating such things as human consciousness and understanding, and these variables are not readily measurable. The investigator's own interpretation may confound the issue.

Despite the methodological problems, we hope exploratory research is undertaken. To the extent that interpretations are a central function of organizations, any insight, however meager, will enhance our understanding of organizations.

PRACTICAL ISSUES

1. *What prescriptions or guidelines for improving success are suggested by the interpretation system approach?* We suggest two prescriptions. First, the job of

management is to interpret, not to get the work of the organization done. Our model calls attention to the need to make sense of things, to be aware of external events and cues, and to translate them into meaning for organizational participants. Managers are actively involved in this process and are responsible for it. Managers may do interpretations intuitively, without realizing the role they play in defining the organization and its role for other participants. One prescription, then, is for managers to understand and take seriously their role as interpreters.

The other useful aspect of the model is that it provides a comparative perspective for managers. The model calls attention to possibilities they may not have thought of before in terms of interpretation system strategies. If managers have spent their organizational lives in a discovery-oriented interpretation system, using relatively sophisticated monitoring systems, they might want to consider modifying these activities and going to a more subjective approach. Perhaps discovery-oriented managers would do as well to consider intuition and hunch in certain situations, and to launch test markets instead of market surveys. Passive test avoiders might be encouraged to try breaking the rules to see what happens. The value of any comparative model is that it provides new alternatives. Managers can then understand where they are as opposed to where they might like to be. They may improve their performance by adopting different interpretation strategies.

Counterintuitive recommendations would include (a) leap before you look; (b) complicate your organization; (c) do not diagnose until the cure is completed; (d) indecision ensures flexibility; (e) ambivalence is the optimal compromise; and (f) mind dominates over matter.

2. *What diagnostic tools could managers use to monitor success?* Managers would have to monitor interpretations rather than more traditional indicators (expenditures, profits) of success. They would have to spend time learning the perceptions of participants throughout the organization and how participants enact their role and the role of the units for which they are responsible. Specific diagnostic tools would be in-depth interviews that would lead to the construction of organizational worlds, perceived roles in the larger organization, completion of modified Kelly personal construct tests (Shaw & McKnight, 1981), or perhaps labels could be sorted and developed for events that occur. Research would be required to develop monitoring devices about interpretations. The devices that would be used by managers would be analogous to monitoring devices developed by scholars to understand interpretation systems. Progress in one arena will add to progress in the other. The needs of scholars and managers are similar in this respect.

3. *What trade-offs, dilemmas, or dysfunctional consequences might be experienced by managers using this approach?* There are many dilemmas and trade-offs in the interpretation system framework. Organizations cannot do everything. Possible dilemmas include the generality–simplicity–accuracy dilemma, the dilemma

between believing past experience and doubting the relevance of past experience, the dilemma that inquiry to see if something exists actually makes it exist whether it did before or not, and the dilemma that you will know what you have done only after it is too late to do things differently. Dilemmas are woven into organizations, people, and events. Things appear just as they seem *and* exactly the opposite. Paradoxes are inevitable in an overdetermined world that is examined by people with bounded rationality and vested interests. To view such a world as instinctively punlike is not to play with language. Rather it is to evoke an image within the language that points simultaneously at both the absolute necessity for interpretations and their inevitable failure to provide more than a momentary glimpse of multiple realities. Effective organizations have both high and low absentism, both cohesion and conflict, both efficiency and waste. Limits are indigenous to organizational life. Some measures of effectiveness hide these dilemmas more fully for longer periods than do others. But the dilemmas are there and they are durable. To manage them is necessary to the attainment of effectiveness in interpretation systems. That is why interpretation systems need to be understood more fully, fleeting though each interpretation may be.

REFERENCES

Bougon, M., Weick, K. E., & Binkhorst, D. Cognition in organizations: An analysis of the Utrecht Jazz Orchestra. *Administrative Science Quarterly*, 1977, 22, 606–639.

Boulding, K. E. General systems theory: The skeleton of a science. *Management Science*, 1956, 2, 197–207.

Braybrooke, D. The mystery of executive success re-examined. *Administrative Science Quarterly*, 1964, 8, 533–560.

Bruner, J. S., Goodnow, J. J., & Austin, G. A. *A study of thinking.* New York: Wiley, 1956.

Cameron, K. Assessing organizational effectiveness in institutions of higher education. *Administrative Science Quarterly*, 1978, 23, 604–632.

Clark, P. Personal communication. Queen's University, Kingston, Ontario, 1978.

Daft, R. L. The evolution of organizational analysis in ASQ, 1959–1970. *Administrative Science Quarterly*, 1980, 25, 623–636.

Fernandez, J. W. Symbolic consensus in a Fang reformative cult. *American Anthropologist*, 1965, 67, 902–929.

Garfinkel, H. *Studies in ethnomethodology.* Englewood Cliffs, N.J.: Prentice-Hall, 1967.

Geertz, C. *The interpretation of cultures.* New York: Basic, 1973.

Goodman, P. S., & Pennings, J. M. (Eds.). *New perspectives on organizational effectiveness.* San Francisco: Jossey-Bass, 1977.

Hall, R. H. *Organization: Structure and process.* Englewood Cliffs, N.J.: Prentice-Hall, 1977.

Heider, F. *The psychology of interpersonal relations.* New York: Wiley, 1958.

Huck, S. W., and Sandler, H. M. *Rival hypotheses: Alternative interpretations of data based conclusions.* New York: Harper and Row, 1979.

Keesing, R. M. Theories of culture. In B. J. Siegel (Ed.), *Annual Review of Anthropology*, 1974, 3, 73–97.

Levi-Strauss, C. *The savage mind*. Chicago: University of Chicago Press, 1966.

McKelvey, B. Organizational systematics: Taxonomic lessons from biology. *Management Science*, 1978, *24* (13), 1428–1440.

Manning, P. K. Semiotics and loosely coupled organizations. Unpublished manuscript, Michigan State University, 1979.

March, J. G., & Simon, H. A. *Organizations*. New York: Wiley, 1958.

Pondy, L. R., & Mitroff, I. I. Beyond open systems models of organizations. In Barry M. Staw (Ed.), *Research in organizational behavior*. Greenwood, Conn.: JAI Press, 1978.

Price, J. *Organizational effectiveness*. Homewood, Ill.: Irwin, 1968.

Shaw, M. L. G., & McKnight, C. *Think again: Personal problem-solving and decision making*. Englewood Cliffs, N.J.: Prentice-Hall, 1981.

Steers, R. M. Problems in the measurement of organizational effectiveness, *Administrative Science Quarterly*, 1975, *20*, 546–548.

Steinbeck, J. *The log from the Sea of Cortez*. New York: Viking, 1941.

Thorngate, W. "Ingeneral" vs "it depends": Some comments on the Gergen-Schlenker debate. *Personality and Social Psychology Bulletin*, 1976, *2*, 404–410.

Wallace, A. F. C. *Culture and personality*. New York: Random, 1961.

Weick, K. E. *The social psychology of organizing* (2nd ed.). Reading, Mass.: Addison-Wesley, 1979.

Yuchtman, E., & Seashore, S. A systems resource approach to organizational effectiveness. *American Sociological Review*, 1967, *32*, 891–903.

WALTER R. NORD

A Political–Economic Perspective on Organizational Effectiveness

The study of organizational effectiveness is plagued by many of the problems that are common to most topics studied in the field of organization behavior. Although the problems are common, they seem to be more severe in the treatment of effectiveness. Some of the problems are definitional; some are methodological. For example, Cameron (1978) noted that despite 50 years of research on the topic, we still do not know what organizational effectiveness is. Coulter (1979) observed: "There seems to be little consensus on how to conceptualize, measure, and explain effectiveness [p. 65]." Hannan and Freeman (1977, pp. 106–131) went so far as to assert that the concept is not researchable. Connolly, Conlon, and Deutsch (1980) summarized the matter well— "The field of organizational effectiveness research appears to be in conceptual disarray [p. 211]." Because effectiveness is often viewed as the bottom line measure of performance, this chaotic state of affairs about such a major dependent variable is indeed troublesome.

Though some of the disarray is due to factors such as measurement problems and resource limitations that afflict most research on organizations, the treatment of effectiveness is made more chaotic by the fact that it causes a number of difficult value and political issues, which in studies of other topics can remain latent, to become manifest. In essence the definition of effectiveness requires some explicit normative statement about *what* the organization should be doing for *whom*. These are not matters that can be easily dispensed with by

95

ORGANIZATIONAL EFFECTIVENESS
A Comparison of Multiple Models

pointing to the need for further research, better methodology, etc. Instead they raise some provocative questions about the basis of legitimacy of various goals. Typically these issues have been obscured from inquiry by accepted institutional arrangements (McNeil, 1978) and are not resolvable by positivistic methods of inquiry.

Adequate treatment of effectiveness requires new and more encompassing approaches than those that dominate mainstream organization behavior (OB). These approaches need to *incorporate* the value and political issues rather than either implicitly or explicitly omitting them. Such approaches are best described by the term *political economy.* As Elliot (1978) noted, they assume that politics and economics cannot be distinguished except "as alternative . . . ways of looking at society . . . [p. 107]" and that economic activity needs to be thought of "as a power system as well as an economizing process [p. 107]."

This chapter is a preliminary attempt to develop such an approach. I shall begin with a brief review of some of the literature that has pointed to the importance of value judgments in the treatment of effectiveness. Second, I shall outline a perspective derived from critical theory and welfare economics that I believe can provide the basis for a more comprehensive approach. I shall then attempt to describe some of the theoretical and research issues that the political economics perspective suggests deserve priority. Finally, I shall speculate about possible implications for academics and practitioners.

VALUE ISSUES IN CONCEPTUALIZING
ORGANIZATIONAL EFFECTIVENESS

Support for the earlier assertion that the value issues are closer to the surface in the study of effectiveness than they are in other topics treated by organizational behaviorists comes from a number of recent contributions that have acknowledged the need to define organizational effectiveness from the perspective of a variety of constituents. Campbell (1977, pp. 13–55) and Goodman and Pennings (1977, pp. 1–12) suggested that the particular criteria chosen in studies of effectiveness reflect value judgments and represent political economic decisions. Similarly, Scott (1977, pp. 63–95) observed that any set of criteria will represent the preferences of some interest groups more than it does the preferences of other people. He suggested we deal with the problem by specifying the normative basis of our choice of criteria and then build knowledge from comparisons based on various premises. Dubin (1976, pp. 7–13) observed that the meaning of organizational effectiveness viewed from inside the organization cannot be reconciled with the view from outside the organization. He agreed with Scott on the need for being explicit about what viewpoint is being taken at a given time. Though some scholars, including Cummings (1977, pp. 56–62), Keeley (1978), and Perrow (1977, pp. 96–105) have followed the general approach suggested by Scott and Dubin of specifying interest groups and criteria of interest, they too recognized that the choice is, at least to some extent, arbitrary. A variant of this approach, employed by still other writers, such as Cameron (1978) and Connolly, Conlon, and Deutsch (1980), is the multiple constituency approach, which attempts to specify all the criteria that might be used to evaluate effectiveness. Another version of the multiple constituency approach was adopted by Katz and Kahn (1978). They recognized the multiple constituency argument but sought to deal with it by defining the goals of external constituents as constraints and then concluding that "organizational effectiveness consists of maximization within these constraints [p. 254]." This approach is less satisfactory because in essence it "solves" the value problem by moving it outside the boundary of organizational theory. The "solution" proposed in this chapter is the opposite of Katz and Kahn's; the present approach seeks to expand the boundaries of organizational theory to incorporate the value issues.

A second criteria of research on effectiveness that demonstrates the centrality of value issues is the charge that the research has focused almost exclusively at microlevels—what Scott (1977) called "microquality variables." Support for this point is strong. Almost all of Campbell's (1977, pp. 13–55) 30-item list of effectiveness criteria and Steers' (1977) briefer list of adaptability, flexibility, productivity, job satisfaction, profitability, and resource acquisition are of this nature. Absent from such lists of microeffectiveness criteria are what Scott called macroquality criteria, which treat how effectively organizations provide for the community at large.

Most treatments of organizational effectiveness have ignored macroquality criteria and proceeded as if greater microeffectiveness is preferable to less without discussion of the extent or process by which such effectiveness benefits society. Some writers have asserted that microquality effectiveness is desirable because it contributes to survival of the organization but provide no rationale for why the survival of a particular firm is desirable. In short, most treatments of organizational effectiveness have failed to meet what Silverman (1970) considered to be a necessary criterion for any organization theory—the specification of the relationship between organizations and larger society.

It appears that the development of macroquality approaches are inhibited by the absence of intellectual and research traditions within the organizational literature that legitimate or encourage the study of dependent variables that are not closely related to the interests of people or groups rather directly associated with a firm or focal organization. A number of perspectives might be useful in developing a macro perspective. In this chapter I will advance a political economic view based on concepts from critical theory and welfare economics.

CRITICAL THEORY AND WELFARE ECONOMICS

Critical theory and welfare economics are not necessarily closely linked although there are important points of convergence. For present purposes, their somewhat polemical position vis-à-vis the dominant models in their disciplines and their convergence on analysis of society as a whole are two of their important similarities.

Critical Theory

During the last 5 to 10 years a critical theory of organizations has received an increased amount of attention. (See Allen [1975], Benson [1977], Clegg & Dunkerley [1977], Heydebrand [1977], Goldman & VanHouten [1977], and Nord [1974, 1977].) Although it is difficult to describe critical theory in a few words, several of its central features have been well summarized by Heydebrand (1978).

> A critical theory of organizations ought to address a number of issues. First, it ought to be "critical" in the sense of revealing the historically embedded, partial, and ideological nature of organizational theories rather than treating such theories merely as more or less adequate reproductions of immediately perceived phenomena.
>
> It follows from this expanded notion of "critical" that organizations themselves should be viewed as part of a larger sociohistorical context and as embedded in specific modes of production, political economies, and sociohistorical processes. . . . Thus such concepts as power, control, rules, resources, production, goals, output or effectiveness cannot be neutral technical terms describing nearly universal social relations; they are, above all, ideological terms relevant to political positions and strategies within specific historical settings and struggles [p. 640].

This perspective highlights a number of issues. First, it encourages us to take the ideological basis for any definition of effectiveness as problematic and to examine the historical process through which currently dominant criteria won out over other criteria. Second, as the nature of the historical processes reveals that existing social patterns and institutions were created by human activity and choice, they take on a less absolutist appearance. Consequently, the existing patterns appear as rather arbitrary arrangements and subject to inquiry and change. Third, as the existing goals, rules, structures, and criteria for evaluation come to be seen as outcomes of a process of struggle in which certain interest groups won out over others, not necessarily because they were more efficient or more rational but because they were more powerful, the criteria of the losers in these struggles gain new prominence. Finally, although not fully reflected in Heydebrand's summary statement, the critical view is wholistic in its emphasis. As Benson (1977) noted, from such a perspective an observer considers organizations and other social systems as interpenetrating totalities and views conventional boundaries as arbitrary phenomena that must be distrusted.

In short, critical theory provides a perspective that can help reduce the impact of existing social patterns on our perceptions and consequently open us to new, more wholistic options. Clearly it still retains many elements of its Marxist roots. However, when it is used as an analytical tool, as it appears to be in the organizational literature, it becomes a rather conservative Marxism—if it is Marxism at all. Though it tends to emphasize many features of what Gouldner (1980) described as "critical Marxism," it does not stress the revolutionary aspects. Moreover, it is certainly very different from Gouldner's "scientific Marxism," in which the collapse of the capitalist system is viewed as an inevitable consequence. As such it is a useful intellectual perspective although many critical theorists would argue that given its low commitment to *praxis*, it is not really critical theory at all.

Welfare Economics

According to Scitovsky (1951), welfare economics is concerned with assessing the efficiency of the market economy and comparing its efficiency with that of planned economies. In this context efficiency refers to the effectiveness of the economic system in employing scarce resources to satisfy the needs of the whole community. Generally this perspective draws heavily on the market as a mechanism to allocate resources but stresses the limitations of the market process for maximizing human welfare when considerations such as equity, justice, and joint consumption effects are included as criteria.

Welfare economics and critical theory provide complementary perspectives for considering the macroquality effectiveness of organizations. Throughout this chapter I will argue that these two frameworks help us to see how the micro- and macroquality criteria of organizational effectiveness are frequently in tension with each other.

From elementary economics it can be argued that under the conditions of perfect competition (e.g., many small firms, informed consumers, easy entry into the industry, etc.) the so-called invisible hand operates to constrain organizations to use resources in ways that contribute to the welfare of members of society. Under these conditions there is some reason to assume a strong, positive correlation between the effectiveness of individual firms and the well-being of society. After all, according to this model, because the ineffective firm will not satisfy the needs of society (i.e., consumers), it will not gain enough resources to survive. Thus macroquality effectiveness is produced because microquality effectiveness is assured.

Unfortunately, as welfare economists (e.g., Scitovsky, 1951) have long recognized, the model of perfect competition provides a poor description of the modern economy. Moreover, even if the model did describe reality well, the operation of the individual firm would fail to provide for an efficient allocation of resources when considered from the perspective of the whole.[1] In addition, the modern firm is affected by so many factors, including government regulation, unionization, monopoly power, and corporate profits taxes, so that efforts to increase the effectiveness of individual firms on microquality dimensions will have less impact on the welfare of the whole than is often assumed. In fact, the impact can often be quite negative; Milton Friedman's (1962) discussion of the American Medical Association (AMA) provides a useful example.

Friedman observed that the AMA has been very effective in its own terms. It has promoted the interests of its members; it has ample resources; it has strong political influence. Moreover, it has helped promote high quality medical service. Entry into the profession is restricted to an elite group of students, and generally high quality training is assured. As a result, Friedman said that we have "Cadillac" medical service. However, from the point of view of society as a whole, because consumers have no alternative to Cadillac quality and price, there is a severe misuse of resources. Many possible consumers are not served and others pay exorbitant rates for services that do not require Cadillac training. In short, the AMA would be highly effective when evaluated in terms of most of Steers' (1977) and Campbell's (1977, pp. 13–55) microquality dimensions but less effective in serving the medical needs of the community. Thus it is clear that the sum of the effectiveness (if it could be calculated) of each organization within the population of organizations within a social system is not an accurate index of their effectiveness in serving the needs of society.

If the effectiveness of each individual firm cannot be counted on to advance the welfare of the totality, what options are available? One part of the answer is to consider the effectiveness of the total set of organizations taken together; I shall call this approach the "population perspective of organizational effectiveness."

THE POPULATION PERSPECTIVE OF
ORGANIZATIONAL EFFECTIVENESS

Instead of looking only at the effectiveness of organizations one by one and assuming that the effectiveness of organizations for serving society can be

---

[1]Throughout this chapter, I shall refer to the welfare of the "whole," the "totality," or society as a whole. In all cases I am referring to the sum of individual satisfactions rather than to some abstract collectivity as these terms sometimes imply.

obtained by summing the effectiveness of the individual organizations on criteria relevant to these individual units, the population perspectives directs attention to the effectiveness of the entire set or family of organizations in contributing to the welfare of the community. Consequently, it focuses on an expanded set of criteria for conceptualizing effectiveness.

The idea of looking at the effectiveness of families of organizations or the entire population of organizations was suggested by Weick (1977) and Pondy (1977, pp. 226–234), who note the advantages of diversity within a population of organizations in facilitating innovation and adaptability. Pondy, in particular, stressed the value of diversity for protecting individuals from exploitation by reducing the dangers of central control and for promoting individual and organizational development. However, the advantages of the population viewpoint go much further.

A major contribution of the population approach is the introduction of new criteria for assessing effectiveness. It encourages us to go beyond the criteria of microquality analysis and hence, to be more sensitive to outcomes that are not of concern to any one organization but which are meaningful to members of the community as a whole. In this approach, many criteria of effectiveness, which economists and individual firms consider externalities, become of central concern.

The criteria considered in this chapter are a small subset of the relevant ones. In fact, if (as I do) one views organizations as one of the most central institutions in determining the quality of life in our society, all 28 variables employed by Hage (1978, pp. 103–145) to describe the quality of societies are relevant dimensions. My effort here is far less ambitious. The criteria I shall consider here can be treated under three headings: (*a*) provision of goods and services; (*b*) effects of the pursuit of microquality effectiveness on the construction of social institutions; and (*c*) provision of high-quality income-generating opportunities. Though each of these three sets of criteria includes some ideas unique to it, each also overlaps with aspects of the other two sets. The three are treated separately here only to facilitate exposition.

Provision of Goods and Services

Dimensions of this first set of criteria pertain to how well organizations provide for the economic needs of members of the social system. Basically, success on these criteria is evaluated by the extent to which the economic system employs resources to provide goods and services in accordance with the preferences and needs of members of society. More specific measures, such as price, quantity, quality, and variety of goods and services available from a given pool of resources are derived from this more general concern.

Organizations that are effective on microquality criteria (e.g., efficiency, flexibility, productivity) contribute to optimal resource utilization in a number of ways. However, there are also a number of ways (at least under current conditions) that firms that are effective in these terms simultaneously retard optimal utilization. This assertion raises a series of complex economic issues. In this section, I shall consider three of those contradictions.

PRODUCER BEHAVIOR AND IMPERFECT COMPETITION

A major source of potential problems is the rational behavior (rational in a microquality sense) of firms under conditions of oligopoly and monopoly. One of the most provocative discussions of these issues can be found in Baran and Sweezy's (1966) book entitled *Monopoly Capital.* Baran and Sweezy described a number of processes through which the behaviors of monopolistic firms contribute to an economically inefficient allocation of resources.

They noted that such firms misallocate resources because a central feature of oligopolistic industries is the virtual elimination of price cutting as a competitive weapon. In the absence of incentives to reduce prices, the achievement of microquality effectiveness (i.e., an organization's profitability, satisfaction of its members, resource acquisition, adaptability–flexibility, etc.) leads to an underutilization and misapplication of resources. Resources become underutilized due to processes that retard production, investment, and innovation. They become misappropriated when the sales efforts take forms other than price competition (e.g., noninformative advertising). A prime example of some of these costs was provided by Fisher, Griliches, and Kaysen (1962) who concluded that over a period of several years the cost of automobile model changes came to approximately 25% of the total cost of the automobiles. Resources also misallocated from a social welfare perspective as firms devote their surplus resources to philanthropy and charitable matters or to such items as corporate offices, airplanes, etc., which Baran and Sweezy saw as the modern equivalent of the potlach in which people are dazzled and awed by conspicuous waste and to satisfying the personal objectives of their managers for power and growth. Numerous other economists, including ones from very diverse perspectives (e.g., Friedman [1962], Galbraith [1973], and Marglin [1975]), have made similar observations.

So far I have considered only the *costs* of the absence of price competition. However, the welfare effects of monopolistic firms are not all negative. For example, to the degree that the capital market is competitive, at least part of the value of a firm's surplus will be reflected in shareholder earnings. Second, Baran and Sweezy observed that, because a major source of power is efficient production, firms are strongly motivated to reduce production costs. Third, by comparison with small competitive firms, large firms often have the technical expertise to be more efficient. Fourth, it is possible that expenditures on model changes and noninformative advertising permit optimal-size production runs.

Finally, there is no way to say that the total welfare of society is not improved by the enhanced enjoyment of products that may result from things such as model changes. Of course, there is also no way to demonstrate that these things improve welfare under present conditions because of a second feature of monopoly capitalism—the erosion of consumer sovereignty.

CONSUMER SOVEREIGNTY

If resources are to be allocated optimally for serving the needs of members of society, then consumer preferences must be effective in controlling the decisions of producers. Economists call this control, which operates most effectively under the conditions of perfect competition, consumer sovereignty.

Before examining consumer sovereignty, it is important to note that even if the market is operating perfectly, the welfare economists tell us that due to inequalities in income distribution and the failure of the so-called rational consumer to take into account the effects of his/her purchase decisions on others, society's needs may not be well served. As Scitovsky (1976) noted, traditional economic reasoning is misleading by its tendency to ignore so-called externalities. Scitovsky wrote:

> While national product provides an estimate of the worth of market goods and services to those who buy them, those goods and services often yield satisfaction or give pain to third parties as well. . . . Those so-called external economies and diseconomies are not considered part of the economic product because the people affected neither pay nor are compensated for them, but they clearly add to and detract from human satisfaction [pp. 85–86].

Scitovsky added:

> the performance of the economy cannot be judged by the size, growth, and distribution of the national product alone. As important, or perhaps more important, is the economy's ability to produce the economic product with a maximum of beneficial and minimum of harmful accompanying side effects [p. 105].

Scitovsky also suggested that because economics treats only those aspects of human satisfaction that pass through the marketplace, it omits or gives too little weight to sources of satisfaction (e.g., personal service, advice, enjoyment from interaction with friends) but by tradition or custom are given free. Thus, even if consumer sovereignty in the marketplace were fully operational, under current arrangements individual consumers still could not control the allocation of resources to maximize total economic welfare.

Generally, however, the term *consumer sovereignty* is not used in connection with these collective welfare effects but refers to the ability of consumers to control producers through the normal market mechanism. Though the total welfare effects are central to our evaluation of the population of organizations, for the time being I will focus on the more traditional, narrower view. As we shall see, it is at this level that some of the contradictions between the pursuit of microquality and the conditions that are necessary to permit a market system to allocate resources in an economically efficient way are most apparent.

All organizations are constrained, to some extent, by consumer needs and tastes. However, work from organization theory (e.g., Thompson, 1967) and economics reveals that firms that are effective on microquality dimensions devote considerable effort to protecting their core functions from all sources of uncertainty—including variations in consumer tastes. These efforts include a number of tactics: sales efforts with individual consumers; advertisements designed to mold tastes; and efforts to mold institutional environments and social networks that define standards and social priorities in ways to shape the demands for products or services that the organization seeks to provide (Meyer & Rowan, 1977). In short, although constraints exist, organizations can often increase their microeffectiveness by reducing consumer sovereignty.

Another means for managing consumer preference is through limiting the availability of alternatives. Scitovsky (1976) argued that, in our society, total social welfare is inhibited because two factors—uninformed consumers and the decline of market competition—combine to reduce the number of alternatives available. Consequently, there is a collective bias to mass produce goods because each individual producer seeks to tap a relatively large segment of the market.

The limitation of alternatives has mixed consequences for the effective allocation of resources. On the one hand, restriction of alternatives contributes to the efficient processing of resources because it allows the technical advantages associated with economies of scale to be achieved. On the other hand, the reduction of alternatives means that important sources of satisfaction and consumer power are lost. For example, as Scitovsky has argued, there is a bias against novelty in production. Because producers prefer longer runs and fewer sources of major uncertainty, consumers are deprived of novelty. Under norms of microrationality, producers prefer to provide variety through model changes and changes in fashion rather than by producing an array of diverse goods more or less simultaneously. (The recent history of the U.S. automobile industry is an example of how producers became divorced from consumer preferences. Model changes represented only minor innovations in most cases. Consumer sovereignty was only "re-established" through foreign producers.)

Lindblom (1977) took a similar stance. He observed that under current conditions consumers tend to have only veto power. Product initiative is with the producers and they control the alternatives available. To the degree there is a conflict between the preferences of consumers and producers, producers' preferences for offering a few basic alternatives and offering alternatives with a short life span are apt to win out.

Consumer sovereignty is also reduced by the development of producers who, for a variety of reasons, are much more knowledgeable about their products than are most potential consumers. As the expert power of the producers comes to dwarf that of consumers, producers exercise even greater control. The knowledge gap is so great that Lindblom (1977) observed that producers often are able to get away with deliberately misrepresenting their products, at the expense of the consumer's welfare.

> The rules and incentives of market systems encourage sellers to resolve any doubts they have about the safety of their products in favor of profits rather than health of customer in all those circumstances in which injury to his health cannot be definitively tied to use of the product. The labeling of pharmaceuticals with obfuscating neologisms and the continued resistance of the food industry to adequate indication of additives on packaged foods drown us in evidence both of consumer incompetence and of corporate energy to preserve so splendid a source of earnings. The magnitude of the phenomenon is indicated by the possibility, now that new chemical food additives are developed every day without much testing of long-term consequences, that the major diseases of the affluent peoples of the world will from now on be man-made epidemics [p. 152].

From a population or macroquality perspective, informed, effective consumers are a necessary condition for organizational effectiveness. Accordingly, one criterion for evaluating the effectiveness of individual firms and sets of firms is their contribution to consumer sophistication and assertion. In contrast, from a microquality perspective, informed consumers are often more of a problem than a criterion of success.

One final challenge to consumer sovereignty posed by microquality effective organizations can be found in the work of Karpik (1978, pp. 15–68). Karpik suggested that there are two fundamentally different economic forms that are often conflated by organization theorists. On the one hand, there is "classical capitalism." In this form similar organizations compete with each other to sell fairly homogeneous goods; the outputs of each organization are ready substitutes for those of their competitors. Because in these industries price and volume of production are key in determining economic success and success is controlled by final consumption, it seems reasonable to assume that consumer needs to exercise at least some influence over the allocation of resources.

Kapik labeled the second economic form "technological capitalism." In technological capitalism the key process is research that generates new products that, for some time, can only be marketed by the organization that was first to develop the product. Karpik argued that in these industries conventional economic theory does not describe the key processes because development of products actually creates consumer wants; in Karpik's words, it "creates human nature." An organization in such an industry is effective by virtue of its success in creating markets—often by political means—which it can serve exclusively. Thus, Karpik argued, in technological capitalism, organizations play political roles; they create the environments they serve and, at least under current institutional arrangements, are not governed by the final consumers. Consequently, the link between their microquality effectiveness and the efficient allocations of resources from a welfare economics perspective is difficult to establish.

Two final points about consumer sovereignty and its relationship to total economic welfare are relevant. First, things are neither black nor white. For example, there is no way to know whether total welfare would be enhanced or reduced in the supply of comfort goods. This issue has been a concern of economists; the macroquality perspective suggests it should be one for students of organizational effectiveness as well. Second, it can be argued that organizations that are effective in getting resources and managing their environments enhance total welfare by making work satisfying and by making the organizations' resources available for the personal use of participants. These benefits may more than compensate for the absence of consumer sovereignty. In fact, Cummings (1977, pp. 56–62) suggested that the availability of organizational resources for achieving member goals is a useful measure of effectiveness. In other words, organizations that are effective on some microquality dimensions (e.g., getting resources) may have slack resources that members can use to their own ends. Consequently, total economic welfare may increase *because* firms control consumer tastes and achieve profits above those that would result from competitive prices. Undoubtedly Cummings has pointed to an important source of satisfaction, but total welfare implications of his argument are difficult to assess.

Implicit in Cummings's argument seems to be an alternative criterion for allocating resources from the economic criterion of marginal productivity. Consequently his position raises a new issue for political economic analysis. Currently an important source of legitimacy for organizations is the belief that they serve consumers. To the degree that organization resources are used to satisfy the interests of their members qua members, the satisfaction of consumers is sacrificed. Cummings's suggestion points to the need to analyze mechanisms that permit access to the control of organizations and govern the distribution of advantages to participants within the organization; in short, it provides an additional reason for considering the effectiveness of modern work organizations as a political as well as an economic issue.

FAILURE AND ECONOMIC WELFARE

It is often assumed that economic efficiency is advanced through a "survival of the fittest" process in which the organizations that are least successful in satisfying the wants of consumers fail and those which are most successful flourish. In many ways this process does contribute to the economic welfare of society. However, its effects are less benign than they are often assumed to be. For one thing, as already noted, in oligopolistic–monopolistic industries, inefficient firms do not necessarily fail. Similarly, as Pfeffer and Salancik (1978) suggested, organizational size itself contributes to survival. The consequences of failure of some firms (e.g., Chrysler) would be so negative for influential groups in society that governments act to keep them in existence. In short, the "survival of the fittest" organizations does not assure that resources will be used in an economically efficient manner.

Moreover, Hirschman (1970) suggested that even if economically efficient firms survive and the less efficient firms fail, resources still may be wasted. Hirschman observed that there are a number of marginal firms whose effectiveness is only a little too low to permit their survival. If these organizations are dismantled, all the benefits from the "sunk costs" (e.g., administrative work that was invested in the firm and in planning for the future) cease providing any benefits to society. Further, the dislocation of individuals and the unemployment that results have substantial psychological and social costs that are not represented in normal economic calculations. Similarly, many of the capital resources (e.g., building, certain machines, etc.) have little or no salvage value and those that do have salvage value may stand idle for years. All of these outcomes reduce the effectiveness of the total population of organizations in utilizing the resources of society.

Of course, I do not wish to imply that firms should always be saved from failure. However, I am suggesting that we consider more of the real costs in our analysis of the effectiveness of a family of organizations. The failure of an organization to achieve a high level of microquality effectiveness does not mean that society is best served by instantaneously dismantling the organization.[2]

SUMMARY–CONCLUSIONS

Students of organizational effectiveness have implicitly accepted microquality effectiveness as a worthy social objective; in this section I have treated some of the problems in accepting this objective as a starting point. In particu-

---

[2]Economic cycles are a related matter. As will be discussed late in my treatment of unemployment, some economists have argued that economic cycles are deliberately induced in our economic system to force discipline and efficiency. To the extent this argument is valid, the costs of economic cycles must appear in the debit column in evaluating organization effectiveness.

lar, I have tried to show a number of conflicts between microquality organization effectiveness and the effectiveness of the population of organizations in providing for economic welfare. To the degree that these contradictions are real and result in serious misallocation of resources, measures of microquality effectiveness cannot be the only criteria for evaluating the contribution of an organization to society's economic well-being. Consequently, students of organization effectiveness need to be more circumspect about the economic and philosophical reasons for taking microquality effectiveness as a worthy goal than they have been in the past.

Organizational Effectiveness and the Construction of Social Institutions

So far I have considered how the population approach can alter our perception of what organization effectiveness is by examining economic criteria. In doing so, it became apparent that modern organizations have political as well as economic consequences. In this section I shall argue that some of the most important effects of organizations are on our political institutions and that these consequences must also be incorporated in evaluations of their effectiveness. Microquality analysts often overlook these consequences; macroquality analysts see them as being far more central. These consequences include the shaping of: the criteria used in evaluating social choices; institutions that create a "suitable" work force; government and of governmental processes and the "possible" governance processes in society.

CRITERIA USED IN SOCIAL CHOICES

Though the organizational literature has become concerned with how organizations create larger environments, sociologists such as Marx and Weber pioneered describing the general historical processes involved. Recently writers in the organizational literature, including Meyer and Rowan (1977), McNeil (1978), Brown (1978), Aldrich (1979), and Zeitz (1980), have discussed ways in which organizations create their environments by influencing the issues viewed as decisionable and the criteria used in making decisions.

Of these approaches, the work of McNeil, Brown, and Zeitz comes closest to the macroquality perspective advocated here. Building on the work of Max Weber, McNeil focused on how the needs of organizational elites for control become embedded in social institutions. For example, McNeil observed that the norms of rationality play a central role in the struggle for control of institutions and resources through their influence on the premises of decision makers and the legitimation of certain criteria as the appropriate ones to employ in making decisions. Similarly, Brown observed how rationality can be used "as a prospective rhetoric for closing off unwanted alternatives and advancing one's own agenda [p. 371]." Zeitz argued that other organizations have become important elements in the environment of any given organization and consequently organizations are becoming "increasingly 'political' as they develop conscious strategies to control other organizations [p. 77]."

The macroquality perspective calls attention to the: relative nature of the criteria used in making the legitimating social choices; utilitarian philosophy that seems to underlie microquality analysis; value of considering social as well as individual utilities for evaluating a political economic system; and consequences of organizations on society. It is sympathetic to examining the impact that organizations have elsewhere in the social system and considering indices of those outcomes as part of the assessment of effectiveness of the population of organizations. The discussion of five of these outcomes that follow makes it clear that microquality effectiveness has been purchased at a substantial cost.

CREATION OF A SUITABLE WORKFORCE

Historians have analyzed a number of ways in which organizations have influenced the development of social institutions that have produced a disciplined workforce suited to the needs of the factory system. E. P. Thompson (1967) and Pollard (1965) have described how property relations, systems of power, and religious institutions functioned in England to socialize a workforce that was suited to industrial discipline. Gutman (1977) described a parallel process in the United States. Daniel Rodgers's (1978) analysis of the work ethic in the United States pointed out a number of ways in which the needs of organizations for a disciplined work force were served by a number of intellectuals, social reformers, and religious leaders who helped to create a social doctrine that papered over the inherent contradictions between the demands of modern industry and the requirements of a free, democratic society. Linder (1970) suggested some of the recent costs of the emphasis on work. Overall, it is clear that modern organizations are only viable if a suitable workforce exists. The process through which such a work force has been (and continues to be) shaped was a harsh one and institutionalized a number of constraints on the opportunity of individuals to exercise free choice about many aspects of life at work and outside the workplace.

DIRECT INFLUENCE ON NATURE OF THE GOVERNMENT

A number of historians have discussed how members of the American business elite influenced governmental structures and policies in ways that contributed to the success of certain forms of organizations and to the failure of others. Two of the most important treatments of this process have been written by Weinstein (1968) and Kolko (1963). These writers have argued that in the early 1900s a coalition of members of the business elite and government officials developed a legal climate and comprehensive ideology that was suited to the dominance of large corporations. Although this process cannot be adequately summarized in a few sentences, Weinstein argued persuasively that leaders of giant corporations and financial institutions consciously developed a form of liberalism that enabled them to have their interests fully interwoven with natural policies. He showed how the leaders of large businesses self-consciously shaped institutional adjustments to their needs and supported political ideologies that, though preserving the ideology of free enterprise from the attacks of the socialists, provided the climate for the emergence of the large corporation over small firms.

Kolko (1963) analyzed the same period in American history and came to parallel conclusions. He argued that, contrary to popular belief, the actions of the Federal government between 1900 and 1916 were not motivated to increase economic competition but rather to protect business firms from the uncertainty introduced by competition. He wrote:

> the dominant tendency in the American economy at the beginning of this century was toward growing competition. Competition was unacceptable to many key business and financial interests, and the merger movement was to a large extent a reflection of voluntary, unsuccessful business efforts to bring irresistible competitive trends under control. . . . As new competitors sprang up, and as economic power was diffused throughout an expanding nation, it became apparent to many important businessmen that only the national government could rationalize the economy [p. 4].

Kolko documented the development of "political capitalism," in which a number of important businessmen played important roles in the political process of establishing the intervention of the national government in the economy. Corporate leaders supported the move to national control of key economic problems, which reduced the insecurity introduced by democratic processes operating at the state level. Also at the national level, business leaders helped to advance a number of political measures that created an environment in which internecine competition and erratic economic fluctuations were greatly reduced. By World War I, Kolko argued, a politically based federal bureaucracy was in place that served to rationalize the economic system that allowed corporations to function in a secure and predictable environment. Finally, Kolko observed that these decisions represented class interests and gave no attention to alternative forms of organization that might have given more emphasis to democratization of the work situation. According to Kolko, "The rationalized, dominated, and essentially totalitarian decision-making process is not a consequence of forces inherent in industrialism but in political capitalism [pp. 302–302]."

In sum, the forms of organization that are effective, perhaps owe a great deal more to the nature of these political decisions and a great deal less to considerations of technological efficiency than is often assumed. The nature of these political environments is an appropriate domain in which to evaluate these forms.

DE FACTO GOVERNANCE

In the previous section, I focused on certain rather deliberate efforts of organizations to shape government. However, organizations have influenced the actual governance process by activities that are not related directly to the state. They act as governments themselves—with respect to broad societal matters and to the lives of their members.

A number of political scientists who have analyzed the consequences of modern organizations on the governance of society have concluded that contemporary work organizations create serious problems for the existence of a society that seeks to govern itself democratically. Dahl (1970) observed that some business firms have annual budgets that are larger than the GNP of many nations. Given the magnitude of the resources involve, decisions made by organizations are of great import to society as a whole. Moreover, through the philanthropic and political activities noted earlier, business leaders influence many activities of other institutions of society, including universities and cultural and political activities. In short, organizations are performing functions and making decisions about matters and in ways that are in tension with some fundamental assumptions about how our democratic institutions are supposed to operate. Among other things, they are influencing: which departments in universities get funded; which political positions and candidates get high levels of exposure; what criteria are used in elementary and secondary schools (Callahan, 1962); and, as noted earlier, what criteria are used to evaluate social policy (McNeil, 1978). In the words of political scientists such as Merriam (1944) and Lakoff and Rich (1973), organizations are "private governments."

Whether or not these quasi-governmental activities (e.g., lobbying and attempts to influence public opinion) and other activities that are often labeled "social responsibility" (e.g., contributions to the arts) do or do not contribute to the microquality effectiveness of the organization is debatable. However, this is not central to this chapter. What is important here is the relationship of these activities to the essence of democratic political institutions, in which the "one-man, one-vote" system is supposed to symbolize equal influence of individuals in the governance process. Organizations can be viewed as social tools (Perrow, 1972); one of the uses of these tools is the amplification of the political power of those who control them.

The effects on our political institutions of this concentration of power in the hands of the business elite are substantial. Lindblom's (1977) analysis is persuasive. He observed that the huge political clout of business organizations stems from their ability to provide financial resources for political causes, their administrative structures and human resources, which allow them to be effective politically, and their ready access to information and to influential people and government officials. As a result, business leaders are usually able to obtain a sympathetic hearing for their position. Moreover, because the viewpoint of business is fully incorporated in current ideology, the political message of business can be effective merely by reinforcing what the individual citizen learned during childhood; the message of business requires no action on the part of the ordinary citizen—it merely requires that the average person do nothing. Though in many ways society may be better off if business organizations have strong influence on particular economic and social matters, the issue here is over process rather than substance. One of the latent consequences of effective organizations as we currently define them is the decline of democratic control due to concentration of economic and political power. Lindblom (1977) summarized the issues succinctly—"The large corporation fits oddly into democratic theory and vision. Indeed, it does not fit [p. 356]."

In our terms, at least under present arrangements, microeffectiveness by individual organizations constrains the democratic process of governance. Clearly, this point is most relevant to describing large business organizations, although it also would seem to apply to smaller firms who via coalitions can exercise substantial influence, which can result in decisions that seem to run contrary to popular preferences. (Many people might say the influence of the National Rifle Association on handgun control is an example of such a coalition.)

Although mainstream research on organizational effectiveness has not incorporated the implications of the work of Dahl, Lindblom, and Lakoff and Rich, in recent years organizational theorists have begun to address some of these matters. Perrow's (1972) view, already noted, that organizations are "tools" that are controlled by the rich to achieve a variety of personal goals is one example. Mintzberg (1979) observed that large corporations concentrate great power in a few hands. They appear to be less subject to market forces, and their managers may be less subject to stockholder control than in the past. One of the consequences of this concentration of power within the corporation is, according to Mintzberg, "the concentration of power in spheres outside the corporation. Unions federate and governments add agencies to establish countervailing powers—ones to match those of the corporations [p. 427]." Moreover, Mintzberg observed that the control system employed by large, divisionalized organizations often induces them to act "at best, socially unresponsively, at worst, socially irresponsibly [p. 424]." In sum, by concentrating resources that can be used for control, microquality organization effectiveness can contribute to a process of societal governance that is de facto nondemocratic and to decisions that give little weight to important social consequences.

Parallel effects have been noted at the individual level where critics have suggested that current organization forms limit the operation of democratic processes by their ability to make decisions that have major consequences for their members through nondemocratic processes. For example, Pateman (1970) observed that managers of both large and small organizations unilaterally make decisions that affect the day-to-day lives of people more profoundly than do most decisions made by public governments through processes that are more democratic in form. More recently, a number of writers have observed that work organizations often seem to violate "basic human rights." Though this has long been an argument of the trade unionists, Ewing (1977) and others have pointed out that employees often do not enjoy basic civil liberties at work. Freedom of speech and protection through due process are some notable examples. Ewing described this area as "the black hole in human rights." The microquality approach tends to ignore such issues, perhaps because it tends to take the legitimacy of current forms of organizations as given. However, analysis guided by a political economic framework is concerned with how organizations influence democratic processes and individual rights throughout society—including the experience of members within organizations.

THE "POSSIBLE" POLITICAL GOVERNANCE PROCESS

Not only do current organizational forms that are effective in a microquality sense contribute to a governance process that is in reality nondemocratic, but they also may stimulate other processes that *reduce* the *possibility* of developing a governance process that is democratic. These outcomes stem from a number of factors, including size and consequences of bureaucratic forms on individual development.

First, consider size. If in fact the pursuit of microquality effectiveness leads to organizations' being larger in terms of the number of employees, this pursuit may contribute to a reduction in the ability of individuals to have an impact on issues of import to them. One source of this decrement is rather direct—as the size of a coalition or social system increases, the average influence of each individual in the system decreases (Coleman, 1973; Schumacher, 1973). In addition, once again consider Mintzberg's (1979) assertion that large organizations stimulate the development of other large organizations. Consequently, not only may large organizations be less susceptible to influence by individuals, but also, following the arguments of Coleman and Schumacher, they may lead to further decrements in influence by individuals by stimulating the growth of other large organizations. An obvious example of this process is the growth of large trade unions and the emergence of industry-wide bargaining in industries where a few large firms dominate the national market. As a result, individual union members exercise less influence over issues of importance to them. Similarly, managers at local levels may find it more difficult to have the contract they must administer suited to their particular situation.

The potential influence of individuals can also be reduced by the effects of organizational processes on the psychological functioning of individuals. In much the same way that organizational control in the marketplace leads to the development of consumers who are unable to exercise power, the inability of workers to exercise control in the work place leads to their political inefficacy elsewhere. Argyris's (1973) review of the literature related to "personality and organization theory" summarized several studies that suggest that the nature of work in many modern organizations contributes to the development of passive, politically impotent individuals. The work of Israel (1971), Kohn and Schooler (1973), and Ouchi and Johnson (1978) suggests similar conclusions. More recently Antonio (1979) argued that the emphasis on rationality, scientific progress, and reliance on experts engenders a set of feelings and beliefs that renders the ordinary citizen powerless. The impact that work organizations have on the ability of individuals to act as effective citizens helps to determine the type of governance process that is possible and ought to be included in assessing effectiveness. Though conventional microquality analysts have been concerned with individual satisfaction and psychological and physical health, they have tended to focus on these criteria primarily as they relate to the performance of people in organization roles. Macroquality analysis focuses on these criteria but takes the consequences organizational processes have for the ability of individuals to play roles outside the work place at least equally seriously.

THE "POSSIBLE" ECONOMIC GOVERNANCE PROCESS

The means used by organizations to achieve microquality effectiveness have consequences on the development of individuals that constrain their abilities to govern economic as well as political processes. Earlier I noted a number of ways in which organizations operate overtly to reduce consumer sovereignty in the marketplace by exercising monopoly power and controlling information. In this section I shall focus on the more covert impact of organizations on the potential of individuals to be informed, influential consumers.

Scitovsky (1976) showed how work and socialization for work can limit the possibility of consumer sovereignty. He argued that the emphasis on time and effort reduction at work has dysfunctional consequences on the ability of people to be effective consumers because when these concerns are carried over to consumption, they lead to people choosing comfort over stimulation. Moreover, as each consumer attempts to reduce the time and effort devoted to shopping, he or she becomes a less effective consumer in the sense that one often purchases goods that are higher in price and/or lower in quality than would be the case if he/she spent more time and energy shopping. When the opportunity cost of one's time is taken into account, from the point of view of each individual, it is often efficient to pay the premium price or accept the inferior goods. However, one consequence of this behavior is to reduce the discipline that consumers as a collectivity exercise over producers and sellers. The failure to exercise this discipline results in consumer goods being inferior and/or more expensive than they need be.

The pursuit of microquality effectiveness by modern organizations has shaped the educational system in ways that have further reduced the ability of members of society to govern the economic system. Following Meyer and Rowan (1977), educational systems may be best understood as the institutionalization of social values. The inclusion and exclusion of certain topics from curricula in our educational institutions are, at least partially, responses to the interests of work organizations to have graduates who are effective producers. As Meyer and Rowan contended, a primary goal of our schools has become to train people to be effective in their production roles but not necessarily in other roles. Consequently, activities that train people to enjoy novelty, to appreciate a wide variety of stimuli, to be good conversationalists, and to be informed consumers tend to get little emphasis.

In *The Harried Leisure Class,* Linder (1970) provided some useful illustrations of this process. Linder argued that the emphasis placed on training for production constrains the ability of people in our society to enjoy leisure. One correlate of economic growth is an increased focus on allocating time to accomplish things rapidly and efficiently. This emphasis induces a trained incapacity for the enjoyment of "things for themselves" and of cultural activities that require patience and leisure to be appreciated. If people are socialized into the types of time orientations demanded by efficient work rather than in ones suited to a variety of consumption activities, than their ability to obtain life satisfaction from available resources may well be reduced. They do not have the "tools" to be effective consumers and, because they are predisposed to allocate their time and energy to work activities, they "overlook" other activities which might yield total satisfaction.

In short, there are a variety of social processes inducing people to become poor consumers and, therefore, ineffective governors of the economic system. The importance of these shortcomings from a macroperspective is magnified when energy and other physical resources are scarce and the consumer is "artificially biased" to prefer goods that are expensive in terms of these resources over those that are less expensive. (One of Linder's central arguments is that as the opportunity costs of leisure increase, one adjustment is to intensify leisure by consuming more goods simultaneously, such as by putting a television set in the car.) Consequently, greater demands are placed on finite physical resources. On the other hand, suppose with a little more training in being a "good conversationalist" a typical family would enjoy an afternoon with each other in the backyard as much as a trip to an amusement park. The savings in energy could be considerable. However, because microquality effectiveness is oriented to goods that pass through the market place, it seems reasonable to hypothesize an institutionalized bias against such "goods" as conversation with family members, which are by custom free.

In this section I have suggested that organizations play a central role in determining the nature of existing as well as possible social institutions. Evaluation of organizational effectiveness is incomplete and misleading unless these outcomes are included in the evaluation, as they are if a macroquality perspective is employed.

Population Perspective on Effectiveness in Providing Work

A number of microquality criteria deal with the contribution of the organization to the satisfaction of needs of employees. Some of these criteria are viewed as ends; others are viewed as important because they contribute to other criteria of effectiveness (e.g., *job satisfaction* → *lower turnover*); many of the criteria are viewed as both ends in themselves and means to other ends. However, because consideration of the effects of organizations on the quality of life, both on and off the job, has been guided by a microquality perspective, many elements have been either examined by organizational behaviorists in an incomplete manner or ignored by them entirely.

Although the insights of Marx and Durkheim seem to dwarf more recent contributions, Argyris (1973), Braverman (1974), Eyer and Sterling (1977), Gardell (1976), Israel (1971), Kanter (1977), and Nord (1977) are a few of the many modern writers who have examined the effects of the nature of work on society. In this chapter (with the exception of Eyer and Sterling's article, which is apt to be least known to students of organization effectiveness) I shall not attempt to review this work in any depth. Rather, I will focus on a few ways in which the population approach highlights and/or adds dimensions to this work. The issues are complex and can only be treated briefly.

UNEMPLOYMENT

An important difference between the micro- and macroquality approaches in evaluating the quality of work life is that the microquality perspective focuses on people who are employed by individual organizations; consequently it tends to omit many elements of work life that *fall between* organizations. A prime example involves the provision of opportunities for work.

Although unemployment would seem to be a major criterion for evaluating organizational effectiveness, it has received surprisingly little attention in our literature. The negative impact of unemployment on the quality of life a society provides is clear. In addition to the obvious loss of salaries and wages (some of which through costs of unemployment insurance are paid by firms) and the waste of human resources, there are other more subtle costs. Brenner (1976) summarized a number of the personal consequences.

> Incorporated in this personal sense of loss . . . is the necessity of adapting to separation from fellow workers who probably constituted a major dimension of the person's closer relationships. The individual has an investment of training, seniority, and emotional ties in his work. These emotional ties are not only to persons, but to the image of the job itself since for a great many persons the job defines the individual. Also lost is the opportunity for achievement that was potenitally connected with the job. Hopes are destroyed, and the individual is frustrated and anxious about the future [p. 92].

He added:

> The combined impact of loss of employment and loss of associated income can have profound implications for community life. In the case of the family, substantial changes may be necessary in its pattern of functioning and in its lifestyle. It is possible for patterns of relationship in the family, including relations between husband and wife to change, and also for patterns of authority, governing relations between parents and children [pp. 92–93].

These costs of becoming unemployed are included in macroquality evaluations of effectiveness. So are the costs borne by the thousands of people who have become so discouraged by their inability to find work that they are no longer counted as unemployed by the government must also be considered.

Typically unemployment is labeled as an economic problem—which it is. However, it is also a problem that indicates that current organizations are less effective in providing for human needs than they might be. From the macroperspective, unemployment is also an index of organizational effectiveness.[3]

TURNOVER

Both micro- and macroquality analysts are concerned with the effects of turnover although they emphasize different aspects. The microquality analyst tends to focus on how turnover may reduce efficiency, increase training and recruitment costs, and perhaps lower morale of employees who remain. The

---

[3]Of course, this point is deceptive because the average costs of production in terms of resource utilization and labor costs are most likely to increase if a firm hires a greater number of "marginal" employees. Though things are not so simple as I have portrayed them, the general point that some of the costs of unemployment are quite properly attributable to the nature of the organizations in society seems valid.

macroquality analyst would share these concerns but would raise some others. On the one hand, as we shall see, the macroquality analyst would see *voluntary* turnover as a sign that individuals have attractive options and thus would view it as an indicator of effectiveness of the population of organizations. However, the macroanalyst would also be concerned with certain costs of turnover for individuals and society, which occur beyond any particular organization. For example, the psychological costs of leaving one organization and entering another become relevant. Moreover, as Ouchi and Johnson (1978) observed, patterns of stable and patterns of unstable employment are associated with quite different types of organizational control systems and quite different types of organizations (Type A versus Type Z). These two types of organization may have sharply different consequences for life beyond the workplace. Organizations where employment tends to be long term (Type Z) are apt to have more of the humane characteristics discussed by McGregor (1960) as well as the potential for achieving more of "the goal congruence and democracy of interpersonal relations described by Argyris (1957) and Likert (1961) [p. 311]." Although Ouchi and Johnson acknowledged the tentativeness of their conclusions, they suggested that Type Z organizations can be an important source for the moral integration in the lives of individuals and society. These issues are relevant criteria for the measurement of effectiveness.

FREEDOM OF CHOICE AND THE QUALITY OF WORK LIFE

Although as Dahrendorf (1979) observed, the number and quality of alternatives an individual can choose from are not synonymous with a high quality of life, the number does contribute to the quality of life in important respects. The microquality perspective appears to give little attention to opportunity for choice. This is an important omission. The number of alternatives available has at least one direct and several less direct consequences for the quality of work a population of organizations provides.

An increase in the number of employment alternatives has the direct effect of increasing the likelihood that individuals will be able to find positions that match their desires and skills precisely. Other things being equal, this improved matching should contribute to greater satisfaction. In addition to this outcome, increments in the number of alternatives have less direct effects as well.

A major source of power for employees to influence employers to provide satisfactory work is the opportunity for "exit" (Hirschman, 1970). Of course, the viability of exit depends, in part, on both an informed labor market and the availability of alternatives that can be elected at relatively low costs. As Lindblom (1977) observed: "Freedom depends on the character of alternatives . . . exchange best supports freedom when every party can choose among offers that do not greatly differ in value from each other or from no exchange at all [p. 99]." Thus, from the macroperspective, the population of organizations may be considered effective in providing satisfactory work when unemployment is low and voluntary turnover is high.

It appears, however, that exit has become an increasingly more difficult option to exercise, and, consequently, microlevel treatments that ignore the role played by alternatives may overestimate the effectiveness of current forms. For example, as Braverman (1974) observed, one consequence of modern capitalism and Taylorism has been the decline of alternative types of work. Thus, the "free labor market" allows one to choose only among identical jobs. Choice has been reduced further by the difficulties of establishing and sustaining a small business. Moreover, as Foy and Gadon (1976) noted, the United States is characterized by rather high levels of unemployment relative to other nations. Foy and Gordon attribute the comparative willingness of Scandinavian employers to invest in expensive quality-of-work-life projects to the tight labor market conditions. Finally, as so many central life concerns (e.g., health insurance and retirement benefits) have come to depend on membership in one particular organization, exit has become an increasing less attractive source of power to the individual.

From the macroperspective, the opportunity to make informal choices among varied *types* of work is an indicator of the quality of life and one which may be in conflict with microquality effectiveness. The absence of alternatives places employees and those seeking employment in a position of low power vis-à-vis employers. The consequences of this unequal power relationship for the quality of life are additional criteria for evaluating the effectiveness of current organizations.

Of course, the availability of viable alternatives by itself is meaningless unless there is an informed labor market. As with consumer sovereignty the availability of information and the development of individuals who obtain and use this information is a necessary condition for an effective free labor market. In other words, an informed labor force is a criterion of the effectiveness of a population of organizations. In some, but not all ways, such an informed labor market would contribute to microquality effectiveness as well.

ALTERNATIVES AND NONTRADITIONAL WORKERS

The concern with providing alternatives and facilitating choice raises a number of other matters. Students of job design have focused on some of them—the number and character of the tasks which make up a job. More recently students of careers (e.g., Sarason, 1977) have focused on others—the opportunity to change not only jobs, but to change careers. Also in the recent past a great deal of attention has been given to various groups of people (e.g., women) for whom the current population of organizations has failed to provide meaningful roles. For example, career opportunities for people who find it difficult to work a normal 40-hour week are severely limited. Microquality analysis often leads to the evaluation of innovations such as flextime on a narrow set of criteria. Macroquality analysis suggests a far broader set of criteria. (See Gardell [1976] for a fuller discussion of these issues.)

Taking the provision of alternatives as a goal sheds a new light on responses to another major segment of the population—the so-called secondary labor market (e.g., minorities, the urban poor, teenagers, occupants of traditionally female occupations, older workers, workers seeking less than 40 hours per week jobs). Normally, providing employment for members of the secondary labor market has been viewed as a source of *constraint* on effectiveness. From the macroquality perspective, a new view emerges: The satisfaction of the interests and the effective utilization of the secondary labor market are *criteria* of effectiveness. The provision of good jobs for all members of society can be viewed as one measure of the effectiveness of organizations in performing one of their major functions—providing places to work.

CONSEQUENCES BEYOND THE WORKPLACE—
HEALTH AND STRESS

In addition to directing attention to opportunities for work, the population perspective encourages a very broad view of the effects of work on other aspects of people's lives. A number of the psychological and sociological consequences noted by writers such as Argyris (1973) and Israel (1971) have already been noted. More recently attention has focused on physical health as well.

In a fascinating paper, Eyer and Sterling (1977) argued that the structure of work-related activities in modern industrial societies forces individuals into patterns of behavior that produce stress and physical illness. In particular, stress-induced illness can be attributed to such factors as: economic cycles, the size of cohort groups competing for positions, and pressures that exist at certain key points in the career cycle (such as between 15–25 and 55–65). Moreover, Eyer and Sterling argued (as did Marx) that the development of commodity production under competitive capitalism has resulted in demands for continuous improvements and efficiency in productivity that have been achieved through development of a flexible labor force (i.e., a workforce that can be moved about as new opportunities for investment and profit develop); the development of chronic, competitive striving among individuals; and the breakdown of family and kinship systems. These conditions lead to a number of costly outcomes. Eyer and Sterling wrote:

> This chronic, competitive striving, the central adaptation for success under capitalism, is synonymous with chronic stress since it requires and generates constant physiological arousal. This primary adaptation is seen in extreme form in the coronary-prone behavior pattern described earlier.

> There are, of course, those who fail to adapt or for whom the cost of adaptation is very high. The cost takes myriad forms: alcoholism (8 million Americans), withdrawal into chronic illness, such as ulcer, mental "illness," and suicide [p. 17].

Based on medical data from several nations, Eyer and Sterling concluded that the frequency of stress-related illnesses has grown as societies have industrialized. Because these patterns seem to have continued in such advanced industrial nations as Canada, Sweden, and the United States, it appears, although one cannot be sure, that such ill effects are in part a function of industrialization, not merely of *industrializing*.

Features of a modern industrialized economy may have similar effects. Economic cycles are a good example. Brenner's (1976) conclusions from his study of cycles within the U.S. economy closely parallel those of Eyer and Sterling. Brenner found support for the rather traditional view that inflation, unemployment, and decreased income, have clear deleterious effects on measures of mental and physical health and criminal aggression. Moreover, he reported that though abrupt economic changes, regardless of direction, produce pathological effects, undesirable changes (e.g., income loss, unemployment) produced more serious consequences.

Though the work of Brenner and Eyer and Sterling is far from conclusive, it does suggest some criteria for organizational effectiveness. Individual organizations that achieve microquality effectiveness at the expense of the health of their members would seem less effective than ones that have positive or even neutral effects on physical and psychological health. Similarly, *ceterus paribus,* a set of organizations that produces a given level of goods and services but leaves a large portion of the available pool of human resources unemployed, given the social consequences of unemployment, can be considered to be less effective than a set that is in other ways identical but provides higher levels of employment. Moreover, due to the influence of change on stress, fluctuations in unemployment and price-levels may be an indicator of the ineffectiveness of a population of organizations.

Unfortunately, it may be that in our economy microquality effectiveness *requires* economic cycles. Crotty and Rapping (1975) have argued this point strongly. They suggested that economic cycles are a necessary occurrence in our economic system because, among other things, the downturns force discipline and efficiency on organizations: Thus, recessions are inevitable in our society, given the current unplanned economy. Though this is a statement about our political economy, if it is true, it is also a statement about the effectiveness of our family of organizations.

Another economic source of stress is inflation and it too is, in part, a product of the nature of organizations. Though improvement on microquality criteria (e.g., productivity) can help combat inflation, the current population of organizations contributes to inflation in a number of ways that have little to do with productivity. For example, conventional economics makes it clear that monopolistic and oligopolistic markets contribute to high price levels. However, the roots of inflation may be sociological as well as economic.

In a collection of papers edited by Hirsch and Goldthorpe (1978), inflation was viewed as a sociological problem as well as an economic one. Taken together, the contributions in this volume argue that an important source of inflation is the influence of rising expectations that flow, at least in part, from the competitive ethic that characterizes capitalism. However, when these expectations cannot be met, and there is no consensus as to the appropriate distribution of income, there is a potential for crisis. Hirsch and others suggest that often inflation is a way out of the crisis. Inflation is not deliberately chosen; it merely is the result of not taking any action that would involve an explicit choice among conflicting interests. It is important to recognize, as at least some contributors to the Hirsch and Goldthorpe volume do, that these dynamics are not necessarily limited to capitalist systems; the problem is more general. It is mentioned here not to suggest that a solution exists but rather to indicate that the level of expectations that are generated by a system (and perhaps required to motivate members of the population to productive activity) relative to the resources available to meet these aspirations may be an important indicator of the effectiveness of a population of organizations.

HUMAN RELATIONSHIPS OUTSIDE THE WORKPLACE

The pursuit of microquality effectiveness has a number of potentially negative consequences on the quality of nonwork life. For example, Nord (1977) argued that satisfying, motivating work and the development of individuals who are dedicated to the organization may be instrumental to achievement of microquality goals; however, the effects on families and others and the ability of the individual to play other social roles may be extremely costly when assessed from a macroquality perspective. Similarly, some organization practices may reduce the opportunity for individuals to develop meaningful interpersonal relationships. Consider, for example, job transfers. Although Brett (1980, pp. 99–136) concluded that "folklore" seems to overstate the negative effects of mobility on the social relationships of teenagers, Pinder (1981, pp. 281–298) has argued that the transfer policies of many companies cause significant and unnecessary social dislocation for employees and their families. (Kanter [1977] suggested that, in fact, a major reason *for* many transfers is this very disruption which, by reducing a manager's social bonds to people and groups outside the organization, increases the probability that he/she will be loyal to the corporation.) Obviously, much is unknown about what magnitude of effects organization actions have for life outside the workplace. The macroview suggests this is a major area for future inquiry and a source of criteria for evaluating effectiveness.

The pursuit of microquality effectiveness often means that organizations place, intentionally or not, a number of costs of certain practices on individual employees and consumers. One such transfer of the costs, both in terms of time and money, is travel to and from the workplace. Some of the costs of current forms of organization that depend on moving people in large numbers are also borne by society more generally through its investment in roads and other forms of transportation. As Paul and Percival Goodman (1960) observed, it might be more cost effective from a societal perspective to move work to people rather than move people to work. A somewhat analogous transfer of costs occurs on the consumption side where due to lack of alternatives consumers must spend their time and other resources coming to and waiting for the producer or seller. Many organizations have enough power relative to their customers to treat the customer's time as a free good. The use of warrantees that minimize production time at the expense of consumer time to take advantage of the service is one rather obvious example of this process. The assessments of organization forms and activities must include analysis of all the resources that make them viable; much microquality analysis fails to do so.

One final issue will serve to define one of the more extreme implications of the type of analysis stimulated by the population viewpoint. Scitovsky (1976) argued that the design of productive activities has consistently resulted in the removal of physical effort from work. Though many of these changes have been desirable, Scitovsky suggested that such developments have costs as well. For example, too little physical exertion is as undesirable as too much. Evaluation of the effectiveness of work design requires consideration of all its effects. These effects go beyond the organization and might include their contribution to the physical well-being of the worker and might be measured in terms of the amount of nonwork time and energy required to keep physically fit.

SUMMARY–CONCLUSIONS

Again, the issues are complex, but the theme is consistent. Normal criteria of microeffectiveness are incomplete and misleading as indices for evaluating the effectiveness of organizations in providing for a high quality of life *in* the workplace. Moreover, microquality criteria give inadequate attention to the consequences of work on life *outside* the workplace and to the consequences of current structure for people who fall in the gaps between organizations. Finally, a microquality focus institutionalizes measures and thought patterns that obscure the macroquality costs of current methods. As with the other areas treated in this chapter, the macroquality perspective directs attention to a number of dimensions for expanding our analysis of the quality of work life and making substantial contributions to human welfare.

CONCLUSIONS

This chapter is directed primarily to students of organizations rather than to managers. Consequently, most of the implications I shall discuss are apt to be of more interest to academics. However, I shall conclude by suggesting that the major theme of this chapter has important implications for managers as well as for their critics. The implications that I draw are in direct response to the questions posed by the editors of the volume.

Conceptual Implications

1. What are the major theoretical predictions or hypotheses that derive from your perspective regarding relationships between effectiveness and other organizational variables (e.g., structure, technology, information processing, individual satisfaction)?
2. How does your perspective expand our understanding of the behavior of organizations?
3. Does the definition of organizational effectiveness change when considering different types of organizations (e.g., public–private, professional–industrial, large–small) or different stages of development (e.g., early stages, institutionalized states, decline)?

The most important conceptual implications have been drawn throughout the chapter. I have tried to show that the achievement of microquality effectiveness cannot be assumed to be an optimal strategy for promoting the well-being of members of society as a whole. Consequently, the dimensions often used in studies of effectiveness are a narrow subset of the possible criteria. Moreover the process through which the criteria have been chosen has not been a purely intellectual–scientific one. Rather, the choice has been heavily influenced by current assumptions about the role organizations play and ought to play in our social system. These assumptions themselves are influenced by (and play a part in) on-going political–economic processes. Throughout the chapter I have argued that one implication of this position is that the set of criteria used to define organization effectiveness needs to be expanded.

Second, if the choice of criteria is a political–economic one as well as a scientific one, then investigators employing any set of criteria need to make the basis of their choice clear and to deal explicitly with the allocation of costs and the distribution of benefits involved in pursuing and achieving these criteria. Making the basis of choice explicit will involve stating one's value judgments clearly. Analyzing the distribution of costs and benefits will involve specifying some model of the political–economic system one assumes to be operative.

A third set of conceptual implications involves a great expansion in what is conceived to be the scope of organization theory. It is generally acknowledged that organizations have pervasive effects on society and the lives of individuals. Consequently, the study and design of organizations are, for many practical purposes, the study and design of society. In fact some historians (Galambos, 1977, pp. 3–15) have suggested that the study of organizational history may provide a centralizing theme for understanding American history. Similarly it appears that the contemporary concerns that are typically labeled as social or economic, or moral problems are, in some measure, organizational problems. For example, inflation, low productivity, poor production quality, and high unemployment can be viewed as stemming from economic or political sources. However, they can be viewed as organizationally rooted as well. In addition to the arguments of Hirsch, the ability of organizations to realize and maintain or distribute slack can be an important source of inflation. Similarly managerial tactics and decisions that result in low employee commitment can reduce output and quality. Moreover, as Pfeffer (1978) and others have suggested, managers choose technology for "political" as well as "rational" economic reasons. To the degree that labor intensive technologies are rejected for other than economic reasons, it is possible that the unemployment is partially an organizational, not a purely economic issue. Consequently these and a host of other "social" problems can be viewed as within the province of organization theory rather than resting only in economics or psychology. Recognizing the appropriateness of these topics for the organizational theorist would open up a variety of exciting areas for inquiry and quite possibly increase the importance of organization theory in influencing social policy.

In addition to analysis of these important social problems, the broadened view of effectiveness could lead organization theorists to contribute to the analysis of our current institutions and to designing ways of making them more effective in coping with contemporary and future problems. For example, it appears that resolution of many contemporary problems requires new types of institutions that can cooperate to deal with complex interdependencies. Our current organizations seem incapable of making such decisions; in fact they frequently impeded such decisions. Modern organizations and our view of what constitutes effectiveness often neglect the role that cooperation among individuals and social units can play in attaining the well-being of society and its members.

Two recent books have shown the nature of this problem. Wiebe (1975) argued that American society is governed by an institutionalized practice of achieving our individual objectives through rather parochial interest groups. We have few institutions that support decisions that are "in the common good." Similarly Thurow (1980) has argued that many of our current economic and social problems (e.g., energy, inflation, slow economic growth, and the environment) are so difficult to solve because our political economic system is not capable of allocating losses in zero-sum situations. Someone must bear the costs involved in solving all of these problems but our institutions function primarily to allow potential losers to prevent themselves from paying the costs. Thurow observed:

> At the end of the 1970s our political economy seems paralyzed. The economy is stagnant, with a high level of inflation and unemployment. Fundamental problems, such as the energy crisis, exist but cannot be solved. We have lost the ability to get things done [p. 24].

> Lacking a consensus on whose income ought to go down, or even the recognition that this is at the heart of the problem we are paralyzed. We dislike the current situation, we wish to do something about our problems, but we endure them because we have not learned to play an economic game with a substantial zero-sum element [pp. 24–25].

In the future, society will need organizations that can work together to get things done. Helping to design organizations that are capable of cooperating and helping to build interorganization networks seem to be important tasks to which organizational theorists can contribute. The population approach with its macroquality focus appears to be a useful framework to stimulate and guide such work. Examples of the form some of these efforts might take can be found in Taber, Walsh and Cooke (1979) and Gricar (1981, pp. 403–420).

Of course, interorganizational networks are not necessarily effective in either macro or micro terms. In fact they may be very ineffective when evaluated by the efficiency criteria we normally apply to organizations. On the other hand, because they are made up of a variety of different organizations, they are more likely to match the diversity of interests that must be satisfied to meet macrolevel criteria. It would be pollyannaish to assume that they will represent all the relevant interests although the ones discussed by Taber, Walsh and Cooke, and Gricar were able, at least for a short time period, to provide for rather broad representation. Nevertheless it is probable that over time such networks will develop orientations, routines, and distributions of power that will reduce their contribution to macroquality criteria. In fact they can be expected to become powerful units that pose formidable barriers to other interests. The study of these developments should be both interesting and fruitful for organization research and theory.

Finally, students of organization should be stimulated by the population view of effectiveness to broaden their definition of the quality of working life to include consequences outside the work place—not only for employees, but for their families and other nonemployees. Such effort might become very broad indeed. They involve some fundamental matters including: What is the nature of a decent society? (Moore, 1968, pp. 401–418); what is justice? (Rawls,

1971); and even "what is the good life?" These questions are well beyond normal microquality analysis. However, they are beyond it, not because they are philosophical or value laden, but because they are obscured by or at least remain latent in microquality analysis. Again, the macroquality approach encourages the analyst to be explicit about how organizations affect the quality of life of the population. The concept of "life chances" (Dahrendorf, 1979) might provide a useful starting point for such conceptual advances.

Methodological Issues

1. What are the major indicators (criteria) of organizational effectiveness using your perspective?
2. How would one test the efficacy of your approach compared to other approaches to effectiveness?
3. What are the major methodological issues of operationalizing effectiveness using your perspective (e.g., those relating to levels of analysis, data collection, predictors, key variables)?

The major implications for research methods of the population perspective stem directly from two features of the critical, political economics. First, from this viewpoint, important aspects of science itself are seen as expressions of a political–economic process. Second, the political–economic view encourages the expansion of our intellectual base and a broadening of the set of constituents considered in evaluating effectiveness.

The fact that science is not value free is widely acknowledged. What researchers take as problematic, what they are supported to study, and what criteria they use in evaluating effectiveness all reflect extra-scientific matters (e.g., cultural values, the interests of potential benefactors, and the personal values of the researcher). Moreover, the results of scientific research are used by interest groups to advance their causes. On the other hand, the absence of research also has policy implications to the degree that decision makers are apt to assign heavy weights to criteria on which data are available and overlook criteria on which little information has been collected. Because both the origins and results of research are in part political, the political–economic approach calls on researchers, at a minimum, to make their values explicit. Second, as I have suggested elsewhere (Nord, 1980) the need for something analogous to strategic planning by members of the scientific community might be indicated. Third, because the availability of information is itself a factor that influences decision making, it seems useful to contemplate the development of a host of indices that reflect as many aspects of human existence as organizations effect. In a sense I am suggesting that we develop "dithering indices."

By calling for the development of dithering indices I am following the ideas of

Turner (1966) who observed that British scientists often attached vibrators to their equipment to keep shaking it up so that mechanical parts that needed to operate freely did not stick together. (He suggested these devices are analogous to kicking a piece of apparatus to make it work.) In the present context, we need new indices to shake up our complacency with such indices as GNP or productivity as measures of human well-being. Students of organizational effectiveness would seem to be able to make substantial contributions to human well-being by developing, administering, and publicizing a set of indices that would lead to other criteria of effectiveness attaining greater weight in the minds of the public and decision makers, as well as providing a basis for understanding the trade-offs between micro- and macroquality effectiveness.

Finally, the political–economic view calls for an expansion in our overall approach to the acquisition of knowledge. By calling attention to the role played by history in defining legitimate criteria and in determining the viability of organization forms, the political economic view demands that historical and philosophical approaches be included in our work. This call, in combination with the value issues just suggested, indicates the value of the methodological discussions of Habermas (1973) and other critical theorists in helping to define modes of inquiry. The application of critical theory may be particularly useful in the case of organization networks where a major part of the problem is to develop and apply knowledge that makes sense to people who often hold conflicting values and objectives. Positivistic science is likely to be seen as one approach—but not the only valid approach—to knowing.

Implications for Managers

1. What prescriptions or guidelines for improving success are suggested by your approach? Are there any counterintuitive recommendations?
2. What diagnostic tools could managers use to monitor success using your approach?
3. What trade-offs, dilemmas, or dysfunctional consequences might be experienced by managers using your approach?

Does the political economic approach to effectiveness offer anything of value to today's managers? On one level the answer is probably not—there is little here for managers to draw on to improve performance on microquality criteria. Moreover, the perspective may generate a great deal of frustration. Because the difficulties in combining micro- and macroquality effectiveness are substantial and their resolution is generally beyond any individual organization, the political–economic view will undoubtedly be a cause for tension and call into question rationalizations that many managers may have made in their pursuit of microquality effectiveness.

On another level, the answer is yes—the political–economic view may be very important to the manager because it encourages the manager to examine the basic sources of the legitimacy of his/her organization and the processes through which legitimacy and other sources of power came into being and have been sustained.

The political–economic view should help the manager to avoid the blind spots induced by a purely economic perspective. The battle for control takes place on many dimensions and in many areas. Today managers seem to think about and to argue for the merits of the goals of their organizations on primarily economic grounds. Clearly, it is in the economic arena that current forms can be best defended. However, future battles are apt to take place in other areas. Though managers may struggle to keep the battle contained, they need to understand that their adversaries will be striving to move the fight to new territory. Managers may be successful in containing the battle, but I suspect that it will become increasingly difficult to do so. The political implications of the pursuit of economic goals under the ideology of capitalism and a competitive economy are bound to become more apparent.

As society's problems become increasingly complex, the need for interorganizational cooperation seems bound to grow. One alternative is a government or some supra-organization system that attempts to manage the complexity and force the cooperative efforts. A second course is to institutionalize criteria and processes within organizations that permit them to preserve their autonomy and legitimacy while serving broad human needs. Probably the first alternative is the easiest to conceptualize: I suspect the second is more desirable.

Though neither of these solutions is apt to be particularly attractive to most managers, the political–economic perspective on which they are based should help managers to understand why they are (at least as their rhetoric suggests) so constrained by government regulation and under attack by various interest groups. The application of this perspective makes it very clear that organizations are playing political–economic roles and managers who attempt to interpret reality through a purely economic perspective will never understand it.

Unfortunately the political–economic view of effectiveness developed in this chapter makes it clear that it will be difficult for managers to develop organizations that are effective in a macroquality sense. The perspective makes it quite clear that modern organizations are designed and driven to achieve microquality as opposed to macroquality effectiveness. Moreover, it makes it clear that the microperspective serves ideological–political functions by legitimating certain goals and activities. In the future it is likely that managers will encounter increasing pressure to change these goals and activities or else to develop a more convincing ideology to defend them. The political–economic framework may be a place to start.

The real payoff? Most likely, however, the real value of the political– economic view will not be for academics or managers at all, but for those who will challenge managers and policymakers to develop more macroeffective organizations. The perspective can provide a framework for organizing knowledge and for stimulating inquiry and action that will show how tenuous the link is in modern society between microquality organization effectiveness and societal welfare. Moreover, it will make the ideological functions served by the application of an economic paradigm to the study of organizations—whether that application is explicit or merely tacit. In short, it provides a new way for understanding the complex, pervasive set of consequences organizations have in modern society and hopefully for modifying them to promote human welfare.

ACKNOWLEDGMENTS

This chapter has benefitted from insightful comments of Sharon Tucker, Jerry Steinman, Peter Frost, Jess Yawitz, Ralph Stablein, and Kim Cameron. Their help is gratefully acknowledged.

REFERENCES

Aldrich, H. E. *Organizations and environments.* Englewood Cliffs, N.J.: Prentice-Hall, 1979.
Allen, V. L. *Social analysis. A Marxist critique and alternative.* London: Longman, 1975.
Antonio, R.J. Domination and production in bureaucracy. *American Sociological Review,* 1979, *44,* 895–912.
Argyris, C. *Personality and organization.* New York: Harper, 1957.
Argyris, C. Personality and organization theory revisited. *Administrative Science Quarterly,* 1973, *18,* 141–167.
Baran, P. A., & Sweezy, P. M. *Monopoly capital. An essay on the American economic and social order.* New York: Monthly Review Press, 1966.
Benson, J. K. Organizations: A dialectical view. *Administrative Science Quarterly,* 1977, *22,* 1–21.
Braverman, H. *Labor and monopoly capital.* New York: Monthly Review Press, 1974.
Brenner, H. Estimating the social costs of national economic policy: Implications for mental and physical health, and criminal aggression. Paper No. 5. *Achieving the goals of the employment act of 1946—Thirtieth anniversary review.* Joint Economic Committee, October, 1976.
Brett, J. M. The effect of job transfer on employees and their families. In C. L. Cooper & R. Payne (Eds.), *Current concerns in occupational stress.* New York: Wiley, 1980.
Brown, R. H. Bureaucracy as praxis: Toward a political phenomenology of formal organizations. *Administrative Science Quarterly,* 1978, *23,* 365–382.
Callahan, R. E. *Education and the cult of efficiency.* Chicago: University of Chicago Press, 1962.
Cameron, K. Measuring organizational effectiveness in institutions of higher education. *Administrative Science Quarterly,* 1978, *23,* 604–632.
Campbell, J. P. On the nature of organizational effectiveness. In P. S. Goodman & J. M. Pennings (Eds.), *New perspectives on organizational effectiveness.* San Francisco: Jossey-Bass, 1977.
Clegg, S., & Dunkerley, D. *Critical issues in organizations.* London: Routledge & Kegan Paul, 1977.
Coleman, J. S. Loss of power. *American Journal of Sociology,* 1973, *38,* 1–17.
Connolly, T., Conlon, E. J., & Deutsch, S. J. Organizational effectiveness: A multiple-constituency approach. *Academy of Management Review,* 1980, *5,* 211–217.

Coulter, P. B. Organizational effectiveness in the public sector: The example of municipal fire protection. *Administrative Science Quarterly,* 1979, *24,* 65–81.

Crotty, J. R., & Rapping, L. A. The 1975 report of the president's council of economic advisors: A radical critique. *American Economic Review,* 1975, *65,* 791–811.

Cummings, L. L. Emergence of the instrumental organization. In P. S. Goodman & J. M. Pennings (Eds.), *New perspectives on organizational effectiveness.* San Francisco: Jossey-Bass, 1977.

Dahl, R. A. *After the revolution? Authority in a good society.* New Haven: Yale University Press, 1970.

Dahrendorf, K. *Life chances.* Chicago: University of Chicago Press, 1979.

Dubin, R. Organizational effectiveness: Some dilemmas of perspective. In S. L. Spray (Ed.), *Organizational effectiveness: Theory—research—utilization.* Kent, Ohio: Kent State University Press, 1976.

Elliot, J. E. Institutionalism as an approach to political economy. *Journal of Economic Issues,* 1978, *12,* 91–114.

Ewing, D. W. *Freedom inside the organization.* New York: McGraw-Hill, 1977.

Eyer, J., & Sterling, P. Stress-related mortality and social organization. *Review of Radical Political Economics,* 1977, *9,* 1–44.

Fisher, F. M., Griliches, Z., & Kaysen, C. The costs of automobile changes since 1949. *Journal of Political Economy,* 1962, *70,* 433–451.

Foy, N., & Gadon, H. Worker participation: Contrasts in three countries. *Harvard Business Review,* 1976, *54,* 71–83.

Friedman, M. *Capitalism and freedom.* Chicago: University of Chicago Press, 1962.

Galambos, L. The emerging organizational synthesis in American history. In E. J. Perkins (Ed.), *Men and organizations.* New York: Putnam, 1977.

Galbraith, J. K. Power and the useful economist. *American Economic Review,* 1973, *63,* 1–11.

Gardell, B. Reactions at work and their influence on nonwork activities: An analysis of a sociopolitical problem in affluent societies. *Human Relations,* 1976, *9,* 885–904.

Goldman, P., & Van Houten, D. R. Managerial strategies and the worker: A Marxist analysis of bureaucracy. *Sociological Quarterly,* 1977, *18,* 108–125.

Goodman, P. S., & Pennings, J. M. Perspectives and issues: An introduction. In P. S. Goodman & J. M. Pennings (Eds.), *New perspectives on organizational effectiveness.* San Francisco: Jossey-Bass, 1977.

Goodman, P., & Goodman, P. *Communitas. Means of livelihood and ways of life.* New York: Vintage, 1960.

Gouldner, A. W. *The two Marxisms. Contradictions and anomalies in the development of theory.* New York: Seabury Press, 1980.

Gricar, B. G. Fostering collaboration among organizations. In H. Meltzer & W. R. Nord (Eds.), *Making organizations humane and productive: A handbook for practitioners.* New York: Wiley, 1981.

Gutman, H. G. *Work, culture and society in industrializing America.* New York: Vintage, 1977.

Habermas, J. *Theory and practice.* Boston: Beacon Press, 1973.

Hage, J. Toward a synthesis of the dialectic between historical-specific and sociological-general models of the environment. In L. Lappik (Ed.), *Organization and environment.* Beverly Hills, Calif.: Sage, 1978.

Hannan, M. T., & Freeman, J. Obstacles to comparative studies. In P. S. Goodman & J. M. Pennings (Eds.), *New perspectives on organizational effectiveness.* San Francisco: Jossey-Bass, 1977.

Heydebrand, W. Organizational contradictions in public bureaucracies: Toward a Marxian theory of organizations. *Sociological Quarterly,* 1977, *18,* 83–107.

Heydebrand, W. *Critical issues in organizations.* Steward Clegy and David Dunkerley. *Administrative Science Quarterly,* 1978, 23, 640–645.

Hirsch, F., & Goldthorpe, J. H. (Eds.), *Political economy of inflation.* Cambridge, Mass.: Harvard University Press, 1978.

Hirschman, A. O. *Exit, voice and loyalty.* Cambridge, Mass.: Harvard University Press, 1970.

Israel, J. *Alienation: From Marx to modern sociology.* Boston: Allyn & Bacon, 1971.

Kanter, R. M. *Men and women of the corporation.* New York: Basic Books, 1977.

Karpik, L. Organizations, institutions, and history. In L. Karpik (Ed.), *Organizations and environment.* Beverly Hills, Calif.: Sage, 1978.

Katz, D., & Kahn, R.L. *The social psychology of organizations* (2nd ed.). New York: Wiley, 1978.

Keeley, M. A social-justice approach to job attitudes and task design. *Administrative Science Quarterly,* 1978, 23, 272–292.

Kohn, M. L., & Schooler, C. Occupational experience and psychological functioning: An assessment of reciprocal effects. *American Sociological Review,* 1973, 38, 97–118.

Kolko, G. *The triumph of conservatism.* New York: Free Press, 1963.

Lakoff, S. A., & Rich, D. (Eds.). *Private government. Introductory readings.* Glenview, Ill.: Scott, Foresman, 1973.

Likert, R. *New patterns of management.* New York: McGraw-Hill, 1961.

Lindblom, C. E. *Politics and markets.* New York: Basic Books, 1977.

Linder, S. B. *The harried leisure class.* New York: Columbia University Press, 1970.

McGregor, D. *The human side of enterprise.* New York: McGraw-Hill, 1960.

McNeil, K. Understanding organizational power: Building on the Weberian legacy. *Administrative Science Quarterly,* 1978, 23, 65–90.

Marglin, S. A. What do bosses do? Part II. *Review of Radical Political Economics,* 1975, 7, 20–37.

Merriam, C. E. *Public and private government.* New Haven, Conn.: Yale University Press, 1944.

Meyer, J. W., & Rowan, B. Institutionalized organizations: Formal structure as myth and ceremony. *American Journal of Sociology,* 1977, 83, 340–363.

Mintzberg, H. *The structuring of organizations.* Englewood Cliffs, N.J.: Prentice-Hall, 1979.

Moore, B., Jr. The society nobody wants: A look beyond Marxism and liberalism. In K. H. Wolff & B. Moore, Jr. (Eds.), *The critical spirit. Essays in honor of Herbert Marcuse.* Boston: Beacon Press, 1968.

Nord, W. R. The failure of current applied behavioral science: A Marxian perspective. *Journal of Applied Behavioral Science,* 1974, 10, 557–578.

Nord, W. R. Job satisfaction reconsidered. *American Psychologist,* 1977, 32, 1026–1035.

Nord, W. R. Toward an organizational psychology for organizational psychology. *Professional Psychology,* 1980, 11, 531–542.

Ouchi, W. G., & Johnson, J. B. Types of organizational control and their relationship to emotional well being. *Administrative Science Quarterly,* 1978, 23, 293–317.

Pateman, C. *Participation and democratic theory.* Cambridge: Cambridge University Press, 1970.

Perrow, C. *Complex organizations: A critical essay.* Glenview, Ill.: Scott, Foresman, 1972.

Perrow, C. Three types of effectiveness studies. In P. S. Goodman & J. M. Pennings (Eds.), *New perspectives on organizational effectiveness.* San Francisco: Jossey-Bass, 1977.

Pfeffer, J. *Organizational design.* Arlington Heights, Ill.: AHM, 1978.

Pfeffer, J., & Salancik, G. R. *The external control of organizations.* New York: Harper & Row, 1978.

Pinder, C. C. Mobility and transfer. In H. Meltzer & W. R. Nord (Eds.), *Making organizations humane and productive. A handbook for practitioners.* New York: Wiley, 1981.

Pollard, S. *The genesis of modern management. A study of the industrial revolution in Great Britain.* Cambridge, Mass.: Harvard University Press, 1965.

Pondy, L. R. Effectiveness: A thick description. In P. S. Goodman & J. M. Pennings (Eds.), *New perspectives on organizational effectiveness.* San Francisco: Jossey-Bass, 1977.

Rawls, J. *A theory of justice*. Cambridge, Mass.: Harvard University Press, 1971.

Rodgers, D. T. *The work ethic in industrial America 1850–1970*. Chicago: University of Chicago Press, 1978.

Sarason, S. B. *Work, aging, and social change. Professionals and the one life-one career imperative*. New York: Free Press, 1977.

Schumacher, E. F. *Small is beautiful*. London: Blond & Briggs, 1973.

Scitovsky, T. *Welfare and competition. The economics of a fully employed economy*. Chicago: Richard D. Irwin, 1951.

Scitovsky, T. *The joyless economy*. New York: Oxford University Press, 1976.

Scott, W. R. Effectiveness of organizational effectiveness studies. In P. S. Goodman & J. M. Pennings (Eds.), *New perspectives on organizational effectiveness*. San Francisco: Jossey-Bass, 1977.

Silverman, D. *The theory of organizations. A sociological framework*. New York: Basic Books, 1970.

Steers, R. M. *Organizational effectiveness: A behavioral view*. Santa Monica, Calif.: Goodyear, 1977.

Taber, T. D., Walsh, J. T., & Cooke, R. A. Developing a community-based program for reducing the social impact of a plant closing. *Journal of Applied Behavioral Science*, 1979, *15*, 133–155.

Thompson, E. P. Time, work-discipline, and industrial capitalism. *Past and Present*, 1967, *38*, 56–97.

Thompson, J. D. *Organizations in action*. New York: McGraw-Hill, 1967.

Thurow, L. C. *The zero-sum society*. New York: Basic Books, 1980.

Turner, R. H. Dithering devices in the classroom: How to succeed in shaking up a campus without really trying. *American Psychologist*, 1966, *21*, 957–963.

Weick, K. E. Re-punctuating the problem. In P. S. Goodman & J. M. Pennings (Eds.), *New perspectives on organizational effectiveness*. San Francisco: Jossey-Bass, 1977. Pp. 193–225.

Weinstein, J. *The corporate ideal in the liberal state: 1900–1918*. Boston: Beacon Press, 1968.

Wiebe, R. H. *The segmented society. An introduction to the meaning of America*. New York: Oxford University Press, 1975.

Zeitz, G. Interorganizational dialectics. *Administrative Science Quarterly*, 1980, *25*, 72–88.

WILLIAM H. STARBUCK
PAUL C. NYSTROM

Pursuing Organizational Effectiveness That Is Ambiguously Specified

DEPARTING FROM TRADITION

Operations research and systems engineering combine the goal-oriented and systems-oriented approaches to organizational effectiveness (Campbell, 1977, pp. 29–31). One well-known definition portrays operations research as "the application of scientific methods, techniques, and tools to problems involving the operations of a system so as to provide those in control of the system with optimum solutions to the problems [Churchman, Ackoff, & Arnoff, 1957, p. 18]". Prominent among these techniques and tools is mathematics.

Operations-research analysts and systems engineers characterize effectiveness with mathematical goal functions. Such a function might be

$$g(x, u; \phi),\tag{1}$$

in which x represents a list (vector) of variables measuring an organization's status, u represents a list of control variables, and ϕ represents a list of parameters. A problem in decision or design would be posed in terms of optimization: say, to manipulate the control variables, u, so as to make g as large as possible

$$\operatorname*{Max}_{u} g(x, u; \phi).\tag{2}$$

Such a maximization would usually also allow for various constraints. Some of these constraints

ORGANIZATIONAL EFFECTIVENESS
A Comparison of Multiple Models

$$w(x, u) = 0 \qquad\qquad (3)$$

would describe how the x's change when the u's are manipulated, and other constraints

$$v(x, u) \geq 0 \qquad\qquad (4)$$

would limit the possible values of the u's. Operations-research analysts and systems engineers formulate the functions g, w, and v, and then search for desirable manipulations of the u's.

If the numbers of pages published in professional journals reflect activity, operations-research analysts and systems engineers spend about half of their time formulating problems—deciding what topics to investigate, what variables to include or exclude, what functional forms to use. The great majority of operations-research studies have addressed issues in the internal management of production: what activities to assign to alternative people or facilities, what personnel or equipment to add or delete, and how much to stabilize production rates over time. A small minority of studies have dealt with organizations' transactions with their environments: prices, advertising, credit policies, or tax rates.

Operations-research analysts and systems engineers expend the other half of their time searching for the optima of goal functions. The search techniques are best developed, naturally enough, for completely specified problems having simple goal functions and simple constraints; and the research frontiers lie among incompletely specified problems and complicated relationships.

The concepts of goal optimization and constraints have long played central roles in organization theory (Simon, 1964), and they frame some models of organizational effectiveness (Pennings & Goodman, 1977, pp. 160–171; Steers, 1977, pp. 176–177). However, we doubt that traditional approaches toward optimization afford useful allegories for organizational design or decision making.

Indeed, operations research and systems engineering have failed significantly in representing or facilitating organizational decision making. Although many analysts have prescribed what decisions organizations should make and how organizations should go about making decisions, and although some analysts have described the decisions that organizations actually make, very few analysts have tried to describe how an organization actually makes decisions (Haberstroh, 1960; Radner, 1975; Shumway, Maher, Baker, Souder, Rubenstein, & Gallant, 1975; Williamson, 1970). The prescriptive studies have generally represented humans with endlessly naïve and complaisant mechanisms that follow instructions blindly and do not learn or anticipate. Rarely have analysts portrayed organizations' members as learners (cf. Reeves & Sweigart, 1981).

Such misrepresentations seem to arise from two causes. One is analysts' desire to use algebraic forms of mathematics. What algebra can do is quite limited, and humans and organizations may be too nonlinear, intricate, and iterative for algebraic models to be productive (Cyert & March, 1963; Mintzberg, Raisinghani, & Théorêt, 1976). However, analysts are not constrained to use algebra: computer simulation can solve nonlinear, iterative problems that exceed the capabilities of algebra (Dutton & Starbuck, 1971).

The second cause of oversimplified representations of humans and organizations, the cause this chapter addresses, seems to be the way analysts have approached optimization. The language and concepts of optimization have tended to impose more structure on the ways analysts solve problems than the available information warrants (March, 1976). Because analysts have designated them as constraints, certain relations are assumed to be inviolable. Analysts usually assume that only the variables they have identified as control variables can indeed be manipulated, and that only variables appearing in goal functions have costs and benefits associated with them, and that they have specified with dependable precision the trade-offs among variables in goal functions. More generally, tradition has held that optimization ought to start with the specification of a goal function: analysts should first decide what goals they wish to achieve. Analysts should supposedly identify control variables and constraints later, on the premise that only controls and constraints relevant to the chosen goal function need to be taken into account.

This chapter aims to make the foregoing premises appear less desirable, useful, and necessary. The next section argues that goals not only make unreliable starting points for problem solving, but they do and should arise out of the problem-solving process itself. Two ensuing sections then suggest ways to base decisions or designs on ambiguous foundations—how organizations can pursue multiple, noncomparable, and inharmonious goals that cannot be specified completely. The first of these sections prescribes structural and temporal decompositions of organizational control: it points out potential substitutions among goal functions, constraints, and control variables; and it prescribes optimization through experimental sequences. The second of these sections proposes that experiments should be determined partly by analytical models and partly by mechanistic heuristics. Finally, the last section addresses the integrating questions posed by the editors of this volume.

Only the section titled "Searching Analytically and Mechanistically" tries to innovate. Although the chapter deviates from the mainstream of tradition, its approach does stand upon a substantial intellectual heritage, and it represents the views of a significant subset of operations-research analysts and systems engineers (as well as economists and political scientists). The methodological ancestors encompass a large body of research on experimental optimization, but the two most influential ancestors are unquestionably Box and Draper's (1969) book, *Evolutionary Operation,* and Lindblom's (1959) article "The Science of

'Muddling Through.'" Keen (1977) has also written about untraditional concepts of optimization, but he put less emphasis on experimental methods.

SPECIFYING GOALS AND AVOIDING
THEIR SPECIFICATION

Every organization interacts with an extensive network of social systems,
and the entire network influences evaluations (Aldrich & Whetten, 1981;
Gerlach & Palmer, 1981). That is, the variables appearing in goal functions
express costs, benefits, rewards, punishments, penalties, or satisfactions. Because these appraisals arise, at least partially, through transactions between
social systems, analysts should not isolate a single variable or a single organization as if it were autonomous. Evaluations occur for many variables simultaneously, by transactions taking place throughout the network of social systems, and transactions that take account of potential activities as well as actual
ones.

But managers and analysts cannot solve all problems simultaneously, so they
decompose the entire network of social systems into manageable subsystems.
Managers and analysts can create good decompositions by treating weak interactions as if they do not occur, and the solutions to these simplified problems
generally suffice for short time intervals (Ando, Fisher, & Simon, 1963; Starbuck, 1973).

Making Variables Constant and Constants Variable

One prevalent method of decomposition is to treat values as parameters,
determined exogenously with respect to the organization being managed. For
example, value environments evaluate the inputs and outputs to organizations
(Rhenman, 1972), and analysts often assume that these value environments do
not depend on actions taken by the organizations being managed. The ultimate
untenability of these assumptions is exposed by observing that value environments are composed almost entirely of organizations, each of which supposedly
exerts no effects on the others. Yet these assumptions can yield accurate
approximations if the specific organization being managed is an extremely small
portion of the total network—that is, if the organization's value environments
resemble perfectly competitive economies.

Analysts should, however, rarely assume that values do not change with
organizations' actions. One reason is that virtually no operations-research analysts or systems engineers work for small organizations operating in industries
with perfectly competitive structures. But even a very small organization may
be able to influence values in its immediate neighborhoods. Indeed, most adver-

tising agencies and lobbying organizations are small. An organization can also choose among environments—choosing where to locate, what products to develop, which customers to serve, how to advertise, whether to obey laws, and so on (Champagne, Neef, & Nagle, 1981; Comanor, Kover, & Smiley, 1981; Morrill, 1981; Nystrom, Hedberg, & Starbuck, 1976; Starbuck, 1976; Weick, 1979; White, 1981). For instance, churches decide whether to engage in missionary activities and, if so, where; and police departments allocate manpower among traffic control, crime prevention, and pursuit of violators.

Because value environments do depend on choices and activities by the organizations inhabiting them, managers and analysts confront hierarchies of increasingly general problems. Suppose analysts start by formulating a goal

$$\underset{u}{\text{Max}}\ g(x, u; \phi), \tag{2}$$

where u is a list of control variables and x is a list measuring an organization's status. One of the x's may denote time. The parameters ϕ express the comparative value consequences of changes in the x's and u's: Analysts treat the ϕ's as parameters only because they are more stable than the x's and u's, and not because they are absolutely constant. Over the long run, the ϕ's depend on the x's and u's, so choices made will eventually feed back and cause the ϕ's to shift. That is, designs and decisions will alter the values that appear in goal functions.

In principle, the analysts can generalize problem (2) by adding relations that predict the changes in values. To do this, the analysts identify some auxiliary equations describing the dependence of the ϕ's on the x's and u's; say

$$\phi = p(x, V), \tag{5}$$

where V represents an augmented list encompassing u plus control variables that can influence p but not g. The original problem would then appear to be

$$\underset{V}{\text{Max}}\ g(x, V). \tag{6}$$

But there are parameters in the functions p as well

$$\phi = p(x, V; \psi), \tag{7}$$

so the augmented goal should be written

$$\underset{V}{\text{Max}}\ g(x, V; \psi). \tag{8}$$

This generalized problem may be a better problem than the original, or a worse one. The ψ's ought to be more stable than the ϕ's, and hence the generalized problem should yield solutions that work for a longer time. But the generalized problem may be too complicated to solve, or it may be so complicated that it can only be solved approximately.

In practice, analysts do and should do very little of this kind of generalization. One reason is that the updating of analyses, policies, and structures limits the benefits of generalization: parameters can take on new values each time an analysis is updated. Another reason is that it is quite easy to pose problems that are too complicated to solve accurately. Yet another reason is that attempts at generalization are error-prone. Analysts derive their equations from the theories that managers use in everyday practices, and such theories are distorted by generous quantities of ideology and fantasy, including a propensity to assume that today's world will persist indefinitely (Beyer, 1981; Sproull, 1981; Starbuck, 1976; Tumin, 1964). If value parameters change gradually over long time spans, the changes are difficult to observe, and the equations describing these changes are very difficult to specify.

Most importantly, people have difficulty anticipating their reactions to situations they have not yet experienced. Analysts try to characterize alternative organizational configurations, including configurations that have never occurred. To some extent, analysts' excellence depends on their imagining what no one has previously thought of, let alone tried out (Hitch, 1966). Then to choose among these alternatives, analysts try to capture their characteristics in goal functions. Even analysts who consider only their own personal likes and dislikes would be unlikely to predict realistically how they would react to a policy or structure they have struggled to imagine. And analysts must normally try to predict the reactions of other people: a board of directors, the customers for a product or clients for a service, a parliament or legislature, the employees who must implement a policy, competing organizations, or the residents of a region. Like the analysts themselves, these people generally have to experience a situation before they can say how much they like it (Hirschman & Lindblom, 1962). Moreover, evaluations by collectivities of people raise many additional problems: organizations are generally deficient in communication channels for formulating and expressing collective preferences, and the mere existence of communication channels does not resolve disagreements.

Resolving Disagreements and Avoiding Their Resolution

Whenever several people express preferences, the people may disagree, and disagreements become highly probable when alternatives are numerous and rather similar and when many, heterogeneous people express preferences. Analysts can ordinarily assume that disagreements exist (Landau, 1973; Wildavsky, 1972), even though people may not be voicing these disagreements (Hirschman, 1970).

People resolve disagreements through governance mechanisms. Because organizations differ in the degrees to which their governance mechanisms are persistent, stable, accepted, clear, equitable, dependable, internally consonant, and so on, analysts' first challenge is to detect what governance mechanisms exist and what properties they possess. Analysts brought into an organization as outside consultants frequently misperceive governance mechanisms, because the organizational members who guide the consultants seek to enhance their own centrality and seek to gloss over their organization's incongruities and lack of cohesion. Outside consultants often become ploys in intraorganizational power struggles (Rhenman, 1972). Analysts who are permanant members of the organizations they are designing may deceive themselves by thinking of governance mechanisms as they wish they were—wise, knowledgeable, rational, technically sophisticated, altruistic, and the like (Bjørn-Andersen & Hedberg, 1977).

After observing what governance mechanisms exist, analysts should choose strategies for supplementing, reinforcing, or replacing them (Lindblom, 1959; Scott, Mitchell, & Peery, 1981). For example, if governance mechanisms are virtually nonexistent, analysts might install majority voting, or they might act as benevolent despots and resolve value disagreements by doing what they personally believe is best. If the governance hierarchy is well-established, analysts might choose to adhere regularly to the desires of the top managers, or they might avoid explicating some choices in order to favor the predicted preferences of people low in the hierarchy. Procedures and communication channels can be added that help organizational members express and resolve disagreements, but an organization's members cannot resolve disagreements founded upon equally legitimate goals. Because a highly fragmented organization may be unable to formulate and pursue any collective goals whatever, and because a monolithic hierarchy may be unable to diagnose and correct its own failings, the variables appearing in a goal function should include properties of the governance structure (Box & Draper, 1969; McNulty, 1964; Nystrom *et al.*, 1976; Stymne, 1972).

Value disagreements among people reflect the general impossibility of formulating a single, completely adequate goal function. Within a cohesive organization, only a minority of disagreements emanate from differences in members' self-interests. Rather, the organization is struggling to pursue a multiplicity of legitimate and important, but partially noncomparable and partially inharmonious, goals; the organization's members fall into conflict in consequence of the goals' disharmonies and noncomparabilities. Analysts seeking to formulate a goal function confront these disharmonies and noncomparabilities. Any single goal function is, at best, a one-dimensional projection of values that are ordered along several dimensions (Afanasyev, 1971). If analysts reduce all values to one goal function, they ignore numerous disharmonies among goals (Bjørn-Andersen & Hedberg, 1977; Cameron, 1978).

One major research focus within operations research and systems engineering is multiple-criteria decision making: Analysts are searching for methods of choice that tolerate inharmonious goals (Starr & Zeleny, 1977). For example, logical analyses can rule out some inferior (dominated) alternatives before the problems are presented to people, so that the people do not argue about irrelevant issues. However, politically neutral analyses cannot resolve serious value disagreements, or even modify them significantly. Analysts have to take political positions, and they cannot avoid injecting their own values into designs (Nystrom & Starbuck, 1977; Scott, 1977; Vickers, 1973).

Analysts ought to adopt two policies. First, analysts ought to be conscious of their own values, and since their values affect their designs, analysts should make their values explicit. Second, when an organization's members disagree with one another about goals that the analysts regard as equally legitimate, analysts should avoid eliminating these disagreements by projecting the members' values into a single goal function. Trade-offs should be made between goals only if the goals are mutually congruous or hierarchically arrayed. Equal and inharmonious goals should be preserved by means of policies or structures that exclude no legitimate goals and that tolerate value disagreements (Churchman, 1968; Hedberg, Nystrom, & Starbuck, 1976; Starbuck, 1975).

DECOMPOSING CONTROL STRUCTURALLY AND TEMPORALLY

In order to preserve inharmonious goals, managers and analysts have to decompose organizational control, because a unitary, integrated control system will constantly encounter its internal inconsistencies and then try to reconcile them. Decompositions ought to involve both structural and temporal dimensions, and they should exploit the substitutability of goals, constraints, and controls (Simon, 1964).

Exchanging Constraints for Diversity

Most constraints—in organizations and in design problems—are partially arbitrary, and arbitrary constraints can become goal functions and control policies. Conversely, goal functions and control policies can become constraints.

Optimization problems originating in a real organization may involve as many as eight kinds of constraints. Two kinds are definitional identities and logical inequalities (such as the requirement to keep slack variables nonnegative): such constraints must never be violated because they underlie a problem's formulation. All other constraints can be violated under appropriate circumstances.

Many equality constraints, the ones sometimes called plant equations, describe a modeled organization (Plant, 1968). These descriptive statements can, of course, be altered by changing the organization's methods; and because these statements are usually no more than approximations obtained by observing past behavior, the organization may never adhere to them precisely. Similarly, most inequality constraints are descriptive statements—statements about maximum work loads or plant capacities, for instance—that can be altered when justifications exist (Box & Draper, 1969; Seashore, 1977, p. 188). Mathematical-programming studies normally estimate the improvements in goals that could result from altering inequality constraints because analysts have found that constraint changes are usually possible and are often worth their costs.

Still other constraints, of both the equality and the inequality varieties, represent control policies. For example, analysts seeking to solve the problem

$$\underset{u}{\text{Max}}\ g(x,\ u) \tag{9}$$

could decide to divide the full control vector into two subsets, u_1 and u_2. If solving the subproblem

$$\underset{u_1}{\text{Max}}\ g(x,\ u_1,\ u_2) \tag{10}$$

produces the statements about u_1

$$\begin{aligned} w_1(x,\ u_1,\ u_2) &= 0 \\ v_1(x,\ u_1,\ u_2) &\geq 0, \end{aligned} \tag{11}$$

the analysts can define a new problem

$$\underset{u_2}{\text{Max}}\ g(x,\ u_1,\ u_2) \tag{12}$$

subject to the constraints given in statements (11). Because these constraints are introduced for analytic purposes, they can be altered by redefining the subset u_1 (Mesarović, Macko, & Takahara, 1970).

This process of generating control constraints illustrates two points about the decomposition of control in organizations. Firstly, goals are being pursued sequentially rather than simultaneously. In the general case, maximizing the function g demands manipulation of the whole set of control variables u, not merely a proper subset. The subset u_1 could control g only within a subspace of g's domain, and so u_1 could pursue only a subset of the goals represented in g. Manipulation of u_1, as indicated in problem (10), amounts to pursuing a subset of the organization's goals initially, on the assumption that the remainder of the organization's goals can be pursued later.

Secondly, while analysts are working on the new problem (12), they have given up direct control over u_1; they have delegated control of u_1 to the constraints (11). Of course, competent analysts can discover functions w_1 and v_1 that faithfully and accurately fulfill their assigned responsibilities, and the analysts can, in any event, resume direct control of u_1 whenever they please. However, delegation of responsibility need not be a fanciful pencil-and-paper exercise. Managers may find it difficult to repeal real-life delegations of responsibility to actual organizational subunits, and higher-level managers cannot depend on the subunits to do what they themselves would do.

Note that decomposition of control stimulates the creation of constraints, such as statements (11). Many of the constraints that purportedly describe an organization originate in delegations of responsibility. These appear as constraints because the bosses make them constraints, but the bosses can revise or repeal such constraints. In the meantime, such constraints afford one means by which the bosses hope to control their subordinates' behaviors.

A boss who delegates responsibility must decide whether to describe the assignment in the form of an optimal goal such as (10), leaving it to the responsible subunit to determine how to optimize this goal, or whether to use constraint statements such as (11) to specify how the subunit should behave in different situations, or whether to combine the two approaches. Assigning only an optimal goal allows the subunit to feel personal involvement with the task, and to bring to bear its own expertise and close familiarity with the subproblem, but makes it difficult to evaluate the subunit's performance, because a superior has no way to decide whether the subunit is actually optimizing its goal function. Specifying behavioral constraints allows a superior to monitor the subunit's performance—because the superior can decide whether the subunit is satisfying the constraints—and substitutes the superior's expertise for the subunit's expertise.

Superiors almost always believe they have more expertise, or at least more wisdom, than their subordinates. Consequently, constraints are popular control media, and their popularity rises as lower hierarchical levels are reached. Yet control by means of constraints frequently produces surprising results. A few years ago, for example, the Boy Scouts of America discovered that membership quotas assigned during their Boypower Campaign had induced some officials to enroll and pay dues for imaginary scouts. One time, the chief executive of a major corporation instructed the manager of his firm's largest plant that he would lose his job if the plant produced more than 12% waste. Neither the plant manager nor anyone else knew how this constraint could be met. So each day when waste reached the 12% limit, the plant began dumping waste into empty railroad cars that were waiting for the finished product. After the railroad cars had been filled, the plant manager started selling the waste to scrap dealers. But the sales proceeds could not be reported on the corporate books because the sales amounted to admissions that the plant was violating its waste constraint. The plant manager kept proceeds as cash in his desk . . . until he had a heart attack and his replacement inherited a desk stuffed full of money.

The optimal reliance on constraints or behavioral rules to control subunits' actions depends on past learning and the subunits' and superiors' developing capacities. Delegation requires skill on both sides. Many organizations in decline, and many of those that appear stable, have lost their effectiveness primarily because they have been deceived by their successes (Nystrom *et al.*, 1976). Organizations fail to detect shifting environments when they rely on programmed responses, do not challenge prevailing myths, and stop planning sequences of experiments (Hedberg *et al.*, 1976).

Formulas (9)–(12) describe an absurdly simple decomposition: there are just two hierarchical levels, with one subunit on each level, and both subunits pursue one mutual goal. Even with two hierarchical levels and a single superior, several subordinates could pursue distinct subgoals. The control vector could be divided into several subsets u_1, u_2, u_3, . . . , and each subset of controls could be assigned a different goal function:

$$\text{Max}_{u_1} g_1(x, u_1, u_2, u_3, . . .)$$
$$\text{Max}_{u_2} g_2(x, u_1, u_2, u_3, . . .)$$
$$\text{Max}_{u_3} g_3(x, u_1, u_2, u_3, . . .) \tag{13}$$

and so on. For example, a marketing subunit might manipulate product prices and advertising, and a production department might decide production schedules and choose raw materials.

This modest complication highlights the need for coordination. In order to act effectively, the subunit that manipulates u_1 must know what decisions are being made about u_2 and u_3. For example, before it can make sensible decisions about raw materials and production schedules, the production department needs to know what advertising claims the marketing department is making. To maximize the autonomy of subunits, analysts should try to identify subgoals and control subsets that minimize such cross-product interactions. Where interactions cannot be eliminated, the analysts can base coordination on predictions of how subunits will solve their subproblems (Dirickx, Jennergren, & Peterson, 1973). But predictions err. Managers would have to be omniscient in order to make a decomposed organization behave exactly as they prefer. Organizations with the good fortune to include omniscient managers ought to let them make all of the decisions, not squander their time predicting the actions of fallible subordinates.

Some operations-research analysts have, in fact, fallen into this trap. For instance, decomposition schemes for large-scale programming problems have stimulated prescriptions for how an organization should be divided into subunits and how subunits should coordinate with each other (Jennergren & Müller, 1973; Kydland, 1975; Mesarović *et al.*, 1970). Such prescriptions have characteristically assumed so much knowledge by the managers at central headquarters that decentralization becomes needless deception: the models portray subunits as making hypothetical choices over and over again until they finally hit upon choices that the top managers could have made initially, and neither the top managers nor their subordinates take account of the ways their mutual games previously turned out.

A potential advantage of decomposition is lessened dependence on the wisdom and expertise of top managers. However, top managers will retain dictatorial powers as long as instructions from superiors to subordinates are supposed to be logically congruous with each other and congruous with a unified, overall goal function. Logically incongruous instructions give subordinates the freedom to reconcile incongruities, and so allow subordinates to use their own wisdom and expertise. Tolerance of logically incongruous instructions also gives superiors the freedom to pursue disparate goals that may not mesh together smoothly, so an organization can discover new goals. Provided the organization has a supportive ideology, one effective structure for generating incongruous instructions is a matrix organization in which each subordinate has two or more superiors who pursue divergent goals (McCann & Galbraith, 1981).

Decompositions that create distinct goals for each subunit's performance make it difficult for the subunits to perceive whether they are pursuing harmonious goals. Decompositions that convert performance goals into behavioral constraints make mutual comparisons across subunits nearly impossible. Without analytic assistance from sophisticated information systems, superiors may be unable to evaluate the logical congruence of their subordinates' behaviors. Congruent decompositions are usually difficult to determine deductively (Jennergren & Müller, 1973); and partly because of errors and unintended deviations from plan, inductive inferences are even more tenuous than deductive ones.

Creating Opportunities by Optimizing Incrementally

Decomposition should generally involve a temporal dimension. In the decomposition described by formulas (9)–(12), for example, the goal function was first optimized with respect to u_1 and then optimized with respect to u_2 afterward. Temporal decompositions create multitudinous options for making substitutions between goals, constraints, and controls.

One cluster of options arises from making substitutions between the controls applied at different times and the constraints imposed at different hierarchical levels. Statements (10) and (11), for instance, inferred some rules for optimizing with respect to u_1; these rules could thereafter constrain a subordinate hierarchical level. A partly analogous decomposition occurs in most procedures for optimizing by means of experimental searches: a goal function is first optimized with one subset of control variables, then these controls are held constant while another control subset is manipulated. Some search procedures nest iterations so that a goal function is optimized with respect to lower-level controls before each experiment with controls on the next higher level. Although iterative nestings more closely approximate solutions in algebraic form, they finely tune controls that may turn out to have been comparatively ineffective (Beveridge & Schechter, 1970; Box & Draper, 1969; Box, Davies, & Swann, 1969; Mesarović *et al.*, 1970; Wilde, 1964).

Temporal decompositions also open up options for substituting constraints for goals (Simon, 1964). In the most extreme instance, the problem

$$\underset{u}{\text{Max}}\ g(x,\ u) \tag{9}$$

would be translated into:

Find u such that
$w(x,\ u) = 0$
$v(x,\ u) \geq 0.$ $\tag{14}$

The constraints $w = 0$ and $v \geq 0$ would be constructed to make g large, and successive iterations would attempt to modify these constraints so as to increase g. A less extreme translation would constrain some control variables and attempt optimization with respect to others. For example,

$$\underset{u_1}{\text{Max}}\ g_1(x,\ u) \tag{15}$$

subject to constraints of the form (14). As before, successive iterations would seek to increase the overall goal g by altering the constraints $w = 0$ and $v \geq 0$.

These iterative optimization methods strongly resemble the previously mentioned procedures for experimental searches. Both groups of iterative methods rely heavily on heuristics, and both may fail to achieve improvements with every iteration.

The methods appear even more similar when opportunities are considered for transforming constraints back into goals. Because experimental searches involve the risk that some trials may violate constraints, and because considerable resources may be expended testing for potential constraint violations in advance, some search procedures replace constraints with penalties. Actions can violate constraints in principle, but constraint violations elicit penalties that are large enough to assure that the experiments are appraised as unsatisfactory (Beveridge & Schechter, 1970; Box *et al.*, 1969). Thus, experiments focus on a surrogate problem that has both constraints and goal function different from the original problem, but heuristics make the solutions to the surrogate problem converge toward solutions to the original problem.

An analogous, but inverted, idea can guide intracorporate transactions: The divisions of a corporation would be free to buy outside instead of using each other's products, but intracorporate transactions would take place at prices differing from those in external markets (Jennergren, 1981). Intracorporate transactions would be fostered by transfer prices that are artificially high for selling divisions and artificially low for buying divisions. This method would modify the divisions' goal functions in lieu of imposing constraints.

Optimizing Incrementally by Satisficing

Iterative methods, at least some of them, break actions or structural changes down into small increments so that effectiveness improves gradually. This is usually good even when analysts believe that they know how to optimize effectiveness immediately. Approaching an optimum gradually may appear to substitute suboptimal performances for optimal ones, but changing an organization as quickly as possible yields less benefit in the long run than does decomposing abrupt changes into increments distributed through time. Abrupt changes undercut coordination among subunits, expose desirable disharmonies among goals and assignments, impede experimentation, break down subunits' autonomy, waste energies in emotional reactions to stress, and stimulate undesirable conflicts among people and goals. By contrast, incremental changes can leave intact most activities and perceptions, can disclose only marginal conflicts, can leave time for learning from experiments, can reserve capacity for exploiting unexpected opportunities, and can enable an organization to maintain a stable concept of its destiny. Abrupt changes can nearly always be decomposed in such fashion that benefits lost through delay are more than offset by the savings from avoiding hostilities, demotivation, wasted energies, ill-founded rationalities, and foolish risks (Braybrooke & Lindblom, 1963; Cartwright, 1973; Day & Tinney, 1968; Hedberg et al., 1976; Miller, 1982; Vickers, 1959).

However, the most essential prerequisite for adopting iterative procedures is a confession of uncertainty by the analysts and their bosses (Jones, 1975). Abrupt changes to optimality appear impractical to analysts who admit they not only do not know how to optimize, but do not know exactly what goal function to optimize or what constraints to observe. Uncertain analysts ought to behave conservatively in the sense that attempted innovations deviate only incrementally from tradition (Braybrooke & Lindblom, 1963; Hirschman & Lindblom, 1962; Lindblom, 1959). An organization should not be inadvertently pushed into an extremely disadvantageous, and possibly irreversible state; and new information about the organization and its environments should be integrated with the analysts' existing perceptions (Starbuck, 1963a). In other words, uncertain analysts should satisfice instead of optimize (Radner, 1975; Simon, 1955; Starbuck, 1963b).

Satisficing relaxes the logical associations among subgoals. One reason is that people interpret nonmonotonic, erratic movements toward an optimum as noisy progress, and noise can conceal divergent movements toward different goals. Another reason is that satisficing replaces a few goal functions by many constraint-like specifications of satisfactory behavior—to find out whether these satisficing criteria are congruous would require many comparisons among relations involving diverse variables. Yet another reason is that satisficing people expect to revise their perceptions, beliefs, and goals, so they hold weak expectations about how congruent simultaneous behaviors should be and how comparable behaviors should be from one day to the next (Hedberg, 1974).

Thus satisficing provides opportunities for analysts to incorporate inharmonious or noncomparable goals. Indeed, even omniscient analysts might use search procedures to camouflage temporal decompositions in which organizations pursue partially incongruous goals sequentially. Without camouflage, efforts to pursue incongruous goals sequentially would reveal the incongruities, and would repeatedly confront an organization's members with their value disagreements. Such confrontations can yield benefits when means exist for resolving conflicts, but conflicts debilitate when bringing them forth only arouses antagonisms, or suppresses constructive dissent, or undermines confidence.

Both temporal and structural decompositions replace statements about goals with behavioral rules that look like constraints: such behavioral rules can encourage superiors to look over their subordinates' shoulders, and they can reduce subordinates' feelings of personal involvement with their tasks. So analysts ought to beware that constraint-like rules do not become so prevalent as to undermine the evaluative diversity they were installed to protect (Hedberg *et al.*, 1976). Indeed, this is a central dilemma in organizational design.

SEARCHING ANALYTICALLY
AND MECHANISTICALLY

The preceding sections make a number of points:

Because organizational actions affect an organization's value environments, organizational actions alter the very goals the actions were intended to optimize. People make unreliable predictions about their future evaluations of possible consequences, and people disagree about the values of actual consequences. Value disagreements often reflect the existence of noncomparable and inharmonious, but nonetheless legitimate and useful, goals for an organization. Governance mechanisms for resolving disagreements almost always have vague outlines; and for several reasons, analysts should try to manipulate governance mechanisms.

People can replace goal functions with constraints that are sequentially modified, and conversely, constraints can become reward or penalty functions. Once they have been adopted, control policies turn into constraints. But controlling with constraints is unnecessary because control responsibilities can be delegated to subunits. So control policies can also become modifications of goal functions.

Analysts ought to behave as if goal functions, constraints, and control variables are ambiguously specified and always modifiable. And analysts should protect the existence of inharmonious, multiple goals—by concealing the disharmonies, by preventing unnecessary confrontations, by promoting awareness that diverse viewpoints help an organization see its errors, and by creating structural and temporal decompositions.

Optimizing Suboptimally

The foregoing implies that analysts should not see organizational policies and structures as challenges to deductive inference, in which the analysts try to marshall data about values and organizational properties and then try to deduce optimal solutions. A deductive approach puts analysts in the position of first expending much time and resources to make policies or structures flawless, and then publicly arguing the certainty of their policies' or structures' success. If these arguments persuade, both the analysts and the people who support them place personal stakes on the policies' or structures' success: they are biased against evidence that the policies or structures contain defects, and they may resist attempts to evaluate effectiveness (Campbell, 1969; Landau, 1973; Wildavsky, 1972). Because every organization's inherent ambiguities imply that flaws must be numerous and inescapable, deductive policies and structures tend to turn into persistent monuments to irrationality.

Analysts should place little trust in their prior knowledge and beliefs; they should not attempt to specify a single optimal solution (Starbuck, 1963b). However, designers should not just muddle through. Muddling through is a strategy that looks only one step ahead (Lindblom, 1959). One step is an inadequate horizon: efficient learning requires that steps be taken in patterned clusters, significant innovations should be planned, and organizations can benefit from formulating long-run goals. Organizational policies and structures should be sequences of experiments (Hedberg, Nystrom, & Starbuck, 1977; Nystrom & Starbuck, 1977, Sackman, 1967).

Analysts should plan sequences of temporary and suboptimal policies or structures that elicit information about an organization and its environments, thus providing bases for long-run improvements (Box & Draper, 1969; Taylor & Vertinsky, 1981). Conceptually, any single policy or structure should be embedded in a family of successive policies and structures. Although specific successors may degrade the organization's effectiveness, clusters of successors should evolve toward higher effectiveness. Suboptimal policies and structures should be tried out to gather information because the value of information counterbalances losses incurred by delaying optimality. Consequently, one higher-level design problem should become: how much suboptimality does information gathering warrant? But this problem too should be embedded in a still higher-level problem. Costs of search depend on the search procedures used, and search procedures should be based partly on analytical models describing an organization and its environments. Better models permit more efficient searches, ones entailing smaller losses caused by extremely suboptimal designs, and ones converging more rapidly toward global optima (Beveridge & Schechter, 1970; Wilde, 1964). So, how much suboptimality do potential improvements in analytical models warrant?

Searching Mechanistically as Well as Analytically

One conjecture is that organizations ought to base searches on mechanistic heuristics as well as analytical models. Analytical models depend heavily on the model builders' existing knowledge, beliefs, and prejudices. Insofar as analytical models dictate search directions, the findings tend to confirm prior knowledge and beliefs, surprises become less probable, and surprises tend to be so extreme that they are rationalized and do not alter prior beliefs. Managers and analysts should expect to be surprised . . . a little bit at a time.

Dependence on prior knowledge and beliefs weakens drastically when experimental alternatives are generated by mechanistic heuristics developed for computers and control systems. For example, Box's "complex" method avoids redundant observations, and it adjusts to shifts in the permissible domain for experimentation (Beveridge & Schechter, 1970; Box et al., 1969); although the method's efficiency depends on the goal function being linear, the method's memory is so short that linearity is usually a plausible local approximation. Emphasis on short-term memory is one benefit of using mechanistic heuristics. Yet mechanistic heuristics do not effectively shift from one search mode to another when the shape of a goal function alters (Beveridge & Schechter, 1970; Box & Draper, 1969; Wilde, 1964). Nor can mechanistic heuristics make inductive leaps and totally reformulate problems (Watzlawick, Weakland, & Fisch, 1974). So managers and analysts ultimately have to exercise their own best judgments about when to exercise their own best judgments.

REAPING BENEFITS FROM AMBIGUITIES

This section expands on some key ideas, interweaving strands in order to address the editors' questions about contributions to theory, to research, and to practice.

Because organizations encompass ambiguous, partially noncomparable, and inharmonious goals, organizational designers should beware of imposing an unrealistic and harmful coherence. Organizations can benefit from diversity and conflict, so these should be preserved and even fostered. The same can be said concerning concepts of organizational effectiveness. Distinct academic disciplines will inevitably yield partially noncomparable and inharmonious

ideas about organizational effectiveness. Certainly, operations-research analysts and systems engineers espouse ideas that diverge from those of sociologists
or psychologists, but divergence does not mean that some ideas are wrong, for
the world is sufficiently complex not only to accommodate but to benefit from
conflicts between ideas.

Defining Effectiveness Effectively

1. "What are the major theoretical predictions or hypotheses that derive
   from your perspective regarding relationships between effectiveness and
   other organizational variables (e.g., structure, technology, information
   processing, individual satisfaction)?"
2. "How does your perspective expand our understanding of the behavior of
   organizations?"
3. "Does the definition of organizational effectiveness change when considering different types of organizations (e.g., public–private, professional–industrial, large–small) or different stages of development (e.g.,
   early stages, institutionalized stages, decline)?"

Research on multiple-criteria decision making may foreshadow future shifts
in ideas about organizational effectiveness. Some operations-research analysts
have abandoned multiattribute utility theory and have begun developing alternative theories "based on the notion that a utility super-function is not only
unknown or extremely difficult to measure but also not a very useful conceptualization of the decision-making process [Starr & Zeleny, 1977, p. 21]." Keen
(1977) identified seven directions of change in concepts of optimality: (1) from
single to multiple criteria, (2) from absolute to situational judgments, (3) from
synoptic to incremental analyses, (4) from efficiency to effectiveness, (5)
from convergence to divergence, (6) from objectives to constraints, and (7) from
economic to political criteria. Keen (1977) asserted that "there can be no
absolute definition of optimality; any such conception must be contingent on
the type of problem involved, on the decision makers' purpose, ability and needs
and on the context of the problem [p. 53]."

Judgments about organizational effectiveness generally tell one more about
the judges' implicit theories than about the organizations being judged. This
chapter points out the value in actions that conventional wisdom often labels as
ineffective. Benefits can arise from accepting goal disagreements, shifting attention from one goal to another, using sophisticated forecasting techniques
while distrusting their forecasts, questioning strategies and procedures that
have clearly succeeded, altering constraints that define acceptable behavior,
and lowering goals after failures or unsuccessful searches. Such actions sharp-
en perceptions, encourage experimentation, and foster improvements.

Judgments about organizational effectiveness generally undervalue information, discovery, and learning. Effectiveness that falls below the best performance attainable is nevertheless desirable if it includes information about better criteria or better methods. Conversely, superficially optimal effectiveness is actually undesirable if it forecloses learning. The managers of successful organizations quite often inflict crises on their organizations by deciding that they have already attained optimal effectiveness and that they know how to attain it (Nystrom et al., 1976). As Chisholm quipped, "Any time things appear to be going better, you have overlooked something [Bloch, 1977]."

Judgments about organizational effectiveness also tell one about the judges' values and political affiliations. Most operations-research projects have been conducted by analysts who, consciously or unconsciously, supported the interests of dominant elites such as technocrats and top managers. The analysts may well have been missing opportunities to serve wider clienteles. Bjørn-Andersen and Hedberg (1977) found that designers of management-information systems made numerous assumptions about what top managers wanted without actually consulting the top managers, and that the designers perceived numerous constraints that did not actually exist. Friedlander and Pickle (1968) found very weak correlations among various stakeholders' judgments about the effectiveness of small business firms: their results suggest that stakeholders' interests do not compete directly, so that it is possible to satisfy one type of stakeholder without dissatisfying others. Perhaps operations-research analysts, systems engineers and other organizational designers could serve the interests of customers, governments, low-level employees, and stockholders without damaging the interests of dominant elites.

Managers and analysts should beware of judging effectiveness reflexively with the same goal functions that have been used to make decisions or to create designs. Such judgments are blind to the flaws that inhere in the goal functions, and experience has frequently shown this kind of effectiveness to be like the Emperor's new clothes. But this is a difficult issue to confront: if analysts could see how to improve a goal function, they would have chosen the better goal function in the first place. Also, an organization is unlikely to keep records about variables that were left out of goal functions.

Indeed, organizational records emphasize financial and numerical data.

Predictions about empirical relationships between organizational effectiveness and other variables incorporate all kinds of assumptions about whose perceptions and values should count. For example, we might predict that highly effective organizations tolerate dissension, reward experimentation, and cherish transience (Hedberg et al., 1976). Such a prediction presumes that more effective organizations avoid crises and last longer, and it places no importance on keeping specific people in superior positions. But managers would favor different criteria of organizational effectiveness; top managers generally place high values on remaining in superior positions, and they like the status quo; lower-level managers often trade off long-run adaptability in order to gain immediate results that pay off to them personally in bonuses or promotions.

Learning By Teaching

1. "What are the major indicators (criteria) of organizational effectiveness using your perspective?"
2. "How would one test the efficacy of your approach compared to other approaches to effectiveness?"
3. "What are the major methodological issues in operationalizing effectiveness using your perspective (e.g., those relating to levels of analysis, data collection, predictors, key variables)?"

Neither understanding nor designing will benefit greatly from attempts to measure empirical relationships between organizational effectiveness and other variables without disturbing these relationships. One reason is that the term *effectiveness* subsumes too many disparate phenomena, not all of which can be measured. Another reason is that people evaluate those attributes they have learned to monitor, applying values they have learned, so evaluations of effectiveness depend on training and experience. Descriptive studies disclose only what people have learned, not what they could have learned or what they should have learned. Because organizational designs mold experiences, managers and analysts are teachers, and they ought to think about what they can and should teach about effectiveness. What kinds of organizations should people learn to judge as being highly effective?

Effectiveness is obviously not the only learned and perceived characteristic of organizations. Behaviors, structures, technologies, and environments are all rather arbitrary. Different people perceive them differently, and people can learn to perceive them differently than they now do. People can select and enact them, and people can learn how to select and enact them. For example, each organization (whatever that means!) inhabits numerous environments simultaneously. Different organizational subunits interact with different environmental elements; and even within a single subunit, different people hold different perceptions. In fact, members' perceptions of their organizations' environments correlate virtually zero with objective measurements of those environments (Downey, Hellriegel, & Slocum, 1975; Tosi, Aldag, & Storey, 1973). Yet some members' beliefs and expectations have demonstrable effects on their organizations' environments.

One consequence of this multiplicity of organizational realities is that the answers to questions depend strongly on who is asked and how they are asked. Relationships discerned in some members' perceptions may not characterize the perceptions of other members. For instance, exit interviews with members who are leaving an organization would likely yield models of organizational effectiveness that contrast with those of the dominant elites (Hirschman, 1970).

This multiplicity also nurtures opportunities for managers and analysts to teach. Merely passing out a questionnaire calls the respondents' attention to the queried issues and implies that their opinions deserve respect (Rhenman, 1972). Feeding back respondents' opinions reinforces these effects; and depending on how the opinions are presented, feedback can manufacture consensus, dissension, new perceptions, expectations, goals, integration, differentiation, love, or hate.

Because managers and analysts do teach and cannot avoid teaching, they should think carefully about what they want to teach. Analyzing the reasons for his success in running the Nazi armaments industry, Speer (1970) observed:

> We owed the success of our programs to thousands of technicians . . . to whom we now entrusted the responsibility for whole segments of the armaments industry. This aroused their buried enthusiasm . . . . Basically, I exploited the phenomenon of the technician's often blind devotion to his task. Because of what seems to be the moral neutrality of technology, these people were without any scruples about their activities. The more technical the world imposed on us by the war, the more dangerous was this indifference of the technician to the direct consequences of his anonymous activities [p. 283].

Who should make which decisions about what members learn? Members should make most of these decisions for themselves if organizations are to realize their potentialities for self-design and to be compatible with a democratic society. But major decisions and new designs aim to produce situations that deviate significantly from experience, and little meaning should be attached to people's preferences for imagined situations.

Organizational effectiveness affords another instance of the general proposition that prescription has to come before understanding (Starbuck & Nystrom, 1981). The notion that one should understand organizations before one tries to improve them is backwards; someone who relies on passive observation will never understand organizations well enough to formulate useful prescriptions. Organizations' dynamism and flexibility imply that one can better understand organizations by making predictions, instigating changes, and watching the reactions. In order to develop good theories about organizational effectiveness, analysts should at least study the dynamic reactions that occur when spontaneous events perturb equilibria. However, spontaneous phenomena are difficult to disentangle, so analysts can obtain clearer discriminations by instigating experiments themselves. Planned experiments also increase the importance of prediction, which is essential for distinguishing good theories from bad ones. Thus, understanding of effectiveness will come from active efforts to change effectiveness.

Practicing Deviant Practices

1. "What prescriptions or guidelines for improving success are suggested by your approach? Are there any counterintuitive recommendations?"
2. "What diagnostic tools could managers use to monitor success using your approach?"
3. "What trade-offs, dilemmas, or dysfunctional consequences might be experienced by managers using your approach?"

This chapter puts forth some prescriptions that deviate from conventional wisdom and traditional management principles. Prevailing managerial ideologies extol the virtues of rational decision making in which people first formulate clear, consistent goals and then choose actions to fit these goals. This same rational decision making guides the approaches to optimization prevailing among operations-research analysts and systems engineers. But rational decision making produces bad consequences because the world is not rational. The meaning of rationality is determined by human anatomy, not by the physical and social world. People make goals clear and consistent by suppressing dissent and ignoring complexity, so perceptions grow less realistic and autocracy stifles democracy. Rationalized perceptions lead people to believe that the world is simple enough to predict, yet rationalized perceptions are so unrealistic that they guarantee prediction failures. Clear, consistent goals discourage experimentation and learning and promote stability and complacency (Hedberg et al., 1976). March (1976) pointed out that actions do and should precede goal setting: "Human choice behavior is at least as much a process for discovering goals as for acting on them. . . . One of the primary ways in which the goals of an organization are developed is by interpreting the decisions it makes, and one feature of good managerial decisions is that they lead to the development of more interesting value premises for the organization [pp. 72–80]." Brunsson (1982) has observed that rational decision making impedes organizations' abilities to take actions.

The prescriptions of this chapter include these unusual ones: Do not start problem solving by trying to specify a precise goal function. Do not expect to find a stable optimum. Adopt solutions that permit dissension, particularly about preferences. Foster ideologies that tolerate ambiguity and conflict and that support risk taking and experimentation. Assume that constraints can be changed; consider solutions that violate constraints. Do not insist that instructions to subordinates be logically congruent; let subordinates deal with incongruent instructions by applying their own expertise and wisdom. Decompose large, abrupt changes into smaller ones distributed over time. Delegate some responsibilities in the form of optimal goals rather than constraints on behavior. Do not just muddle through, one step at a time: plan sequences of experiments. Choose some experiments on the bases of analytical models, and other steps on the bases of mechanistic heuristics.

If these prescriptions seem impractical, reflect on the conclusion of a McKinsey & Company study that compared 10 companies chosen for being well-run: Dana, Digital Equipment, Emerson Electric, Hewlett-Packard, IBM, Johnson & Johnson, McDonald's, Procter & Gamble, Texas Instruments, and 3-M. The study concluded that the primary attribute these companies shared was a bias toward action. "Controlled experiments abound in these companies. The attitude of management is to 'get some data, do it, then adjust it,' rather than wait for a perfect overall plan [Peters, 1980, p. 196]."

Support also arises from more abstract research. For instance, a simulation of firms competing in a duopoly found that if decision makers have high aspirations, adaptive processes perform as well as optimizing methods. Neave and Petersen (1980) conjectured that where a problem structure is changing,

> adaptive methods of decision making may well be superior to optimizing models on the grounds of lower setup, implementation, and adjustment costs. For, by the time an optimizing procedure can be found and implemented, the problem structure may have changed, with the result that the implementation of such a study's prescriptions could well prove irrelevant if not damaging to the firm [p. 821].

An experimental approach encourages people to monitor effectiveness because actions depend on feedback. Experimental feedback also stimulates people to discover their preferences (Taylor & Vertinsky, 1981). However, organizations ought to make explicit efforts to monitor (a) problem-solving techniques and (b) the range of information considered when evaluating effectiveness. Problem-solving techniques should change enough to show that people are learning, yet remain sufficiently stable for most problems to be solved with routines. Grinyer and Norburn (1975) found that more profitable firms use wide ranges of information when they appraise their effectiveness, whereas less profitable firms concentrate on financial information. As Smith (1976) noted, financial information is biased "in favor of the obvious and the short term [p. 751]."

Operations research and systems engineering possess an unfulfilled potential to aid organizational decision making by inventing simple, approximate solutions to complex problems. Doing this involves clustering problems into general categories and then generating a simple approximation for the family of solutions in each category. Such analyses could benefit from mathematics, which facilitates precise generalization and error analysis. Work of this type has been done by Baumol and Quandt (1964), Hay and Holt (1975), and Hirzinger and Kreisselmeier (1975), among others, but these studies have been rare. The overwhelming majority of operations-research and systems-engineering studies have sought complex solutions to simple problems.

> A well designed organization is not a stable solution to achieve, but a developmental process to keep active [Starbuck & Nystrom, 1981, p. xx].

REFERENCES

Afanasyev, V. G. *The scientific management of society.* Moscow: Progress Publishers, 1971.

Aldrich, H., & Whetten, D. A. Organization-sets, action-sets, and networks: Making the most of simplicity. In P. C. Nystrom & W. H. Starbuck (Eds.), *Handbook of organizational design* (Vol. 1). New York: Oxford University Press, 1981. Pp. 385–408.

Ando, A., Fisher, F. M., & Simon, H. A. *Essays on the structure of social science models.* Cambridge, Mass.: M.I.T. Press, 1963.

Baumol, W. J., & Quandt, R. E. Rules of thumb and optimally imperfect decisions. *American Economic Review,* 1964, *54,* 23–46.

Beveridge, G. S. G., & Schechter, R. S. *Optimization.* New York: McGraw-Hill, 1970.

Beyer, J. Ideologies, values, and decision making in organizations. In P. C. Nystrom & W. H. Starbuck (Eds.), *Handbook of organizational design* (Vol. 2). New York: Oxford University Press, 1981. Pp. 166–202.

Bjørn-Andersen, N., & Hedberg, B. L. T. Designing information systems in an organizational perspective. In P. C. Nystrom & W. H. Starbuck (Eds.), *Prescriptive models of organizations.* Amsterdam: North-Holland, 1977. Pp. 125–142.

Bloch, A. *Murphy's law and other reasons why things go wrong.* Los Angeles: Price/Stern/Sloan, 1977.

Box, G. E. P., & Draper, N. R. *Evolutionary operation.* New York: Wiley, 1969.

Box, M. J., Davies, D., & Swann, W. H. *Non-linear optimization techniques.* Edinburgh: Oliver and Boyd, 1969.

Braybrooke, D., & Lindblom, C. E. *A strategy of decision.* New York: Free Press, 1963.

Brunsson, N. The irrationality of action and action rationality: Decisions, ideologies and organisational actions. *Journal of Management Studies,* 1982, *19,* 29–44.

Cameron, K. Measuring organizational effectiveness in institutions of higher education. *Administrative Science Quarterly,* 1978, *23,* 604–632.

Campbell, D. T. Reforms as experiments. *American Psychologist,* 1969, *24,* 409–429.

Campbell, J. P. On the nature of organizational effectiveness. In P. S. Goodman & J. M. Pennings (Eds.), *New perspectives on organizational effectiveness.* San Francisco: Jossey-Bass, 1977. Pp. 13–55.

Cartwright, T. J. Problems, solutions and strategies: A contribution to the theory and practice of planning. *Journal of the American Institute of Planners,* 1973, *39,* 179–187.

Champagne, A. M., Neef, M. G., & Nagel, S. S. Laws, organizations, and the judiciary. In P. C. Nystrom & W. H. Starbuck (Eds.), *Handbook of organizational design* (Vol. 1). New York: Oxford University Press, 1981. Pp. 187–209.

Churchman, C. W. *Challenge to reason.* New York: McGraw-Hill, 1968.

Churchman, C. W., Ackoff, R. L., & Arnoff, E. L. *Introduction to operations research.* New York: Wiley, 1957.

Comanor, W. S., Kover, A. J., & Smiley, R. H. Advertising and its consequences. In P. C. Nystrom & W. H. Starbuck (Eds.), *Handbook of organizational design* (Vol. 2). New York: Oxford University Press, 1981. Pp. 429–439.

Cyert, R. M., & March, J. G. *A behavioral theory of the firm.* Englewood Cliffs, N.J.: Prentice-Hall, 1963.

Day, R. H., & Tinney, E. H. How to co-operate in business without really trying: A learning model of decentralized decision making. *Journal of Political Economy,* 1968, *76,* 583–600.

Dirickx, Y. M. I., Jennergren, L. P., & Peterson, D. W. Some relationships between hierarchical systems theory and certain optimization problems. *IEEE Transactions: Systems, Man, and Cybernetics,* 1973, *SMC-3,* 514–518.

Downey, H. K., Hellriegel, D., & Slocum, J. W., Jr. Environmental uncertainty: The construct and its application. *Administrative Science Quarterly,* 1975, *20,* 613–629.

Dutton, J. M., & Starbuck, W. H. *Computer simulation of human behavior.* New York: Wiley, 1971.

Friedlander, F., & Pickle, H. Components of effectiveness in small organizations. *Administrative Science Quarterly,* 1968, *13,* 289–304.

Gerlach, L. P., & Palmer, G. B. Adaptation through evolving interdependence. In P. C. Nystrom & W. H. Starbuck (Eds.), *Handbook of organizational design* (Vol. 1). New York: Oxford University Press, 1981. Pp. 323–381.

Grinyer, P. H., & Norburn, D. Planning for existing markets: Perceptions of executives and financial performance. *Journal of the Royal Statistical Society, Series A,* 1975, *138,* 70–97.

Haberstroh, C. J. Control as an organizational process. *Management Science,* 1960, *6,* 165–171.

Hay, G. A., & Holt, C. A. A general solution for linear decision rules: An optimal dynamic strategy applicable under uncertainty. *Econometrica,* 1975, *43,* 231–259.

Hedberg, B. L. T. Growth stagnation as a managerial discontinuity. Unpublished manuscript, International Institute of Management, Berlin, 1974.

Hedberg, B. L. T., Nystrom, P. C., & Starbuck, W. H. Camping on seesaws: Prescriptions for a self-designing organization. *Administrative Science Quarterly,* 1976, *21,* 41–65.

Hedberg, B. L. T., Nystrom, P. C., & Starbuck, W. H. Designing organizations to match tomorrow. In P. C. Nystrom & W. H. Starbuck (Eds.), *Prescriptive models of organizations.* Amsterdam: North-Holland, 1977. Pp. 171–181.

Hirschman, A. O. *Exit, voice and loyalty.* Cambridge, Mass.: Harvard University Press, 1970.

Hirschman, A. O., & Lindblom, C. E. Economic development, research and development, and policy making: Some converging views. *Behavioral Science,* 1962, *7,* 211–222.

Hirzinger, G., & Kreisselmeier, G. On optimal approximation of high-order linear systems by low-order models. *International Journal of Control,* 1975, *22,* 399–408.

Hitch, C. J. *Decision-making for defense.* Berkeley: University of California Press, 1966.

Jennergren, L. P. Decentralization in organization. In P. C. Nystrom & W. H. Starbuck (Eds.), *Handbook of organizational design* (Vol. 2). New York: Oxford University Press, 1981. Pp. 39–59.

Jennergren, P., & Müller, W. Simulation experiments of resource-allocation decisions in two-level organizations. *Social Science Research,* 1973, *2,* 333–352.

Jones, C. O. *Clean air.* Pittsburgh: University of Pittsburgh Press, 1975.

Keen, P. G. W. The evolving concept of optimality. In M. K. Starr & M. Zeleny (Eds.), *Multiple criteria decision making.* Amsterdam: North-Holland, 1977. Pp. 31–57.

Kydland, F. Hierarchical decomposition in linear economic models. *Management Science,* 1975, *21,* 1029–1039.

Landau, M. On the concept of a self-correcting organization. *Public Administration Review,* 1973, *33,* 533–542.

Lindblom, C. E. The science of "muddling through." *Public Administration Review*, 1959, *19*, 79–88.

McCann, J., & Galbraith, J. R. Interdepartmental relations. In P. C. Nystrom & W. H. Starbuck (Eds.), *Handbook of organizational design* (Vol. 2). New York: Oxford University Press, 1981. Pp. 60–84.

McNulty, J. E. *Some economic aspects of business organization.* Philadelphia: University of Pennsylvania Press, 1964.

March, J. G. The technology of foolishness. In J. G. March & J. P. Olsen (Eds.), *Ambiguity and choice in organizations.* Bergen: Universitetsforlaget, 1976. Pp. 69–81.

Mesarović, M. D., Macko, D., & Takahara, Y. *Theory of hierarchical, multilevel systems.* New York: Academic Press, 1970.

Miller, D. Evolution and revolution: A quantum view of structural change in organizations. *Journal of Management Studies*, 1982, *19*, 131–151.

Mintzberg, H., Raisinghani, D., & Théorêt, A. The structure of "unstructured" decision processes. *Administrative Science Quarterly*, 1976, *21*, 246–275.

Morrill, R. L. How migration and regional development affect organizations. In P. C. Nystrom & W. H. Starbuck (Eds.), *Handbook of organizational design* (Vol. 1). New York: Oxford University Press, 1981. Pp. 238–252.

Neave, E. H., & Petersen, E. R. A comparison of optimal and adaptive decision mechanisms in an organizational setting. *Management Science*, 1980, *26*, 810–822.

Nystrom, P. C., Hedberg, B. L. T., & Starbuck, W. H. Interacting processes as organization designs. In R. H. Kilmann, L. R. Pondy, & D. P. Slevin (Eds.), *The management of organizational design* (Vol. 1). New York: Elsevier North-Holland, 1976. Pp. 209–230.

Nystrom, P. C., & Starbuck, W. H. Why prescription is prescribed. In P. C. Nystrom & W. H. Starbuck (Eds.), *Prescriptive models of organizations.* Amsterdam: North-Holland, 1977. Pp. 1–5.

Pennings, J. M., & Goodman, P. S. Toward a workable framework. In P. S. Goodman & J. M. Pennings (Eds.), *New perspectives on organizational effectiveness.* San Francisco: Jossey-Bass, 1977. Pp. 146–184.

Peters, T. J. Putting excellence into management. *Business Week*, July 21, 1980, 196–205.

Plant, J. B. *Some iterative solutions in optimal control.* Cambridge, Mass.: M.I.T. Press, 1968.

Radner, R. Satisficing. *Journal of Mathematical Economics*, 1975, *2*, 253–262.

Reeves, G. R., & Sweigart, J. R. Product-mix models when learning effects are present. *Management Science*, 1981, *27*, 204–212.

Rhenman, E. *Organization theory for long-range planning.* New York: Wiley, 1972.

Sackman, E. *Computers, system science, and evolving society.* New York: Wiley, 1967.

Scott, W. G., Mitchell, T. R., & Peery, N. S. Organizational governance. In P. C. Nystrom & W. H. Starbuck (Eds.), *Handbook of organizational design* (Vol. 2). New York: Oxford University Press, 1981. Pp. 135–151.

Scott, W. G. Effectiveness of organizational effectiveness studies. In P. S. Goodman & J. M. Pennings (Eds.), *New perspectives on organizational effectiveness.* San Francisco: Jossey-Bass, 1977. Pp. 63–95.

Seashore, S. E. An elastic and expandable viewpoint. In P. S. Goodman & J. M. Pennings (Eds.), *New perspectives on organizational effectiveness.* San Francisco: Jossey-Bass, 1977. Pp. 185–192.

Shumway, C. R., Maher, P. M., Baker, N. R., Souder, W. E., Rubenstein, A. H., & Gallant, A. R. Diffuse decision-making in hierarchical organizations: An empirical examination. *Management Science*, 1975, *21*, 697–707.

Simon, H. A. A behavioral model of rational choice. *Quarterly Journal of Economics*, 1955, *69*, 99–118.

Simon, H. A. On the concept of organizational goal. *Administrative Science Quarterly*, 1964, *9*, 1–22.

Smith, P. C. Behaviors, results, and organizational effectiveness: The problem of criteria. In M. D. Dunnette (Ed.), *Handbook of industrial and organizational psychology.* Chicago: Rand McNally, 1976. Pp. 745–775.

Speer, A. *Inside the Third Reich.* New York: Avon, 1970.

Sproull, L. S. Beliefs in organizations. In P. C. Nystrom & W. H. Starbuck (Eds.), *Handbook of organizational design* (Vol. 2). New York: Oxford University Press, 1981. Pp. 203–224.

Starbuck, W. H. Level of aspiration. *Psychological Review,* 1963, 70, 51–60. (a)

Starbuck, W. H. Level of aspiration theory and economic behavior. *Behavioral Science,* 1963, 8, 128–136. (b)

Starbuck, W. H. Tadpoles into Armageddon and Chrysler into butterflies. *Social Science Research,* 1973, 2, 81–109.

Starbuck, W. H. Information systems for organizations of the future. In E. Grochla & N. Szyperski (Eds.), *Information systems and organizational structure.* New York: de Gruyter, 1975. Pp. 217–230.

Starbuck, W. H. Organizations and their environments. In M. D. Dunnette (Ed.), *Handbook of industrial and organizational psychology.* Chicago: Rand McNally, 1976. Pp. 1069–1123.

Starbuck, W. H., & Nystrom, P. C. Designing and understanding organizations. In P. C. Nystrom & W. H. Starbuck (Eds.), *Handbook of organizational design* (Vol. 1). New York: Oxford University Press, 1981. Pp. ix–xxii.

Starr, M. K., & Zeleny, M. MCDM—State and future of the arts. In M. K. Starr & M. Zeleny (Eds.), *Multiple criteria decision making.* Amsterdam: North-Holland, 1977. Pp. 5–29.

Steers, R. M. *Organizational effectiveness.* Santa Monica, Calif.: Goodyear, 1977.

Stymne, B. *Values and processes.* Lund: SIAR Studentlitteratur, 1972.

Taylor, R. M., & Vertinsky, I. Experimenting with organizational behavior. In P. C. Nystrom & W. H. Starbuck (Eds.), *Handbook of organizational design* (Vol. 1). New York: Oxford University Press, 1981. Pp. 139–166.

Tosi, H., Aldag, R., & Storey, R. On the measurement of the environment: An assessment of the Lawrence and Lorsch environmental uncertainty subscale. *Administrative Science Quarterly,* 1973, 18, 27–36.

Tumin, M. Business as a social system. *Behavioral Science,* 1964, 9, 120–130.

Vickers, G. C. Is adaptability enough? *Behavioral Science,* 1959, 4, 219–234.

Vickers, G. C. Values, norms, and policies. *Policy Sciences,* 1973, 4, 103–111.

Watzlawick, P., Weakland, J. H., & Fisch, R. *Change.* New York: Norton, 1974.

Weick, K. E. *The social psychology of organizing* (2nd ed.). Reading, Mass.: Addison-Wesley, 1979.

White, L. J. How organizations use exchange media and agreements. In P. C. Nystrom & W. H. Starbuck (Eds.), *Handbook of organizational design* (Vol. 2). New York: Oxford University Press, 1981. Pp. 440–453.

Wildavsky, A. B. The self-evaluating organization. *Public Administration Review,* 1972, 32, 509–520.

Wilde, D. J. *Optimum seeking methods.* Englewood Cliffs, N.J.: Prentice-Hall, 1964.

Williamson, O. E. *Corporate control and business behavior.* Englewood Cliffs, N.J.: Prentice-Hall, 1970.

PAUL S. GOODMAN
ROBERT S. ATKIN
F. DAVID SCHOORMAN

7

On the Demise of
Organizational Effectiveness Studies[1]

Organizational effectiveness has attracted considerable research interest ever since organizations achieved a major role in our society. From the early days of industrialization through the era of scientific management, organizational effectiveness (OE) was measured by productivity and/or profits. As more humanistic approaches to management emerged, so did apparently "new" goals of the organization, resulting in an expansion of OE to include individual satisfaction and need fulfillment. More recently, others have argued that OE must be assessed with respect to its impact on the family, on the community and society, and even on the environment. This accelerating movement toward multiple constituencies, multiple causal determinants (independent variables) of effectiveness and multiple measures (dependent variables) of effectivness has obfuscated a clear definition of OE. One result of this situation has been the grail-like search for a unified framework within which to study OE, as though such a find would provide a singular, parsimonious theory that could be tested and supported.

The basic position of this chapter is quite different—specifically, it is our contention that the absence of such a singular theory is likely to continue and studies of organizational effectiveness *per se* are not likely to be fruitful. To explore this contention, five interwoven theses are developed, which then

[1]This research was supported in part by the Buhl Foundation.

ORGANIZATIONAL EFFECTIVENESS
A Comparison of Multiple Models

become the bases for a review of several representative OE studies. Finally, an alternative research strategy is presented with some illustrative studies.

Before we begin, however, one caveat frames the context of our analysis. First, the other chapters in this section all have a disciplinary perspective. Cognitive psychology, industrial psychology, a systems perspective, political economy, and operations research provide their intellectual underpinnings. For reasons of intent this chapter does not adopt such a perspective. The other chapters in this section focus on *substantive* OE issues. A disciplinary perspective provides the foundation for choice of variables and methodologies. By contrast, the present chapter concerns the *process* of doing OE research. This, we contend, is not discipline specific and hence, we have explicitly attempted to avoid a narrow perspective.

BASIC THESES

1. *There is, at present, no singular, parsimonious model or theory of organizational effectiveness.* The "classic" literature examines OE in terms of goals (Cyert & March, 1963; Price, 1968) and organizational systems (Gibb, 1972; Katz & Kahn, 1978), metaphors (Weick, 1977), and processes (Steers, 1977). This list could be expanded easily, if that were a useful activity. However, the very existence of multiple models of OE is likely only reflective of the multiple ideologies and views in organizations extant in the field. Indeed, the use of the word *model* is at best misleading because the literature does not generally provide well-specified models, but tentative and loosely constructed conceptualizations of OE and/or its determinants. Each is so general in its level of specification as to be of limited value in the deductive derivations of testable hypotheses.

2. *The absence of strong theory has nurtured, ad hoc, atheoretical and non-cumulative empirical studies of OE.* As might be expected in the absence of a strong theory capable of producing a definitive set of testable hypotheses, on-going empirical work becomes characterized by a search for what we might call "stylized facts." Such searches are likely guided by the various implicit theories of the investigators and are often encouraged by the convenience of available field sites. This process results in a body of empirical observations, but is not likely to produce a cumulative body of support for any theory (cf. Goodman & Pennings, 1980; Hannan & Freeman, 1977; Steers, 1977 for a similar analysis).

This does not imply that there are no regularities to the research effort. Indeed, it appears as though two classes of OE studies have evolved—outcome studies and determinant studies—with the critical distinction being whether primary attention is on the dependent or the independent variable space.

The former, exemplified by the work of Seashore and Yuchtman (1967) and Cameron (1978), typically take as their charge the identification of the structure of OE. That is, having collected a set of archival and/or perceptual data, rank reduction techniques are employed to determine the dimensions of effectiveness. Such approaches provide no a priori specification of the dimensions of effectiveness, the time period of effectiveness, and so on. The resultant findings, therefore, are likely to be sample specific.

The second class of studies appears principally riveted on the independent variable side (e.g., Glisson and Martin, 1979; Khandwalla, 1973). The generic form of this class appears to involve the following steps: (a) choice of a single measure of effectiveness; (b) identification of a limited set of antecedent variables; and (c) determination of the interrelatedness of the antecedent variables in high- and low-effectiveness organizations. Such approaches usually have a loosely constructed framework about the relationship between the independent and the dependent OE variables. The models generally are not well specified with a careful delineation of exogenous and endogenous variables. The resultant findings are not particularly robust or generalizable.

3. *Hence, it is not likely that there will be convergence on a single theory of OE.* OE may be a unique concept within organizational theory because its definition is particularly sensitive to *value* considerations. Some have argued that member satisfaction (Argyris, 1964) or societal benefits (Friedlander & Pickle, 1968) should be included in the definition of OE. Why this should be the case is never exactly clear. Are not these statements simply value positions with which others might disagree? Others (Pennings & Goodman, 1977) have argued that within a given organization, the dominant coalition would specify the meaning of OE. This, however, is simply another reflection of the value statements of the authors. Given that there are different constituencies with different values about what constitutes OE, there is likely to be little convergence on the meaning of effectiveness.

4. *Hence, rather than continuing attempts to test general theories of OE, we need to concentrate on indepth microstudies of specific organizational outcomes.* Scott (1977) argues this point as follows: "We should not seek explanations of OE in general since it is not clear to what, if anything, the concept refers. Rather we should attempt to develop and test more precise predictions relating particular measures of effectiveness to particular features of the organization or system of organizations [p. 89]." He illustrates this argument in his own research by testing hypotheses about causal determinants of mortality due to a specific type of surgery rather than examining some general notion of hospital effectiveness.

Such a change in focus has several consequences:

1. We reject the need to search for a general OE construct space to provide the basis for the "right set" of effectiveness measures.

2. Rather, we see the selection of the dependent variables as somewhat arbitrary. The selection may reflect the tastes of the researcher, some central topic in the literature or the pragmatic choice of some constituency. There is no need to place this indicator in some general construct space.

3. The principal task is to specify a precise model that explains the observed variability in the selected dependent variable. This "fine-grained model" should consider both exogenous (outside organizational control) and endogenous (within organizational control) independent variables.

4. The model needs to be tested as rigorously as the data and sample size allow.

The most obvious result of this change in focus is the acquisition of detailed knowledge of particular independent–dependent variable linkages, *rather* than of the overall effectiveness of some organization. For example, we may learn what causes differences in crew-level productivity in the underground bituminous coal industry—but we shall not learn if, or why, company X's overall effectiveness is high or low.

A direct corollary of this approach is that it is likely that different models, consisting of different causal variables, will be necessary for different outcomes. The ultimate result of such as series of studies may be the discovery of stylized facts across either disparate organizations or contexts. It is the emergence of these empirical truths that are likely to then provide us with the "stuff" to build more general theories. The interested reader might examine Roberts, Hulin, and Rousseau (1978) who provide a general discussion of many of these issues.

5. *Hence, our final thesis, namely, there should be a moratorium on overall studies of OE.* The study of OE in the molar sense does not produce a tractable research problem. It is unlikely, given the current level of theoretical sophistication in organizational theory, that an adequate theory of effectiveness is attainable. It is also unlikely that any molar study of OE can be conducted given the costs required for generating the appropriate sample, instrumentation, and analytic techniques (see Goodman & Pennings, 1980 for a discussion of the minimal requirements of conducting such a study).

The remainder of this chapter details the rationale behind these five theses statements. To accomplish this, we shall overview six empirical studies. Two of these use outcome approaches, two use determinant approaches, and two are in the tradition advocated by Scott.

The second caveat concerns our choice of studies used to illustrate our analysis. As will be discussed, our overview of the OE literature suggested two dominant types of inquiry, namely, those studies that focus on the measurement of OE and those that consider the causes of OE. For each of these themes we have chosen to review two studies, one well known in the field and one of a more current vintage. Finally, we identified a third, alternative class of studies. The two research projects reviewed here may exhaust this category.

OUTCOME APPROACHES TO OE

Seashore and Yuchtman Study

The focus on organizational outcomes, with its attendant interest in identifying and measuring indicators of OE, is one of the principal approaches in studying OE. One of the classic studies in this area was conducted by Seashore and Yuchtman (1967). Their basic strategy was "[to] start with a large number of variables describing the performance of organizations and then examine the pattern of relationships among them in order to infer the underlying dimensions of performance from this pattern [p. 379]." These underlying dimensions were referred to as *penultimate dimensions*.

Given this position, they collected 76 performance variables from 75 independently owned life insurance agencies. The empirical analysis identified 10 factors (or effectiveness indicators), which are presented in Table 7.1. The meaning of effectiveness for these offices, then, is defined by business volume, production cost, new member productivity, etc. In further analysis, Seashore and Yuchtman demonstrated there was some stability in the factor structure over time.

Our analysis of this study focuses on the degree to which it increases our understanding of OE. Clearly, it provides us with evidence that effectiveness may be multidimensional and that at least some temporal stability may exist.

TABLE 7.1
Performance Factors in Insurance Agencies[a]

Factor	Assigned name
I	Business volume
II	Production cost
III	New member productivity
IV	Youthfulness of members
V	Business mix
VI	Manpower growth
VII	Management emphasis
VIII	Maintenance cost
IX	Member productivity
X	Market penetration

[a]After Seashore and Yuchtman, 1967.

Further analysis suggests that some of these factors are systematically related, perhaps in a weak causal manner, to manage supportiveness power, communication with subordinates, and the amount of total control.

We remain, however, with many questions:

1. To whom do these 10 factors provide an adequate measure of OE? As argued in Thesis 1, multiple OE ideologies exist, each with its own constituency. In the present case, we do not know which, if any, of these 10 factors or their underlying variables would be chosen by agents, customers, or regulators as appropriate measures. It is not even evident which, if any, are used by the agency managers.

2. Are these factors comprehensive? Though Seashore and Yuchtman do provide a multidimensional effectiveness space, it would seem to exclude most noneconomic measures. For example, we know nothing of the individual agency's ability to affect the rate or type of new products developed by the company, nor of the agency's flexibility to modify or "bend" company policy vis-à-vis agent hiring, training, or compensation in order to exploit its local environment.

3. Assuming that the 10 factors were comprehensive and constituent-independent, how do variations in these measures affect OE? The authors acknowledge that agencies (a) cannot unilaterally employ maximizing strategies without potentially depleting the environment; and (b) must jointly optimize across factors by trading off unilateral strategies. Further, they argue that because the firm's ultimate OE criterion can never be assessed, effectiveness can only be addressed by considering jointly the position of the organization on all penultimate decisions. This does not, however, seem to acknowledge the problems of constraints (Simon, 1964) or functional form (i.e., whether variation in an indicator covaries with OE) (Kahn, 1977), nor does it consider whether the trade-offs need to be made simultaneously or sequentially over time.

4. Assuming that variability in these factors is conceptually related to OE, how can we explain variation in these measures? Interpretation of this variation requires linkage to independent variables. The lack of factor score stability over time for several of the factors requires explanation. That provided by the authors is not adequate precisely because there was no a priori specification of a conceptually reasonable causal model. For example, market penetration could vary because of changes in the population or the number of salesmen added to a particular territory. The former cause is exogenous to organization, and by itself, tells us little about the effectiveness of the organization. The latter cause is an organizational act that does provide a context for OE. The failure to identify determinants in this study restricts the utility of this approach in assessing OE.

Proponents of this approach might argue that an outcome taxonomy is, itself, an important goal or a critical first step in model development. To this, we have two responses. First, we find little support in the literature for the "step" argument. Second, structure-driven taxonomies (remember kingdom, phylum, etc.) are not likely to produce scientifically useful ends.

5. Finally, how can we determine the appropriate time frame within which to assess OE? The fiscal or calendar year, used by Seashore and Yuchtman, is not necessarily appropriate for at least three reasons. First, the time-frame choice requires an understanding of the cyclical nature of the phenomenon. Second, resource exploitation implies having certain outcome levels "on hand" at certain well-specified times, which are likely not to be at year end. Last is the problem of aggregation over time. For example, for the variable production per new agent, is it more appropriate to use a year-end measure or an average over the year?

6. Another issue in the OE literature is separating out determinants and outcomes or final and intermediate outcomes. In this study it is not clear whether youthfulness of members and production costs fall into the same class of OE indicator. Is youthfulness of members a cause of production costs or is it an indicators of OE, or both? If usefulness is an indicator of OE, is it a surrogate for adaptability, turnover or some other variable?

Cameron's University Study

Our second example was selected because it represents one of the best recent statements of OE research on indicators. Cameron (1978) interviewed top-level university administrators to tap his/her model of OE as it affected their institution. Some of the questions were open-ended; others asked the respondent to evaluate the relevance of OE criteria derived from the literature. Nine separate groupings, based on an a priori intuitive perspective, evolved from the interviews (see Table 7.2). They are characterized by subjective evaluations and satisfaction judgments, and focus on the student, faculty, administrator, and the organization. The contrast between the dimensions derived by Seashore and Yuchtman (1967) and by Cameron is substantial. Using these dimensions as a basis, Cameron developed a questionnaire and subsequently conducted a reliability and validity study. Our examination of the Cameron study follows the pattern used to analyze the Seashore and Yuchtman study.

1. Are these dimensions comprehensive? Cameron states that nine OE criteria were formed from an a priori intuitive perspective that was influenced by interviews with top administrators. Unfortunately, the theoretical basis of these indicators and their interrelationships were not fully explored. Hence, the degree to which they are generalizable to other universities, other educational institutions, or other organizations is questionable.

2. How do variations in dimensions relate to OE? As in the Seashore and Yuchtman (1967) review, it does not appear as though Cameron has addressed

TABLE 7.2
Dimensions of OE for Institutions of Higher Learning[a]

1. Student educational satisfaction
2. Student academic development
3. Student career development
4. Student personal development
5. Faculty and administrator employment satisfaction
6. Professional development and quality of the faculty
7. Systems openness and community interaction
8. Ability to acquire resources
9. Organizational health

[a]After Cameron, 1978.

the problems of constraints, functional form, or dimensional trade-offs. Cameron does address this question, however, in his validity study by comparing perceptual data (questionnaires) with objective data (archival). Here, too, there are unresolved problems. First, it is not clear how the objective data maps onto OE. Second, only four dimensions received strong validity support, and examination of this research suggests that they account for only about 14% of the variance in the questionnaire data.

3. Cameron uses perceptual reports about the organization (i.e., university) as the appropriate level of analysis. He reports significant differences among universities for his OE indicators, and he also reports that job position of the respondent is not associated with differences in the indicators. The latter finding is particularly important because it suggests that aggregation of the university level may be appropriate.

The theoretical problem, however, is that universities are not unitary systems. At best, they are composed of loosely coupled schools, departments, and other units, each producing different products, with different organizational arrangements, and different types of objectives. By asking organizational officials to rate the degree of students' academic development or professional development of the faculty, one is forcing an aggregation process across fairly diverse institutional arrangements. This point has to be seriously considered before we can understand what OE means in institutions of higher learning. Our position is that the schools or departments within the university are the appropriate units of analysis for most of the dimensions identified by Cameron, not the university. Our guiding rule is not to aggregate across organizational units with different production functions. It is not clear that the environment, input, transformation of, or outputs in an electrical engineering department are the same as those in a drama department. Nor is the production function of the administrative component likely to be the same as the one in an academic department. Aggregating across different units with different production functions confound the interpretation of the relationship between the variables in the production function and the production criterion.

4. We have already argued that variation in outcome or indicator variables are uninterpretable unless we can relate these outcomes to their determinants. Models relating these elements are simply not provided. Is variation on each dimension predictable from the same model or are there multiple models, each linked to one or more of the dimensions? Also, there may be confusion as to whether the nine indicators are clearly measures of OE or perhaps also determinants. For example, educational satisfaction could be a predictor of students' academic development. Ability to acquire resources probably influences the quality of faculty. The key issue, however, is that we cannot interpret variations of students' academic development as a measure of OE until we understand the controllable and uncontrollable variables that affect this dimension.

5. Again, time frames for evaluating effectiveness may vary across dimensions. The measurement period for assessing any of these dimensions is critical. Indicators of educational satisfaction could be gathered after a course or at the end of 4 years of college. Professional development of faculty may be a long-range activity that would require measurement over a series of years. The point is that time frames need to be identified.

Summary

The outcome approach, although prevalent in the OE literature, fails to increase substantially our understanding of OE because (a) the construct space of OE is never carefully delineated; (b) the relationship between indicators and OE is not examined; (c) most outcome approaches do not distinguish between determinants and indicators; (c) no well-specified model is presented for explaining variations in these indicators; and (d) the time frame for the indicators is not specified. These problems are inherent to the outcome approach and in the value-laden concept of effectiveness. No easy solutions seem available.

DETERMINANT APPROACHES TO OE

This class of studies focuses more on determinants of OE (i.e., the independent variables that might "cause" effectiveness) rather than OE indicators or outcome measures. There is quite a range of studies within this class. Some focus on single antecedents (e.g., leadership); others look at multiple antecedents. In most cases, the OE indicators are part of the organization's record system.

Our selection of studies to be examined is, of course, arbitrary. Our criterion is to look at a representative set of studies rather than identifying any particular good or poor study.

Khandwalla's Study of Manufacturing Firms

The first we shall consider was conducted by Khandwalla (1973), who examined the relationship between organizational design and profitability in 79 manufacturing firms. Organizational design was decomposed into (*a*) uncertainty reduction variables measured by the amount of staff support and vertical integration; (*b*) differentiation variables measured by the degree of decentralization of authority, functional departmentalization, and divisionalization; and (*c*) integration variables measured by the level of sophistication in management control and the level of participative management. Profitability was measured by averaging the firms highest and lowest before tax rates of return on net worth during the previous 5 years.

The principal findings of the study were that (*a*) none of the organizational design variables were related to profitability; and (*b*) most of the design variables were positively interrelated.

In a further analysis Khandwalla grouped the firms into high- and low-profitability groups and examined the relationship among the design variables. The finding from this analysis was that highly profitable firms exhibited a higher degree of covariation among the organizational design variables than the marginal firms.

Let us examine how this study increases our understanding about OE.

1. Profitability is selected as the indicator of OE. Unfortunately, there is no discussion about the functional relationship between profitability and OE. Also, we would expect that the standards of conceptual profitability would vary considerably within the 79 firms as they represent different industries and markets. Therefore, one would have to determine the profitability of the firm relative to its industry before across-industry comparisons could be made. The problem is that the meaning of profitability across industries and its relationship to OE is not developed.

2. The level of analysis for this research was the firm. Given the selection of profitability as the criterion, this would appear to be the appropriate unit for assessment of OE. This, however, fails to recognize several important nuances concerning analysis. Though the sample is of manufacturing firms, some of these firms are likely aggregates of manufacturing firms, each operating in different markets with different organizational arrangements. The current level of sophistication in organizational theory addresses itself to the gross relationship between a unitary organization and its environment, not to how combinations of different organizations and environments can be aggregated and then related to profitability. The question of what constitutes a firm in this study then has some bearing on the definition of the appropriate level of analysis.

3. This study attempts to link determinants and OE indicators. This link is critical to understanding variation in any indicator such as profitability. The problem with the Khandwalla paper is in the specification of the determinants. Basically he has identified some *possible correlates* of OE, but he has not carefully constructed a well-specified *model* of profitability. Profitability is a function of variables such as capital, technology, labor, and organizational and managerial factors, as well as environmental and market factors. Only by completely specifying the model does interpretation become feasible. For example, it might be that the organizational variables are systematically associated with profitability, but only with that portion of the variance unpredicted by the other (unspecified) elements of the complete model. Even if Khandwalla had found significant associations, the results would still be difficult to interpret due to presence of biased estimators in the underspecified model.

4. Because of financial conventions and government reporting requirements, data such as profitability are reported on an annual basis. This, however, does not mean it is the appropriate time frame. In the Khandwalla study a 5-year period was used. No basis for selecting the 5-year period was given other than it probably was a long enough period to smooth profit variations. The critical problem was that the organizational dimensions were collected at one time period and the profitability data were collected over a longer time period; in particular, the financial information actually preceded the organizational information. Ideally, we would like to collect the organizational information and relate it to subsequent financial performance, in order to make some causal inferences.

Glisson and Martin's Study on Human Service Organization

A recent study by Glisson and Martin (1979) examined the effectiveness of human service organizations. We classified this as a determinant-oriented study because the researchers focus on the affects of centralization and formalization on two measures of effectiveness—productivity and efficiency, Basically, they hypothesize formalization and centralization are positively related to the effectiveness criteria; tenure, size, and organizational age are related to formalization and centralization. The hypothesized model is set up in a path model format to permit analysis of direct and indirect effects on the two criterion variables.

Thirty organizations dispensing different human services (drug abuse, family counseling, welfare, mental health) participated in the study. Four-hundred and eight workers filled out questionnaires measuring the organizational variables. Productivity was measured by the average number of different clients served by each line worker, and efficiency was the number of clients served per week, per $10,000 annual budget.

The principal findings of the study were that (a) centralization is positively associated with productivity and efficiency; (b) formalization has a marginal negative relationship with productivity and efficiency; (c) formalization is positively associated with centralization.

Let us examine what we have learned from this study about OE.

1. The researchers selected productivity and efficiency as their two criteria. As with other studies we have reviewed, there is no statement about the functional relationship between these two criteria and OE, no statement of constraints and no apparent concern with trade-offs.

2. The researchers clearly acknowledge the existence of other goals, some of which may conflict with productivity and efficiency. For example, though centralization may be related to quantity (i.e., productivity) it may also decrease innovation, morale, and negatively affect the quality of services, or the goal of attracting outside funds (by servicing many clients) may conflict with providing quality services. The problem in assessing OE is to take into account multiple goals, especially if the goals are in conflict.

3. Though the number of clients processed per input labor unit may be a measure of effectiveness, it is not clear the unit of analysis—the human service organization—is appropriate. The researchers selected 30 different human service organizations. Some provide correction services, others drug abuse treatment; others provide family counseling. The clients, the funding environment, and the production process are probably quite different across these organizations. It is not clear if one can treat these as conceptually similar organizations (i.e., "human service organization" may be too broad an umbrella). If we had to work with this sample, some kind of careful standardization procedures should be introduced over and above what was suggested by the researchers (Glisson & Martin, p. 29). Aggregating across these different organizational units confounds any interpretation of the relationship between the organizational variables (e.g., centralization) and the effectiveness indicators.

4. Though this research appears to explain productivity in human service organizations, the links between organizational variables and productivity are not well drawn. The major determinants are formalization and centralization. Are these the only variables that explain variation in quantity of clients processed? Quality and professional orientation of the staff, coordination and information-exchange mechanisms, procedures for assigning clients to professionals, and organizational reward systems are some of the endogenous factors that may also affect processing of clients. However, there are also external factors such as size of potential client group, visibility of social organization, and degree of competition among the social organizations that could also explain

differences among these organizations. In addition to not specifying a model of internal and external variables that affect productivity, there are marked differences among the organizations (see preceding number 3) which further confounds this analysis. Because we do not understand the determinants of productivity in this context, it is not clear what the results tell us.

5. In this study, productivity was assessed on a weekly basis to minimize some effects of the difference across organizations. The rationale for selecting this particular time-frame issue is important in evaluating any human service organization. The time frame for assessing the effectiveness of family counseling service, drug abuse treatments, and mental health assistance is very difficult to determine. Failure to identify the time period, which probably varies across services, would confound any effectiveness assessment. The researchers in this study side-step this issue by focusing on quantity of clients processed rather than the quality of the services.

Summary

The determinant approach, although prevalent in the literature, fails to increase our understanding of OE because (a) the relationship between indicators and OE is not examined; (b) generally single indicators are examined without reflecting their relationship with other OE indicators in which they may be in conflict; (c) the models specifying the determinants are typically underspecified and the time frame for estimating the criterion variable is rarely explored; and (d) there is a tendency to interpret indicator information as the same although the organizational units are very different.

AN ALTERNATIVE APPROACH

Our basic argument has been that neither the outcome approach nor the determinant approach has led to a significant, cumulative body of knowledge about OE. An alternative approach would be to move away from effectiveness studies per se in order to develop comprehensive models of single indicators. That is, we reject the idea of identifying the construct space of OE or in examining an indicator from that space. *We are arguing for a moratorium on traditional OE studies.* Rather, we believe that developing carefully specified theoretically derived models for single dependent variables and developing the data sets to test these models are the major research tasks. This is particularly so at the organizational unit of analysis. The result will be studies on satisfaction, productivity, and accidents, *but not on OE.* By restricting the focus, we avoid the problem of specifying the functional relationships between indicators and OE. The focus on OE, per se, has generated a series of problems that have prevented the development of a coherent body of literature.

Our alternative approach, which calls for a "fine-grained" analysis of an organizational dependent variable, is more akin to the determinant approach than to the indicator approach. This is based on our belief that variation in OE indicators is uninterpretable unless this variation is linked to its determinants. Unfortunately, the determinant studies reviewed have not attempted to specify fully the underlying models. They represent more studies of convenience where a few variables of interest are related to some criteria. The critical endogenous and exogenous variables have not been identified. Often the data sets to permit testing causal linkages have not been developed. The appropriate time frames for examining the criteria also are not discussed.

Two studies were selected to illustrate our alternative approach. They *approximate* rather than represent the ideal alternative approach to OE studies.

Scott's Study on Hospitals

Scott, Forrest, and Brown (1976) conducted an intensive study of hospital and control characteristics (structure), service intensity and duration (process), and patient care and costs (outcome). The principal outcome variable, patient care, was operationalized by the rate of inhospital mortality. Expenditure per patient was also considered. Relative to other OE studies of hospitals (cf. Georgopolous & Mann, 1962), these researchers have focused on a limited number of variables. Mortality in this research was further limited to surgical cases. However, even with the specific focus on mortality (only related to surgery), Scott recognized that the mortality variable would have to be further decomposed to be an indicator of hospital care or effectiveness. Examining mortality across hospitals, we would expect variations in rates to be related to *types of surgery* as well as differences in patient conditions. Scott and his associates developed an analytic procedure to standardize the mortality rates based on type of disease and patient condition characteristics. The critical issue underlying the standardization procedures is that studies examining variation in an effectiveness indicator need to control on "input" variables (e.g., patient conditions, difficulty of surgery) that might confound interpreting the effect of organizational properties on the indicator across different organizations. Hospitals with greater prestige may get more difficult cases that may experience higher mortality. The standardization process represents the initial stage in specifying a model.

The remainder of the model focuses on a variety of measures of hospital structure. These included hospital capacity measured in terms of total number of personnel, number of different types of facilities, ratio of residents to medical staff, proportion of surgical staff that was certified, etc., and control structure measured by hospital administrators' decisions in the administrative area, ratio of supervisory to direct-care personnel, and control exercised by surgical staff over new members. The relationship between many of these variables and mortality were identified prior to the analysis. Data were then drawn from an intensive study of 17 hospitals. Only two variables, a measure of staff qualifications and a measure of administrator control, were positively associated with mortality.

Why is the Scott study unique? Why does it fit into our definition of an alternative approach?

1. The study focuses on a limited set of dependent variables. The basic focus is *to explain* variations in mortality (the dependent variable), which was further decomposed into different surgery types.

2. Some consideration is given to examining mortality at different time periods.

3. The level of analysis for this research is the hospital. The important contribution that Scott makes in this research is to recognize that hospitals will differ in terms of patient characteristics and type of work performed. Simply examining mortality rates across hospitals with different input characteristics will tell us little about the quality of care. The standardization procedure, which used 603,000 individual patient records, represents an important theoretical and methodological contribution of this study.

This research attempts to develop models of OE. It begins by postulating a general model of hospital structure, process, and outcomes. Specific models are then developed to relate (a) structure and process; and (b) structure and outcomes. Added to these models, through the standardization procedure, are patient conditions and diagnostic categories. Is the Scott model the definitive model of the impact of hospital structure and mortality? The answer to that is obviously "no." In the theoretical discussion, the researchers do not appear confident in spelling out all the relationships in their model. In the empirical section, the results are at best, mixed. Still, relative to other studies we have examined, this study gets closer to the concept of performing fine-grained analysis of a limited dependent variable. Its mixed success in identifying consistent empirical relationships only points to difficulties in identifying the complex relationships between organizational characteristics and outcomes.

Goodman's Study on Coal Mines

A study by Goodman (1979) examined the effect of an organizational intervention on a variety of OE indicators. Though this study differs from the Scott study in that it assesses the effects of change, both studies purport to explain variations in OE.

TABLE 7.3
Estimated Production Function for Tons of Coal per Week[a]

Variable	Estimate	t statistic
Constant	−689.3	−1.32
Roof	195.9	4.35
Runway	93.6	2.1
Pillaring	89.55	9.8
Actual working time	1.126	18.7
Dummy variable for physical conditions	−0.166	4.6

[a]After Goodman, 1979.

The location of this research is a coal mine in Pennsylvania. An organizational intervention created a new form of work organization in some of the mining sections (work areas) but not in others. (See Goodman, 1979 for the history and nature of the change effort.) The purpose of this research was to assess the effectiveness of the intervention.

In this discussion, we will focus on one of the indicators of OE—productivity. The basic hypothesis was that changes in organizational structure that were compatible with the technological system in mining would increase productivity. Several models were theoretically developed to explain variations of productivity. Because productivity is related to a variety of factors (i.e., the production function), it was necessary to specify the model in order to separate the effect of the intervention from other factors. In coal mining, the following factors can affect productivity; (a) roof and runway conditions; (b) types of mining-pillaring yields higher productivity than does development mining; (c) number of people in the crew; and (d) actual crew time. Seam height, quality of coal seam, and type of machinery can also affect productivity, but these variables were relatively constant because the study was conducted in a single mine.

Table 7.3 presents the estimated production function for a mining section over a 2-year period without consideration of any organizational variables. The dependent variable is raw tons produced per week. Roof and runaway conditions were measured by a rating scale and represent variables over which management has no control. The type of mining is a management decision, and it is measured by the number of shifts using the pillar method. Crew size is affected by management and absenteeism. Average working time is affected by controllable and uncontrollable analysis.

After identifying the general model for productivity, the next step was to estimate whether the new organizational factors would have an independent effect on productivity. Three alternative techniques were used to examine the effect of the organizational arrangements versus the other variables on productivity. (See Goodman, 1979, Chapter 15, for more detail.)

The results suggest that organizational arrangements (holding the other variables constant) contribute over 4 years to positive increases in productivity but the differences are not statistically significant.

Why does this study represent an alternative approach to OE studies?

1. It focuses on a limited set of dependent variables. It does not purport to explain the effectiveness of an organizational intervention but rather the impact of that intervention on a set of indicators.

2. Goodman (1979, Chapter 15) examined the trade-offs among the selected criteria. An intervention was designed to increase productivity and also affect costs, safety, etc. A procedure was developed to reflect some of the trade-offs among these criteria.

3. This study tried to estimate a fairly complete model of productivity. Both endogenous and exogenous variables are captured. The model presented in Table 7.3 is one of four models. Variation in the data is well explained by the models, which are stable over different time periods and over different sections. The models are not unique to that mine and should be generalizable to other coal-mining organizations.

4. Data in this study covered a baseline period (1 year) and a 4-year experimental period. During that period, there were several important, critical historical points such as the start up, the first year's evaluation period agreed to by the union and management, and a critical vote where the union voted against the experimental plan. To make sense of the data, they were analyzed in these different time periods (which cut across calendar years) to determine these effects.

Summary

The alternative approach rejects doing studies of OE. It argues for doing studies of specific indicators such as productivity, safety, or mortality. No attempt is made to link these studies to the construct of OE.

The task of generating these fine-grained models is exceedingly complex. Some people may argue that we are trying to simplify (by focusing on a single variable) a complex situation. Indeed, we are doing the opposite. Mapping the causal linkages with any of the outcome variables is an extremely complex activity. In the Goodman (1979) model, building was conducted over several years before some precise model was specified.

Though the task of fine-grained analysis is intellectually complex, it is not necessarily expensive. Though the Scott (1976) and Goodman (1979) studies are large-scale, expensive projects, this is not an intrinsic characteristic of the alternative approach. With a budget comparable to the expenditures in the cited outcome and determinant studies, Schoorman, Atkin, and Goodman are currently using this alternative approach in investigating certain organizational outcomes in a university setting.

DISCUSSION

In this section the basic arguments raised in this chapter will be reviewed. We will do this by responding to a series of questions raised by the editors of this book, some of which we have combined. Unfortunately, but not surprisingly, most of these questions are inappropriate, given our theme of not doing OE studies.

1. *What are the major theoretical predictions regarding the relationship between OE and other organizational variables?* Our position argues that there are no general or major relationships between OE and organizational variables that have been established theoretically or empirically. We advocate moving from general theories (e.g., contingency theory) toward specific models that relate specific causal factors (determinants) to specific dependent variables (e.g., mortality) in specific settings. The dependent variables are not related to OE. Only after a series of fine-grained analyses about a specific indicator have been done will the empirical regularities necessary to form generalized statements emerge.

Scott's work moves in the right direction. He develops a specific model that relates a set of specific determinants (type of illness, patient characteristics, and organizational characteristics) to a specific dependent variable in a specific setting. It is clear this one study does not afford us the luxury of generating general hypotheses. The study should be replicated to determine why many of the model variables "did not work." Until the model becomes more refined and more robust in terms of validation, no general statements will be possible.

2. *Does the definition of OE change when considering different types of organizations or different stages of development?* In this chapter we have not proposed a definition of OE. Indeed, we are arguing that this is not a useful task given the value-laden quality of the concept and the problems with multiple constituencies.

We contend that outcome studies merely list indicators but do not define OE or state its relationship to the indicators. Also, most of the indicators are derived from a specific set of organizations, which may not be generalizable to other organizations.

The determinant studies we reviewed also did not define OE, and further, they treated their OE indicators as having the same meaning in the context of a heterogeneous population. One study examined profitability over a very hetero-geneous set of human service organizations. It is unclear whether the meaning of these variables would be the same across these different types of organiza-tions. Also, they do not clarify the functional relationship between indicators of OE.

3. *What are the major indicators of OE?* We have argued that there are no general set of OE indicators. On the one hand, OE indicators can be derived from a theory of organization. But there are no generally accepted theories of organization. On the other hand, OE indicators can be derived from constitu-ency value premises. There is no reason, however, to think that the preference of one constituency is better or more valid than another. Hence, multiple preferences, expressed operationally as OE indicators, need to be modeled and examined.

Some writers (cf. Steers, 1977) have generated lists of OE indicators used in a variety of studies. The fact that common indicators appear across different studies does not necessarily imply that they are universal indicators at the operational level of constituencies. It may, in fact, simply be reflective of a common theory held by the researchers.

Our position is to select some organizational outcome of interest. It may reflect some consequences from the input, transformation, or output process of the organization. No assumptions are made about its relationship to OE. No general definitions are presented about our selected outcome variable that is generalizable across all organizations. Our focus is to look at specific definitions of outcomes in specific settings. Note the approach used by Scott. In the hospital study it might appear that mortality would have common meanings. Scott, however, demonstrated that mortality rates have different meanings in the context of different illnesses and different patient conditions.

4. *How would you test the efficacy of your approach compared to other approaches to OE?* We have not presented a substantive approach to OE studies. Rather, we are arguing for a *process* in studying specific outcome variables. In that sense, such a comparison is moot. On the other hand, you can compare the processes by which people approach OE studies. The outcome approach, what-ever the theoretical perspective, is not viable. Simply knowing that there is variation in OE indicators without knowing the causal factors makes in-terpretation of the variation almost impossible. The determinant approach to OE comes closer to our position. However, the studies we have reviewed simply do not specify the model under consideration sufficiently carefully. Rather, they relate *some* organizational variables to an outcome in question. This type of specification leads to biased estimates and uninterpretable results.

5. *What are the major methodological issues in operationalizing effectiveness?* Again, we do not advocate trying to measure OE. The methodological problems confronting our alternative approach are the same as in any social science

research. Develop a good theoretical model. Develop measures of the independent and dependent variables with the appropriate psychometric properties. Utilize the appropriate estimating techniques.

6. *What are the practical implications of our approach?* The practical implications of our position are both simple and powerful. Basically, managers should not use variations in productivity or other indicators to assess effectiveness. That would mean indicators such as sales, income, productivity, accidents, number of units sold, and number of customers serviced by *themselves* are not good indicators. Simply looking at the variations of these variables over time is not useful for policy purposes.

Our basic argument is that variation in these variables are caused by controllable and uncontrollable variables. The controllable variables are those that managers can affect and/or control. In the mining case, if a production section moves into an area of good physical conditions, productivity will increase. Because the quality of the conditions is outside of management control, it is important to interpret the increase in the context of these exogenous factors. Changes in productivity can result from internal organization changes (e.g., new arrangements, new incentive systems, better supervision for external events, changes in general business conditions or modifications in government regulations). Without identifying the source or determinant of the swing in productivity, it is difficult to evaluate the effectiveness of the change or any policy implications. Basically, our approach to OE identifies a process for assessing OE that should be useful to managers.

REFERENCES

Argyris, C. *Integrating the individual and the organization.* New York: Wiley, 1964.

Cameron, K. Measuring organizational effectiveness in institutions of higher education, *Administrative Science Quarterly,* 1978, 23, 604–629.

Cyert, R., & March, J. D. *A behavioral theory of the firm.* Englewood Cliffs, N.J.: Prentice-Hall, 1963.

Friedlander, F., & Pickle, H. Components of effectiveness in small organizations, *Administrative Science Quarterly,* 1968, 13, 289–304.

Georgopoulos, B., & Mann, F. *The community general hospital.* New York: Macmillan, 1962.

Gibb, B. Organizational effectiveness: An open-systems perspective. Ann Arbor: Department of Psychology, University of Michigan, 1972. Mimeo.

Glisson, C., & Martin, P. Y. Productivity and efficiency in human service organizations as related to structure, size, and age. *Academy of Management Journal,* 1980, 23, 21–37.

Goodman, P. S. *Assessing organizational change: The Rushton Quality of Work Experiment.* New York: Wiley, 1979.

Goodman, P. S., & Pennings, J. M. Critical issues in assessing organizational effectiveness. In Edward E. Lawler III, David A. Nadler, & Cortlandt Cammann (Eds.), *Organizational assessment: Perspectives on the measurement of organizational behavior and the quality of worklife.* New York: Wiley, 1980.

Hannan, M. T., & Freeman, J. Obstacles to comparative studies. In Paul S. Goodman & Johannes Pennings (Eds.), *New perspectives on organizational effectiveness.* San Francisco: Jossey-Bass, 1977. Pp. 106–131.

Kahn, R. L. Organizational effectiveness: An overview. In Paul S. Goodman & Johannes Pennings (Eds.), *New perspectives on organizational effectiveness.* San Francisco: Jossey-Bass, 1977. Pp. 235–248.

Katz, D., & Kahn, R. L. *The social psychology of organizations* (2nd ed.). New York: Wiley, 1978.

Khandwalla, P. N. Viable and effective organizational designs of firms. *Academy of Management Journal,* 1973, *16,* 481–495.

Pennings, J. M., & Goodman, P. S. Toward a workable framework. In Paul S. Goodman & Johannes Pennings (Eds.), *New perspectives on organizational effectiveness.* San Francisco: Jossey-Bass, 1977. Pp. 63–95.

Price, J. L. *Organizational effectiveness: An inventory of propositions.* Homewood, Ill.: Irwin, 1968.

Roberts, K. H., Hulin, C. L., & Rousseau, D. M. *Developing an interdisciplinary science of organizations.* San Francisco: Jossey-Bass, 1978.

Scott, R. Effectiveness of organizational effectiveness studies. In Paul S. Goodman & Johannes Pennings (Eds.), *New perspectives on organizational effectiveness.* San Francisco: Jossey-Bass, 1977. Pp. 63–95.

Scott, R. W., Forrest, W. H., Jr., & Brown, R. W., Jr. Hospital structure and post-operative mortality and morbidity. In S. M. Shortell & M. Brown (Eds.), *Organizational research in hospitals.* Chicago: Inquiry Book, Blue Cross Association, 1976.

Seashore, S. E., & Yuchtman, E. Factorial analysis of organizational performance. *Administrative Science Quarterly,* 1967, *12,* 377–395.

Simon, H. A. On the concept of organizational goals. *Administrative Science Quarterly,* 1964, *9,* 1–22.

Steers, R. M. *Organizational effectiveness: A behavioral view.* Santa Monica, Calif.: Goodyear, 1977.

Weick, K. E. Re-punctuating the problem. In Paul S. Goodman & Johannes Pennings (Eds.), *New perspectives in organizational effectiveness.* San Francisco: Jossey-Bass, 1977. Pp. 193–225.

COMPARISONS AND IMPLICATIONS OF
MULTIPLE MODELS OF EFFECTIVENESS

Organizational Effectiveness and Organizational Behavior: A Critical Perspective

This chapter has two purposes. First, the contributions in the present volume of Seashore; Nord; Weick and Daft; Schneider; Goodman, Atkin, and Schoorman; and Starbuck and Nystrom are compared and critiqued through the application of an integrating framework. Second, prescriptions are offered for enhancing effectiveness through the application of selected constructs and findings from organizational behavior. The two sections are intended as relatively independent contributions. That is, the prescriptions are not offered as answers to the critiques of the other contributions in this volume. Rather, these prescriptions derive from a selective use of existing theoretical and empirical bases within organizational behavior.

COMPARING, CRITIQUING, AND INTEGRATING THE PERSPECTIVES

The framework depicted in Figure 8.1 will be used to compare and integrate five of the six perspectives offered in this chapter. The sixth perspective, that of Goodman, Atkin, and Schoorman, will be evaluated, however.

First, the dimensions of the figure will be explained and then the five perspectives will be positioned within the figure, allowing comparison and critiquing of the perspectives to facilitate integration. *Integration* is here defined

187

ORGANIZATIONAL EFFECTIVENESS
A Comparison of Multiple Models

LEVEL OF   Societal   Nord
ANALYSIS

                Organizational   Starbuck and Nystrom   Starbuck and Nystrom
                                                          Weick and Daft

                Social   Seashore

                Individual   Schneider

                                  Rational   Nonrational

                                  DRIVING FORCE

FIGURE 8.1. Perspectives on effectiveness: A comparison matrix. The Goodman, Atkin, and Schoorman contribution, though clearly outstanding, cannot be compared with the other five due to its focus on process rather than content. Goodman, Atkin, and Schoorman presumably concur in this judgment, given their responses to the overarching questions posed by the editors of this volume. (In the figure, driving force can be rational forces that imply that the model subject to the force is linear, causative, expected, relative to accepted dogma and theory, subject to a priori managerial manipulation, and goal oriented. Or they may be nonrational forces that imply ambiguous causation, the unexpected and unpredicted, subject a post facto mangerial rationalization and justification and the absurdity of purpose as a compelling, simplistic explanation for action.)

as arraying the perspectives to highlight their similarities and differences and, most importantly, to note the gaps left by the perspectives in aggregate. As we shall see, major issues and dimensions of effectiveness are left untouched by the perspectives when considered jointly.

The clearest dimension on which to describe perspectives on organizational effectiveness focuses on the level of analysis assumed to be central in the understanding of effectiveness. Four such levels seem to cover the domain. These are arrayed on the vertical axis of Figure 8.1, ranging from most micro (i.e., individual) to most macro (i.e., societal). The central issues confronted by this dimension are:

1. What level of analysis serves to dominate the descriptive statements of the perspective in question?
2. What level of analysis is assumed to be subject to change if one is to take the perspective seriously as a normative model for enhancing effectiveness?

These two components are, in the case of each perspective, isomorphic; that is, description and prescription utilize the same level of analysis within each perspective. It should be noted that this isomorphism is not a necessary condition. Effectiveness can be assessed with outcomes aggregated to the organizational level and thus so defined—though it is clear that these outcomes are influenced by actions exerted at other (e.g., individual) levels of analyses. The horizontal axis depicts a dimension of more subtlety and ambiguity. Yet it is central to understanding the contrasts, and even incompatibilities, among the six perspectives. The essence of this dimension centers on the nature of the processes assumed to be driving units (whether individual, social, organization, or societal) toward enhanced effectiveness.

The framework allows for a contrast between rational and nonlinear (or nonrational) processes. Rational processes assume that units, at whatever level of analysis, are capable of being managed via a priori goals, systematic forecasting, and planning and control systems that emanate from the logical structure of goals and plans. Rational perspectives assume that systems are self-correcting over time through either closed system logics or open system adaptations to and impacts on environments. Nonrational (and frequently nonlinear) processes operate to create a posteriori explanations and rationality. Planning and goal-oriented action have little meaning. These are fictions serving the useful purposes of allowing the imagery of rationality, effectance, and managerial efficacy. Organizational (or unit) effectiveness becomes a "summing up," an "understanding of the past," an "interpretation." Managerial processes are viable in such a perspective. But they are aimed not at *creating* effectiveness but at creating meaning from randomness, from confusion, and from complexity. Management becomes the process of establishing, defining, interpreting, and reinforcing symbols (Pfeffer, 1981).

Nord's analysis, though rejectionist in that it negates the centrality of capitalist notions of effectiveness criteria, is based on rational assumptions. That is, societies can be (and should be) defined and created that will rationally pursue the goals of their members. Objectivity, purpose, planning, feedback, governance, and control each have meaning as a priori constructs in Nord's perspective.

Nord makes a major point of critiquing what he refers to as microquality indicators of effectiveness as insufficient, perhaps even misleading, as assessments of organizational effectiveness. This position provides the most significant contrast presented by the contributions in this volume. That is, the Goodman, Atkin, and Schoorman perspective on the one hand, and Nord's perspective on the other are irreconcilable. Microquality indicators are the only valid indexes of effectiveness in the Goodman *et al.* position. After pointing to several problems with the microquality approach, Nord argues for assessing macroquality indicators by focusing on the effectiveness of populations of organizations in providing economic welfare. Nord never goes the next step needed to give us confidence in the advantages of this macro approach for purposes of the scientific study of effectiveness. That is, he does not show how defining and assessing macroquality (through the construct he labels "families of organizations") will be any easier and less subject to the constraints mentioned for the micro case. The complexities and problems of construct validation, measurement, and evaluation would, in fact, seem to be even greater for the macrolevel outcomes suggested by Nord. Reflect for a moment on the complex dimensionality, inconsistencies, and multiple meanings of the consequences suggested by Nord as indicators of macroquality: "The nature of the criteria used in evaluating social choice, the role of government, the creation of a suitable work force, the nature of the governance process, and of the 'possible' governance process in society [Chapter 5, this volume]."

But Nord's perspective in the analysis is not intended as an alternative scheme for scientific analysis. It is, rather, a political and normative call for change. At times, unfortunately, it is a biased call. This is most clear in Nord's condemnation of business organizations as constraining democratic values: "In our terms, at least under present arrangements, microeffectiveness by individual organizations constrains the democratic process of governance [Chapter 5]." Nord quoted Lindblom (1977) in support: "The large corporation fits oddly into democratic theory and vision. Indeed, it does not fit." The bias is indeed evident. If there is a villain, it is less likely to be business organizations than *large* organizations of a bureaucratic nature, regardless of their economic, political, or social roles. In fact, in many large business organizations, democracy is richer, more fully articulated than in other societal elements. Many mechanisms of democratic influence are most fully exemplified in private sector organizations (e.g., employee ownership, quality of work life, workers' participation, collective bargaining, and union grievance procedures). The *relative* and *actual* (versus theoretical) democratization of business organizations can be seen by merely noting the low participation of the citizenry in the political processes (campaigns, elections) of governmental units even when given the opportunity to reinforce and exercise democratic processes.

Starbuck and Nystrom's perspective is the most rational of the six. It borders on the mechanistic—even sterile. Of course, the insertion of operations research and management science terminology and formats is relatively new in the behavioral science literature on organizational effectiveness. However, in the end, their analysis represents a contemporary version of the early 1900s functional and process approaches to managerial action. The .processes for optimization are straightforward and center on organizational design and strategies of decentralization and delegation. Each aberration deriving from human individual differences within the organization is malleable to managerial logic and intervention. Objective functions are assumed to be the basis for management's influence attempts, and the less influential are assumed to be persuable. Why? Because they are logical in process and are capable of seeing their best interests as compatible, even facilitative, with organizational, a priori, mission, and logic.

There is little new in the Starbuck and Nystrom analysis. Add the management principles of delegation, decentralization, and commensurate authority and responsibility of 50 years ago to a restatement of constraints on maximization and optimization models (cf. behavioral decision theory of 20 years ago) plus a few principles of organizational change developed a decade ago and you have old wine in middle-aged bottles. The prescriptions made for management action, though striking, derive from a frustration with the results created by the very logic espoused by management science techniques. It is because these strategies for enhancing effectiveness do not work that we are led to the unrealistic and unlikely prescriptions offered by Starbuck and Nystrom.

Beneath Seashore's focus on constituents and external control of goals and resources, his framework centers on the ability of a social system's management to identify, co-opt, and manage these dependencies. The emphasis is again on the rational, a priori, linear nature of these processes aimed at effectiveness: "Systemic integrity must exist in sufficient degree of balance among the component factors; goals must be attained to some sufficient degree . . . ; decision and control processes must be sufficiently appropriate and workable to deal with the problems relating to goal structures, systemic maintenance, and the maintenance of a sufficiently efficient goal-oriented input—throughput—output system [Chapter 3, this volume]." The reason Seashore can claim to have captured the integration of the natural system model, the goal model, and the decision-process model of effectiveness is because he has centered his integration on the two features shared by the three models, namely, the assumption of organizational rationality and the assumption of internal (as in the goal and decision-process models) or external (as in the natural system model) dependencies. Beyond those commonalities, Seashore has captured little that is new. He has offered an alternative language for describing the intersection of the three models. Seashore's perspective provides this integration by focusing on the functioning of the *internal* social system of an organization. It is this patterned interaction of the organization's members that achieves the cooptation of constituencies and provides the guidance necessary for effectiveness. The organization is seen as the context, not the unit, of analysis for understanding this internal social system.

Schneider has offered a rich, rational model at the individual level. Though he explicitly advocates an interactionist perspective (between persons and situations), it is the individual's understanding of the settings that provides the E in the famous B (behavior) $= P$ (person) $\times E$ (environment) paradigm. The individual dominates both the P and the interpretation of the E in explaining and modifying behaviors such as effectiveness. As Schneider says: "The central issues in organizational effectiveness are attraction, selection, attrition, and the nature of organizational goals [Chapter 2, this volume]." Each of these four constructs are assumed to be subject to choice, rational planning, systematic assessment, and corrective action if needed in the pursuit of effectiveness. Though goals are not assumed to be uniformly influential over the course of an organization's development, they are constructs that are preplanned, that are real (i.e., they take objective, recognizable forms), and that drive the initial actions of an organization's founders and early leaders. Central to Schneider's concept of organizational effectiveness is the implicit assumption that organizations are *capable* of peering into the future, forecasting, and rationally anticipating through planned actions the events of the future: "In this vein, it was explicitly recommended that organizational effectiveness be defined as the investments an organization makes in constantly assessing its future requirements for viability."

The perspective offered by Schneider is the most useful of the five in terms of easily derived prescriptions for organizational effectiveness. It is clear that to Schneider the demise of organizations is most likely due to the growing domination of "right-types" with the attendent creeping conformity, staleness, and rigidity of thought. Schneider offers solutions to counter these trends. He does not leave us at the abstract level of ambiguous prescriptions as do Nord and Seashore. On the other hand, he does not abandon the search for generalizations and across-organizational prescriptions as do Goodman, Atkin, and Schoorman.

Though Schneider has labeled his perspective as taking a "systems" view, it is more appropriately thought of as an individual-level analysis of organizational effectiveness. This is the case because Schneider's view is a model of the *determinants* (versus outcomes) of effectiveness, and the key determinants are embedded in *individual* goals, learning, perception, and motivation. It is these characteristics of individuals who are attracted to and selected and retained by the organization that, in turn, establish the level of organizational effectiveness.

But Weick and Daft and Goodman, Atkin, and Schoorman are not to be ignored. Theirs are different perspectives. Another dimension along which the perspectives on effectiveness can be compared is the degree to which the perspective presents organizational effectiveness as a definitional or conceptual problem of construct validation (Schwab, 1980). The perspectives reviewed to this point perceive that issue as relatively secondary to an analysis of the means–ends chains to achieve effectiveness at some level of analysis. Weick and Daft and Goodman, Atkin, and Schoorman, from quite different perspectives, focus on effectiveness as an issue of construct meaning and tractability to research endeavors.

Among the six contributions, Weick and Daft's is the only one purely representative of the nonrational, enactment theme on effectiveness. It is not that effectiveness is an unimportant construct; rather, it is one that has little or no meaning a priori. Given that organizations are, above all else, norm-defining and interpreting systems, effectiveness then becomes a construct to be defined and redefined continuously through processes of the management of symbols and negotiation among alternative-meaning systems. To posit a priori goal statements, objective functions, and systematic planning systems is to miss the point. Effectiveness cannot be so posted before action. Rather, it is an emergent concept that yields multiple uses well beyond the assessment of an organization's performance. That is, effectiveness becomes a construct through which meanings and interpretations of an organization's actions are possible.

Finally, Goodman, Atkin, and Schoorman are essentially arguing that the construct of organizational effectiveness cannot be placed with the matrix of Figure 8.1 because it, as a construct, is not amenable to scientific discussion and research. Organizational effectiveness is not an issue capable of being subjected to systematic analysis. The argument is essentially twofold, with only half of the potency of the assertion being given due emphasis by Goodman *et al.* The first, and primary, argument of Goodman *et al.* is that organizational effectiveness as a construct is too broad, too macro, and too complex to be fruitfully understood as a scientific construct. To quote Goodman *et al.*: "Focus (should be) on an in-depth microstudy of a particular indicator such as mortality, productivity . . . *not* on the overall effectiveness of some organization. We advocate such fine-grained analyses of particular indicators, together with documenting the critical determinants, processes, and constraints that explain variation in that variable [Chapter 7, this volume]." The second twist on the construct provided by Goodman *et al.* is the novel and highly practical emphasis on indicators of effectiveness that have been shown to be under the control of those determinants that are endogenous within a micromodel. In Goodman *et al.*'s words: "We cannot interpret variations of . . . a measure of OE until we understand the controllable and uncontrollable variables that affect this dimension." Combining these two thrusts leads Goodman *et al.* to quite the reverse position of Seashore, Nord, and Starbuck and Nystrom with their emphasis on more macro designs for understanding and enhancing effectiveness. To quote Goodman *et al.* again: "We believe that developing carefully specified theoretical models for a *single indicator* and developing the data sets to test these models is a major research task, particularly at the organization unit of analysis." Clearly, Goodman *et al.*, like Campbell (1977) before, are calling for just good old-fashioned, but infrequently practiced, hard work aimed toward construct validation (Schwab, 1980; Schwab & Cummings, 1970). Equally clear is that Goodman *et al.* are arguing that this should precede attempts at grand theorizing about system-wide, macro models of effectiveness. In a concluding and stinging implicit criticism of the perspectives of Nord, Seashore, Starbuck and

Nystrom, Weick and Daft, and even of Schneider to some degree, Goodman *et al.* conclude: "It is only when we generate a cumulative series of *fine-grained analyses about a specific indicator* will we be in a position to offer generalizations [italics mine]."

So, what emerges from this analysis of the six perspectives? The field or study of organizational effectiveness is an arena for intellectual self-indulgence, for the expression of personal streams of consciousness, frequently in the absence of systematic application of the traditional canons of scientific logic and construct development. Clearly the contributions of Goodman *et al.* and, to some degree, Schneider are attempting to move away from this perspective. Perhaps this is one of the reasons the study of organizational effectiveness has drawn the attention of such a diverse array of perspectives and postures. To that extent, the absence of a limiting set of epistemological assumptions and rules of scientific logic and discourse is to be applauded. Creativity has not been constrained. Yet, the study of organizational effectiveness, as reflected in the perspectives included in this volume, remains largely embedded in logical, rational, goal-oriented, a priori models. There are only two entries in the right column of Figure 8.1.

Is the malady one of insufficient attention to the basic canons of systematic, deductive theory development followed by careful construct validation and programmatic research (as stated by Goodman *et al.* and implied by Schneider)? Or is it one of unimaginative, overly rational, constrained conceptualizations of effectiveness both as an outcome and as a process construct (as implied by Nord and Weick and Daft)? The following sections of the chapter discuss these issues from the standpoint of organizational behavior theory.

ORGANIZATIONAL EFFECTIVENESS ISSUES AND PRESCRIPTIONS FROM ORGANIZATIONAL BEHAVIOR

All the inconsistencies, ambiguities, and even cynicism of the study of organizational effectiveness aside, what *does* organizational behavior have to offer organizational effectiveness as a theoretical *and* applied issue? If one were forced (or positively stimulated) to improve the effectiveness of a unit (individual, group, or organizational) and had only organizational behavior as an available tool, what could one say? The following is a personal statement to that end. It is not intended as an assertion about or reflecting all of organizational behavior. Nor is it intended to be descriptive or integrative of all perspectives from organizational behavior.[1]

---

[1]One would have to be both naive and ultra picky to assume that the statement is so intended. Unfortunately, such is occasionally the case among academics.

The most fruitful route to the challenge of organizational effectiveness is to select a perspective on effectiveness and its causes that is fundamental, basic, and central to a variety of approaches to enhancing effectiveness. The definitional implications of this perspective can then be drawn and prescriptions can be presented concerning decision systems and managerial strategies that would enhance effectiveness, given this perspective.

Basic Issues

Any approach to effectiveness would be profited by asking and answering the following questions.[2] Each question will be followed by an answer, the *sum of such answers* representing a unified perspective on effectiveness.

1. *Within what arena of an organization's activity is effectiveness being assessed and pursued? What service, product market, clientele is being considered?*

Answer: The domain of effectiveness is defined by the opportunities provided by an organization to those who are dependent on it. That is, the effectiveness of any unit is best assessed through the number and quality of opportunities provided by that unit *to* those who are dependent on it. This standard, when applied fully and equitably, leads to outcomes that are incorporated into many and diverse models of effectiveness. These outcomes include *sustained* power and control over resources, continued involvement of participants (within organizations, given an organizational perspective), sustained productivity of those on whom the unit is dependent, and humaneness in the unit's relations with others. The distribution and quality of opportunities, *given* the goals of the dependent units, become the arena within which effectiveness is to be assessed. Unequal distribution of opportunities can be expected of course. The processes for resolving such inequalities, if also perceived as inequitable, are also subject to the same criterion (i.e., are opportunities provided for participation in such resolutions for those who so desire?).

2. *Within that area, whose perspective is being assumed when assessing and pursuing effectiveness?*

Answer: The perspective of organizational members, in proportion to their investment in the organization. Clearly, those with greater inputs (experience, effort, performance, and ownership) expect greater influence in defining and assessing effectiveness. Investment is conceived of as both psychological (e.g., commitment as an attitude) and behavioral (e.g., actual effort and performance). When this perspective is not taken, the basis for organizational cohe-

---

[2]These questions are an adaptation of those presented by Cameron in his perspective on the issue of organizational effectiveness (see K. Cameron, "The enigma of organizational effectiveness," in D. Baugher (Ed.), *New Directions in Program Evaluation: Measuring Effectiveness*, San Francisco: Jossey Bass, 1981, pp. 1–3). Cameron deserves no part of the blame for the answers, however.

sion and integration deteriorates (Dachler & Wilpert, 1978; Martin, 1981). Inequitable distributional processes operating at the individual level become the motivational base for relative deprivation among groups and classes that, in turn, frequently generate interunit conflict.

3. *At what level of analysis (aggregation) is the perspective to be viewed in this assessment and pursuit (individual, group, organizationl, societal, across-societal collectivities like OPEC, Common Market, Warsaw Pact, etc.)?*

Answer: The individual is the fundamental building block and the fundamental determinant of effectiveness. Even the most macroperspectives on effectiveness are dependent on and operate through the individual. Clearly, the perspectives of Seashore, Schneider, and Weick and Daft, as reflected in this book, make no sense without this premise. The individual is the building block for higher level models of aggregative criterion functions.

4. *Within what time frame is effectiveness to be pursued and assessed (long-range or short-range)?* Though frequently cited as important, for the question not to be trivial, we must make the tenuous assumption of a causal model that specifies linkages among determinants and consequences of effectiveness over time.

Answer: The short-run is the necessary, but perhaps not sufficient, perspective. Why?

(*a*) Most individuals will not invest efforts that span beyond their usual time horizon (e.g., 1 week or 1 month and, only very infrequently, 1 year or beyond). Thus, results must begin to appear within this time horizon or effort and application of ability will decline. Furthermore, given the importance of a person's immediate time perspective and the shifts in this perspective throughout the life cycle (Katz, 1980; Levinson, 1978), an analysis of effectiveness must hinge on understanding the individual's present time perspective. This is usually, except in periods of life transitions, short-range.

(*b*) The assessment of long-term effectiveness is so confounded by technological, environmental, and organizational changes as to make long-run assessment of questionable meaningfulness. Of course, this is one basis for the pessimistic perspective toward global organizational effectiveness taken by Goodman *et al.* in this volume. It is possible to assess the long-run effectiveness of a unit a posteriori. On the other hand, developing and applying *causal* models of long-run effectiveness are fictitious. If asked, units can generate justifications suggesting the existence and operation of long-range plans for enhancing effectiveness. These are, however, best thought of as rationalizations (Staw, 1980). The action, the causation, and the meaning exist in the accumulation of a series, not always systematically related, of short-range perspectives.

5. *What type of data should be used in assessing effectiveness (objective or perceived—i.e., subjective)?*

Answer: Perceived will be necessary, even desirable, in the most important cases. Why?

(*a*) Most major managerially controllable determinants of effectiveness operate on productive behavior through perceptions and cognitions. These need to be assessed as *leading* indicators of subsequent changes in effectiveness.

(*b*) Measurement of effectiveness, at anything other than the lowest, simplest operating level, requires the use of subjective, judgmentally based data.

6. *What referent should be used in pursuing and assessing effectiveness (absolute performance, performance against a goal, comparative assessment—relative to other individuals, units, organizations—or across time with a single unit)?*

Answer: Goal achievement should be used where possible; otherwise, comparative assessments across organizational outcomes are necessary. This referent will enhance effectiveness *as long as* conditions of competition among units is sustained (Latham, Cummings, & Mitchell, 1981). The other alternatives are less desirable for the following reasons. Absolute performance of a unit tells us little concerning either the external (survival) or internal (efficiency) effectiveness of a unit. This is because absolute performance can be attained through mechanisms that deteriorate and consume opportunities for participants rather than generate them. Performance without comparison against some standard is meaningless as an index of effectiveness.

Performance against an absolute goal as an index of effectiveness is meaningful only when goals can be clearly and reliably specified. The conditions necessary to achieve these criteria are usually present only in the *case of trivial performances* (Latham, Cummings, & Mitchell, 1981; and Goodman *et al.*, in this volume). Comparisons across time within a unit are the only remaining alternative. Of course, there are problems even here. These problems center on careful delineation of comparable units of analysis and appropriate aggregation strategies. At least these problems are amenable to solution (Roberts, Hulin, & Rousseau, 1978).

A PERSPECTIVE

One possibly fruitful way to conceive of an organization and the processes that define it is as an instrument to produce effectiveness. This effectiveness is to be indexed by the degree to which participants can engage in behavior they perceive as instrumental to their goals. From this perspective, an effective organization (or any other unit of analysis) is one in which the *greatest percentage of participants* perceive themselves as free to use the organization and its subsystems as instruments for their own ends.[3] It is also argued that the greater

---

[3]This perspective is elaborated in L. L. Cummings, "Emergence of the Instrumental Organization," in P. S. Goodman and J. M. Pennings (Eds.), *New Perspectives on Organizational Effectiveness*, San Francisco: Jossey Bass, 1977; also in L. L. Cummings, "Toward the Instrumental Organization," the 1980 National Beta Gamma Sigma Distinguished Lecture.

the degree of perceived organization instrumentality by each participant, the more effective the organization. Thus, this definition of an effective organization is entirely psychological in perspective. It attempts to incorporate both the number of persons who see the organization as a key instrument in fulfilling their needs *and,* for each such person, the degree to which the organization is so perceived.

Within this framework, organizational efficiency and profitability become necessary minimal conditions for organizational survival. Efficiency (equated with productivity), profitability, and effectiveness are here distinguished as follows. Each construct can be applied at any level of analysis.

Efficiency = An economic index of the ratio of measured inputs to measured outputs.

Profitability = A particular case of efficiency where the economic index is assessed through return on x; where x can be any number of input constructs (e.g., assets, equity, sales, etc.).

Effectiveness = The aggregation of opportunities provided to the members of the unit (in the case of the individual level of analysis, it is the opportunities provided by the individual to others dependent on that individual; in the case of the organizational level, it is the opportunities provided by organizational membership to the individual). Efficiency and profitability may or may not enhance effectiveness. Under competitive conditions, they are assumed to so contribute.

Efficiency and profitability are not, however, the goals of an effective organization. For an organization to be effective in this instrumental sense, a subsystem must be concerned with showing that performance meets the standards that external and internal constituencies (for example, resource suppliers and customers) monitor. This is necessary to provide the resources needed to make the organization instrumental for its participants. Also, an effective organization would develop a subsystem that buffers this legitimatizing subsystem from the environment in order to produce efficiently outputs that are desired by the environment. These outputs are the mechanisms through which resources are yielded to the organization so that it can become an instrument for fulfilling its participants' needs.

There are several implications of this perspective. To understand and to influence effectiveness within organizations (and of organizations), we need both perspectives, that of the core of participants and that of the legitimatizing and buffer subsystems. However, the legitimatizing subsystem is a servant of and instrument agent for the core. The agents engaged in legitimatizing behavior do, partially and perhaps secondly, buffer the technical core for efficiency, but (and more importantly) their primary mandate is to allow participants to pursue their own motivational–political agendas.

Two measurement implications arise when effectiveness is defined as the percentage of participants who perceive (and the degree to which they perceive) that the organization is instrumental to the attainment of their personal valued outcomes. Measurement would need to focus on participants' perceptions of their present organization as an instrument compared with other organizations (for example, from previous experience) and on participants' perceptions of present (actual) instrumentalities compared with ideal, desired instrumentalities.

This perspective changes the societal functions performed by organizations. Organizations are best assessed as instruments of outcomes, that is, the effective organization is the organization that best serves those who perceive it (relative to other avenues) as a means to their ends. The independent variables typically studied in organizational behavior (leader behavior, structure, task design, technology) will be assessed in terms of their impact on the proportion of participants who see instrumentalities in the organization, on the degree of instrumentality they perceive, and on the number of organizational mechanisms or vehicles they perceive as instrumental to their valued ends. The relevant administrative decisions become: Do we design tasks to maximize instrumental perceptions? Do we structure organizations to maximize instrumental perceptions? Do we select–train leaders to maximize instrumental perceptions? Do we design and implement operations systems to maximize instrumental perceptions?

This perspective suggests at least two areas worthy of our exploration. One concerns the determinants of inconsistencies in perceptions of instrumentalities, given agreed values and strategies for resolving conflicts. These determinants underlie the integration or the segmentation of organizations. They are crucial to our understanding of the cohesion of social units and social systems. The other concerns the determinants of differences in the perceptions of independent variables that are susceptible to administrative action and that cause participants to view their organizations instrumentally (Pierce, Cummings, & Dunham, 1981).

Increasingly, scholars from varying disciplines and orientations are depicting organizations as arenas within which actors play out their own agendas, or as performances without script or program. That is, organizations are seen as being enacted in process (Pfeffer, 1981). These perspectives imply that the criteria of effectiveness and its assessment are multidimensional, time-bound, dynamic, subject to negotiation, and organizationally, or even unit, specific. One implication of these speculations is that it is increasingly likely to be profitable to use research designs of $N = 1$ (cf. Goodman *et al.* in this volume).

Several variants of this design are likely. Two of the more prominent are reversal designs utilizing either natural or contrived reversals, and intensive, longitudinal case studies. Contrary to some commentators, I do not believe that such a focus on individual organizations denies the *possibility* of eventual construction of more general models of organizational effectiveness. This focus does, however, mean that systematic aggregation of rigorous studies of individual organizations is the most profitable route to understanding organizational effectiveness.

Several constructs, each implying issues and decisions for the manager of the future, seem to describe the emerging state of our knowledge of effective organizations as instruments. These are complexity and dimensionality; multiple time perspectives; multiple levels of analysis with the attendant aggregation questions; focus on process versus content; utilization of a comparative perspective in evaluating organizations; and, finally, the role of individuals in relation to the organization. The instrumentality perspective views actors within organizations as a *determinant* of managerial behavior, as agents exerting effects on organizations; also as actors who view themselves as a constituent, as agents who make claims on the organization.

Each of these issues implies decisions and choices. Choices on each of the preceding issues must be seen as necessary for successful management. The outcomes of the choices (for example, what dimensions to assess, what time perspective to take, what level of analysis to use, etc.) impact the style and effectiveness of managerial decision and action. Like Goodman *et al.,* I would argue that assessing effectiveness is a moot issue until one specifies the styles and techniques (the determinants and their use) of managing effectiveness. Attempting to understand and assess an organization's effectiveness without awareness of the choices underlying the determinants of effectiveness in that organization is a sterile enterprise. It is akin to attempting to evaluate and change a habit without knowledge of the stimuli that control that habit. However, these are issues that are not appropriately settled once and forever. They need to be faced and decided at each stage of an organization's growth or shrinkage (Child & Keiser, 1981).

CONCLUSION

What are the implications of this perspective for specific strategies for enhancing effectiveness? This section will explicate these. In addition, it will prescribe actions based on established bodies of knowledge in organizational behavior.

Nearly all definitions of effectiveness, whatever the perspective, involve the assumption that enhancing effectiveness, under competitive conditions, centers on increasing the ratio of outcomes to inputs (i.e., outcomes/inputs). Given this definition, strategies for increasing effectiveness may aim toward holding outcomes while holding inputs constant. The perspective taken in this chapter argues that the latter alternative is both preferred to and more feasible than the former.

There are two fundamental problems with attempts to increase effectiveness by attaining constant outcomes with declining inputs. These problems are particularly severe when the inputs of relevance are human resources. First, such strategies run counter to an economic–political ideology that dictates growth in outcomes as an indication of progress and development. The importance of growth in personal income and assets, in organizational size, profits, and domain, and societal control over resources all reflect the pervasive influence of increasing outcomes as a basic ideology. Generally, efforts advocating no-growth or shrinkage as strategies for effectiveness enhancement have, at best, fallen on deaf ears or, more likely, drawn smiles of disbelief and cynicism. Second, even if constant outcomes were ideologically and politically feasible, reduction of human inputs to achieve effectiveness gains is frequently translated into substantial underemployment and/or unemployment. Such by-products of pursuing effectiveness are not generally politically feasible or societally healthy (cf. Nord, in this volume).

Far more likely and preferable are effectiveness improvements through increased outcomes with constant human inputs. In addition to avoiding the two maladies of the preceding strategy, this approach suggests specific actions that can be taken to enhance effectiveness through personal and organizational management (Latham *et al.*, 1981). In general, each of these strategies focuses on either increasing the fit between persons and jobs (Schmidt, Hunter, McKenzie, & Muldrow, 1979) and/or increasing the focus and persistence of the motivation of individuals through the more intelligent design of reward systems, tasks, and organizational units.

Underlying these strategies are several fundamental ideas derivable from current organizational behavior findings and applications. If one wishes individuals, groups, or organizations to be effective, whatever their roles (e.g., owners, managers, workers—skilled or unskilled), then what are the necessary conditions as indicated by this behavioral knowledge? The prescriptions will be drawn for the individual case. They can be generalized to other units at higher levels of aggregation.

1. Individuals must believe in the fairness of the "system" through which rewards are distributed. If "relative deprivation" is experienced, then any efforts to increase productivity are likely to fall (Martin, 1981).
2. Individuals must believe that the reward systems that they experience are *equitable* when outcomes are compared to inputs across individuals within

social comparison groups (i.e., given no sense of relative deprivation across classes, then individuals must see *individual* comparisons as generating equity) (Goodman, 1977).

3. Individuals must perceive that performance will lead to (cause) rewards. That is, differential rewards must be seen as *contingent on* differential performance. For effectiveness to be enhanced, managerial and personal actions must contribute positively to these contingency perceptions (Cummings, 1975).

4. Given that individuals perceive positive contingencies, then these individuals must believe that either personal ability and/or motivation will be important causes of performance differences between individuals and that the personal application of ability and motivation will not be constrained artificially by technology, organizational design, or managerial style.

5. Finally, individuals must believe that reward distributions can be accumulated over time. Systems of taxation and income and wealth distribution must be conductive to reward accumulation.

Managerial actions, reward systems, job design, organizational arrangements, and information systems that contribute to the preceding beliefs will enhance effectiveness. Those that disconfirm such beliefs will hinder efforts at enhancing effectiveness. Technological advancement and economic policy operate on effectiveness through these individual causes.

Restatements, in different language, of fundamental principles of organization and delegation (cf. Starbuck and Nystrom, in this volume) and the phenomenological reconceptualization of organizations (cf. Weick and Daft, in this volume) do not aid in the enhancement of effectiveness. They are neither new (as in the first case) nor particularly relevant to enhancing effectiveness (as in the second case).

REFERENCES

Campbell, J. P. On the nature of organizational effectiveness. In P. S. Goodman & J. M. Pennings (Eds.), *New perspectives on organizational effectiveness.* San Francisco: Jossey-Bass, 1977.

Child, J., & Kieser, A. Development of organizations over time. In P. C. Nystrom & W. H. Starbuck (Eds.), *Handbook of organizational design* (Vol. 1). New York: Oxford University Press, 1981.

Cummings, L. L. Strategies for improving human productivity. *The Personnel Administrator,* 1975, 20(4), 40–44.

Dachler, H. P., & Wilpert, B. Conceptual dimensions and boundaries of participation in organizations: A critical evaluation. *Administrative Science Quarterly,* 1978, 23(1), 1–39.

Goodman, P. S. Social comparison processes in organizations. In B. M. Staw & G. R. Salancik (Eds.), *New directions in organizational behavior.* Chicago: St. Clair Press, 1977.

Katz, R. Time and work: Toward an integrative perspective. In B. M. Staw & L. L. Cummings (Eds.), *Research in organizational behavior* (Vol. 2). Greenwich, Conn.: JAI Press, 1980.

Latham, G., Cummings, L. L., & Mitchell, T. R. Behavioral strategies to improve productivity. *Organizational Dynamics,* 1981 (Winter), 5–23.

Levinson, D. J. *The seasons of a man's life.* New York: Knopf, 1978.

Martin, J. Relative deprivation: A theory of distributive injustice for an era of shrinking resources. In L. L. Cummings & B. M. Staw (Eds.), *Research in organizational behavior* (Vol. 3). Greenwich, Conn.: JAI Press, 1981.

Pfeffer, J. Management as symbolic action: The creation and maintenance of organizational paradigms. In L. L. Cummings & B. M. Staw (Eds.), *Research in organizational behavior* (Vol. 3). Greenwich, Conn.: JAI Press, 1981.

Pierce, J., Cummings, L. L., & Dunham, R. B. Sources of environmental structuring and participant responses. Working paper, Center for the Study of Organizational Performance, University of Wisconsin—Madison, 1981.

Roberts, K. H., Hulin, C. L., & Rousseau, D. M. *Developing an interdisciplinary science of organizations.* San Francisco: Jossey-Bass, 1978.

Schmidt, F., Hunter, J., McKenzie, R., & Muldrow, T. Impact of valid selection procedures on work-force productivity. *Journal of Applied Psychology,* 1979, *64,* 609–626.

Schwab, D. P. Construct validity in organizational behavior. In B. M. Staw & L. L. Cummings (Eds.), *Research in organizational behavior* (Vol. 2). Greenwich, Conn.: JAI Press, 1980.

Schwab, D. P., & Cummings, L. L. Theories of performance and satisfaction: A review. *Industrial Relations,* 1970, *9*(4), 408–430.

Staw, B. M. Rationality and justification in organizational life. In B. M. Staw & L. L. Cummings (Eds.), *Research in organizational behavior* (Vol. 2). Greenwich, Conn.: JAI Press, 1980.

GARRY D. BREWER

Assessing Outcomes and Effects

> True, from a low materialistic point of view, it would seem that those
> thrive best who use machinery wherever its use is possible with profit;
> but this is the art of the machines—they serve that they may rule.
> Samuel Butler, *Erewhon*, 1873, p. 184

Butler's classic, *Erewhon*, was both an indictment of machines and a reminder that human arrangements must be assessed in terms of their contribution to an overriding goal of human dignity. The reminder is often forgotten in
the headlong rush for increased profits, for maximum efficiencies, or for
heightened effectiveness of instrumental means. Specialization and fragmenta-
tion of effort, seen in the proliferation of subspecialty fields within the social
sciences, offer a possible explanation for such misplaced attention. Buried by
the minutia of ever increasing details, many social scientists lose sight of the
fundamental goal and, as this happens, their efforts become meaningless. The
problem stands out in scientific studies of organizational effectiveness.

Specialists in organization theory have tended to restrict themselves to analyzing systems of justification—often without benefit of, reference to, or
grounding in specific concrete settings. The organization is accepted as a given
while energies are spent to maximize or optimize its performance. Attempts to
clarify or inform the choice of value goals are rare—for those responsible for an

ORGANIZATIONAL EFFECTIVENESS
A Comparison of Multiple Models

effectiveness study or those affected by the study's consequences. If considered at all, the basic goals of those paying for the study usually dominate. Specialists on explanatory models of organizations give minimal attention to normative considerations. Rather, disproportionate attention is given to the identification and collection of "data" of dubious relevance and validity in pursuit of simple, stable, and deterministic representations of a world having few of these attributes. Those who invent and evaluate policy and decision options are commonly absorbed by current, short-range, and narrow preoccupations. And in the absence of an accumulation of experience, such absorption leads to discredited, outmoded, and inappropriate prescriptions (Etheredge, 1981).

A result of all this is clear: The *status quo* and the values and interests it represents are served more than the goal of human dignity (Lasswell & Kaplan, 1950, Intro.).

SOME BASIC PREMISES

The scientific penchant for simplification and precision is rightly called to task for losing "sight of the importance of intentional analyses which unfold some of the richness of human meaning and valuation [Winter, 1966, 266]." The human organism, social scientists continually rediscover, presents formidable obstacles to abstract and simplified theorizing. Indeed, efforts to devise "universal laws" about human behavior and intentions have been nearly as fruitless as they have been distracting of energy and attentions away "from partial inquiries that can illuminate situationally localized problems in empirical ways [Lasswell & Kaplan, 1950, xxiii]."

Another basic message is clear. Values are contextual, not absolute (Ramsay & Outka, 1968). Values can only be assessed with respect to a concrete setting: "A description of a value of a commodity refers to that commodity in its environment. Value is not a property of the commodity in abstract, but of the commodity *in situ* [Smith, 1956, 112]." For instance, making the statement that the workplace should be safe, while superficially appealing, is relatively meaningless without an adequate specification of the time, place, and other circumstances in which this value is sought. Among other circumstances, one must trade-off safety against a host of related, and often competing, values, all of which are rooted in a specific situation. The safety enjoyed by a bank teller, and the means used to achieve it, in mid-town Manhattan certainly differ from that in a branch bank in Harlem. Likewise, the safety attained in the cockpit of a commercial airliner cruising high over mid-America compared with that in a strategic bomber about to penetrate enemy airspace will not be the same. How effective and costly are means taken to assure a safe working place? It all depends, because assessment is uniquely determined and subject to interpretive and perceptual variations that occur in specific circumstances.

Variation becomes most pronounced as one considers or imagines the future. As Boulding (1961) points out:

> Man responds not to an immediate stimulus but to an image of the future filtered through an elaborate value system. His image contains not only what is, but what might be. It is full of potentialities as yet unrealized. In rational behavior, man contemplates the world of potentialities, evaluates them according to his value system, and chooses the "best" [pp. 25–26].

It is in the future, in our attempts to manipulate social systems and human arrangements, that the nexus of human intentionality, situation, and value attains prominence. As Winter (1966) reminds us, "It becomes apparent that historical fulfillment is the decisive perspective for evaluating social policy. The problem of policy is ultimately how the future is grasped and appraised. The essential meaning of responsibility is accountability in human fulfillment in the shaping of the society's future [p. 282]."

This abbreviated discussion is offered as a point of departure for what follows. The ideas introduced are complex, rich, and essential to understanding what the assessment of human outcomes and effects involves and means (Kaplan, 1963; Means, 1969).

PERFORMANCE ASSESSMENT: AN IDEALIZATION

Studies of organizational effectiveness typically strive to create indicators of the direction, magnitude, and desirability of an institution's activities—*institution* here and elsewhere means a "stable pattern of human interactions." Many factors conceivably enter into the construction, application, and interpretation of performance measures (Berk, 1974). Several of these, but far from all, are quantitative in nature (Mantel *et al.*, 1975). A *measurement strategy* is a means by which a set of indicators assists an analyst in observing the activities of an institution and its consequences for the surrounding environment (Coleman, 1979; Poland, 1974).

Performance measures are typically classified as being either absolute or relative—absolute when performance is assessed with respect to some previously defined or ideal feature, and relative when compared to a standard performance or to a comparable aspect of another institution's performance (Child, 1974). Measures are either *direct* or *indirect*. The former evelute performance as expressly as possible, and the latter key on related behaviors—often through the use of surrogate measures (Ostrom, 1974; Webb, Campbell, Schwartz, & Sechrest, 1966). Ideally such measures should be as objective as possible when concerned with quantifiable aspects of performance (Keeney & Raiffa, 1976). However, qualitative aspects also matter and include determinations of "excellence," "satisfaction," and similar hard-to-define and harder-to-measure attributes (de Neufville, 1975, Chapters I, XII; Said, 1974). Data must be accurate and they must be collected systematically. The one-shot approach has traditionally been misleading, and data-gathering and analysis activities require continuing appraisal (Carley, 1981, Chapter 5; Weiss, 1972).

Because multiple objectives characterize the usual institutional agenda, and these objectives are sought through various programmatic activities, there is a requirement to use multiple measures (Lerner & Lasswell, 1951, Chapter I; Provus, 1971). It is crucial to identify and understand the objectives themselves. On examination, many will be ill-considered or inappropriate (Quade, 1975, Chapter 5). Stated and unstated goals for the assessment are also worth detailed analysis (Rein, 1976).

Performance may be assessed in terms of process, response, or impact. The first concentrates on the internal workings of an institution; the second attends to an institution's responses to its surrounding environment; and the last attempts to assess the environment's reactions to an institution's activities (Brewer & deLeon, 1982, Chapter VI; Hatry, 1970).

Finally, performance measurement must be set off against a variety of plausible and potential purposes to be served by the measurement (Campbell &

TABLE 9.1
Specific Elements of Idealized Assessment

Measurement strategy
 Quantitative elements
 Qualitative elements
 Absolute standards of comparison
 Relative standards of comparison
 Direct measures
 Indirect measures
Data type
 Cross-sectional
 Time series
Data treatment
 Systematic collection
 Data validation–appraisal conducted
Assessment purposes
 Identified for analyst, client, others affected
 Measures for each stated–unstated purpose made
 Internal–external staffing
Type of assessment
 Process
 Response
 Impact
Main emphasis
 Outcomes
 Effects

Erlebacher, 1970). For instance, if the assessment is to be made for an agency's internal purposes, then agency staff members will be most likely to be responsible for the work. If the evaluation is part of a general assessment of the sponsoring agency, done on behalf of the "public interest," outside and less directly involved specialists are required. In either case, the evaluator's professional and personal identifications will have important consequences for the type, comprehensiveness, and severity of the evaluation (Clark, 1975; Williams & Evans, 1969).

There are well-intentioned but idealized characteristics of performance assessment (Table 9.1). They are also mostly never observed in practice. Indeed, as is the specific case with studies of organizational effectiveness, there is also mounting disillusionment in the general area of social program evaluation (Cronbach & Associates, 1980; Greenbaum, Garet, & Solomon, 1977; Orlans, 1971, 1975), a condition that stems in no small part from the setting of impossibly high ambitions, from a failure to specify the type and purpose of the assessment, and from a noticeable lack of concern and attention to situational or contextual matters. Each of these points is next illustrated and discussed.

TYPES OF ASSESSMENTS

For most organizations, resources are seldom lavish or, in any event, one usually works to ensure their efficient and effective use. Simple economic efficiency, for instance, can be defined in terms of a single economic entity pursuing its goals in such a way that "no alternative organization [would] yield it a higher payoff when all costs and outputs are taken into account [Shubik, 1978, p. 123]." However, at even this apparently simple level of conceptualization and activity, a variety of meanings and interpretations exists to complicate matters. For instance, such a definition fails to account for the organization's influence on the surrounding environment, for a realistic determination of alternative capital and labor mixes to yield measures of technological efficiency pertinent to the specific setting, for the social consequences of failing to achieve collective or multiperson and multiunit efficiency, for distinctions that exist between short-term and long-run efficiency, for risk and uncertainty, and for the different perceptions and values individuals have about the single economic entity, including their relationship to and responsibility for it (Shubik, 1978). Despite these problems, internal auditing, accountability, managerial and fiscal analyses, and other tools and techniques exist to enhance administrative practice and control. In common parlance, these are referred to as *process* or *internal assessments*.

In contrast, one may also wish to know and assess the consequences for an organization of external demands, threats, and opportunities. For instances, in the case of unexpected conflict or dispute, sacrifices in the total managerial program may have to be made to allow additional monitoring or surveillance. The results, in terms of the outputs of other activities, must be determined. Likewise, how much are high-visibility, short-term problems deflecting attention and resources away from less visible, longer-term, but possibly more significant ones? Such considerations, and the means taken in their resolution, are known generally as *response assessments*.

Determining the consequences of actions (including inaction) on the encompassing environment is a third type generally known as *impact evaluation*. What are the proximate outcomes and longer-range effects of management actions or inactions? Who or what is responsible for successful or unsuccessful results? Can they be recognized and rewarded to enhance and encourage performance, in the first case, or to correct and ameliorate, in the latter? Determining impacts is often very hard to do. Outside and consultative assistance is often required to improve the scope and objectivity of the evaluation. Furthermore, the concept of impact assessment is explicitly comprehensive. One works to determine the impact on the relevant whole of the setting, not simply a few of its routine and commonplace parts. The matter is made more difficult by making appropriate distinctions between spatially and temporally proximate *outcomes* and longer-term, spatially removed *effects*.

Consider an automobile assembly plant. Absolute performance measures can be devised to aid assessment of efficiency and productivity. Were the target goals achieved? In a timely fashion? At least per-unit cost? And so forth. Relative measures, such as, did the plant "measure up" to others in the corporation's scope of business or to those of competitors, may also be applied. More successful and prevalent assessments will be of the process type and hence will stress relatively simple auditing and control tools and techniques. Typically, they will also emphasize direct measurement, save for instances where lagging productivity of inefficient performance fails to yield to it, in which case indirect observations and measurements may be used. In either case, the thing observed and measured will be outcomes, where causal linkages are short and predominantly transparent. Far less time or energy will be spent pursuing individual reactions and concerns about being part of or responsible for the processes, and even less will focus on matters concerning differences between short- and long-term efficiencies.

Response evaluations are considerably harder than process ones. How, for instance, does one recognize and then calculate the consequences of something as prevalent and chronic as worker absenteeism? Workers stay away from work for different reasons. Sickness may be legitimate, but its legitimacy blurs when occurrences are repeated, habitual, or prolonged. Other, illegitimate, reasons exist for not coming to work. But how does one determine such deceptions, decide on ways to cope with them, and assess the costs and consequences to the organization of both absenteeism and the steps taken to control it? Besides trying to understand, come to terms with, or minimize sickness for reasons of efficiency and productivity, management is also confronted with demands to comply with contractual constraints (e.g., healthy and safe working conditions) and with other external demands on its time and attention (e.g., regulations). These and many factors have consequences for operations. What both cause and consequence might be is far more problematic. What are the "costs," for example, that result from management's preoccupation with absenteeism and its consequent lack of attention for other less pressing matters? These may be significant, particularly as they cumulate over time, only to be recognized—too late—as full-blown crises of one sort or another.

Assessing impacts is the most difficult challenge of all. For the auto plant, it is a simple matter to determine the number of employees, their gross contribution to the local economy, the number of automobiles produced within a given period of time, and other such outcomes. But where does one bound the assessment? Who bears responsibility for the heavy economic dependence placed on the plant by local authorities (e.g., municipalities or states), especially in times of market downturn? When and under what conditions is the manufacturer absolved for deaths resulting from automobile use? What are the cumulative impacts, conceived and measured in a variety of ways, of all such deaths? And, what are the costs associated with automobile manufacture as compared with alternative uses of the same resources? How, to carry the point further, does one determine responsibility for environmental degradation that occurs as a consequence of cars and their production? Or, to put it somewhat differently, what is the trade-off between a dollar of profit, one additional job, or one extra car and one additional death, one more unit of pollution, or one more abandoned wreck on a New York City street? These and hundreds of similar questions are relevant to impact assessment.

A main implication of this discussion is to be very specific about the type or form of assessment at hand. As suggested in our hypothetical automobile example, certain types of assessment can be conducted; others are far more difficult; and many may be simply impossible. Even the most cursory experience with real evaluations leads one to believe that expectations outstrip results (Cronbach & Associates, 1980; U.S. General Accounting Office, 1978).

PURPOSES OF ASSESSMENT

Up to this point in the discussion, a fundamental purpose for assessment has been treated implicitly: How much does an observed phenomenon deviate from a norm or expectation for it? Why? Who is responsible? Other purposes exist, however, and their nature and existence often exert great weight in shaping and determining the practice and results of assessment. Robert Floden and

Stephen Weiner (1978) provide a striking inventory of other purposes in their excursion from "Rationality to Ritual: The Multiple Roles of Evaluation in Governmental Process," key points of which are elaborated in the following.

Conflict Management

Evaluation may signal that a program is not immutable and that, indeed, its specific provisions and very existence are still open to debate, amendment, and compromise. In cases where divergence of opinion about a program's utility, direction, and form occur, conflict management purposes serve a critical "cushioning" or "damage-limiting" end: Cushioning in the sense that precise terms and expectations may be modified and aligned with reality, and limiting in the sense that stressful or onerous provisions of a program may be sensed, changed, or contained at something less than open hostility.

Social Change

Dramatic instances of evaluations that have resulted in social change exist (e.g., major scandals that lead to performance assessment and wholesale readjustments), but of greater significance are the cumulative results of hundreds, if not thousands, of routine appraisal activities undertaken continually in the social context. In the case of the reaffirmation of the constitutional rights of several minority groups in the United States, the results of one or a few landmark judicial assessments certainly mattered (e.g., *Brown* v. *Board of Education* in 1954). However, the aggregate social impact of numerous other small assessments made during the period clearly accounts for more in deciding where change originated and why it sustained.

Social experiments, considered as a limited form of performance assessment, have resulted in social change, too. An experiment generally means that a limited program or policy is undertaken to allow observation and measurement of its various outcomes and effects (Riecken & Boruch, 1974; Rivlin, 1971). Some may agree to the experiment and the assessment it engenders as a means to vindicate a preferred option. In time, a pilot or demonstration program may be drawn up, based on the experimental findings, and its mere existence generates experiences, hopes, and dependencies that are more likely to persist—even flourish—than are the raw ideas about and different perceptions of the project that existed in the a priori case (Brewer, 1973a).

For example, in the case of the lengthy, on-going national health insurance experiment being conducted at the Rand Corporation (Newhouse, 1974), a turning point occurred when all the concerned parties stopped discussing broad strategic issues and began to focus on tactical questions (e.g., "How are we going to do this?" and, "What have we gotten ourselves into?"). Similar shifts in emphasis represent at least tacit agreement to investigate and appraise several new alternatives, and that is a necessary, albeit by no means sufficient, first step toward social change. Such change, naturally, is based on observed and measured performance in the controlled setting of the social experiment (Archibald & Newhouse, 1979).

Stimulate Examinations of Assumptions and Behavior

Complacency reduction serves two desirable purposes: Working with those conducting an assessment, to determine what success might be and how to measure or even observe it, program personnel must also clarify their own goals and prejudices. This is healthy. Examination of one's own preferences often leads to a rejection of previous modes of thought and action and to the use of alternatives. Such introspection is essential for one involved in an innovative enterprise, for it leads to increased clarity about what has to be done and how to do it (Brewer, 1980b).

Assessment may allow operational personnel a moment to step back from their day-to-day demands to think about what they are in fact doing and trying to accomplish. Experienced evaluators are seldom surprised by this reaction. It is certainly a valid and beneficial reason for assessing performance, although it has little to do with an idealized view of such. Furthermore, self-examination may happen for those doing the assessment. Heightened self-righteousness and an assumption that everything being addressed is "evil," "corrupt," "wrong-headed," and the like may moderate during assessment, or, one's negative predispositions may intensify in light of the experience. In either case, the act of intervention offers everyone involved a chance to examine pertinent assumptions and to modify behavior accordingly.

Contribute to an Image

Merely assessing performance could enhance the image of the sponsoring organization. This need not be a suspicious or dysfunctional purpose, particularly if the sponsor sincerely wants to understand the organization well enough to make sensible improvements. Doing assessments may also give one a competitive edge—realistically in terms of improved performance and symbolically in terms of enhanced reputation, especially with one's superiors. Distinctions between "sincere" assessment and "whitewash" or "eyewash" efforts done for deceptive or self-promotional reasons must be made. The conventional literature on organizational effectiveness is curiously mute on these other, commonplace assessment reasons.

Displace or Assign Responsibility

Assessments may be used to assign blame. Board of inquiry, trouble-shooters, and "hatchet men" are standard indicators here. Responsibility is a two- or more dimensional idea, though, and an assessment may acknowledge excellence as well as incompetence. Certainly when political judgments against an organization or agency are made, and the hatchet men are loosed, the nature, form, and substance of the assessment will be different from one prompted by more scientific reasons. The conventional literature overlooks this common purpose and practice.

Contribute to Knowledge

The "purest" purposes of performance assessment are related to improved decisions and operations and, more notably, to theoretical advances in the sponsoring academic disciplines. To one unfamiliar with representative work and the tradition of the organization effectiveness "school," a distinctive orientation seems toward the pursuit of methodological, measurement, and theoretical ends. Decision and operation improvements are given less weight, and the other routine purposes and forms of asssessment just listed are scarcely treated at all. But, anyone interested in performance assessment needs to be aware of other possibly significant purposes than just limited academic ones. This discussion sketches several of these less obvious purposes—less obvious to the academic specialists, but certainly quite prominent to anyone having direct experience with the realistic world of performance assessment.

OTHER REALITIES

Many other realistic features exist to limit effectiveness and other assessment studies. Professional standards, integrity, and competence are all in short supply (Brewer, 1973b, 1980a). Indeed there is a legitimate question whether evaluation is a profession or merely the playground for numerous undisciplined and shady operators (Cronbach & Associates, 1980). One consequence, it is alleged, is that assessments are performed more for adversarial purposes than for scientific ones (Orlans, 1975). Because many studies are done under time and resource constraints and pressures, scientific shortcuts and other problems exist to limit and distort findings, or, in Etheredge's (1981) terms, "You want it bad, you get it bad [p. 127]." Many studies have been conducted to discredit or undercut bureaucratic and other competitors (Moynihan, 1970); an attitude that assessment can only hurt one is thus understandably prevalent in both governmental and private organizations. And, finally, common practice and experience are such that evaluation results are usually used selectively to enhance the control of those holding power to a far greater extent than for making organizations more effective—or more attuned to the overall goal of improved human dignity specified earlier.

To this point the discussion has been based on rather general reflections of assessment. A main point of it has been to open up thinking to a wider and more realistic range of possibilities. It would be asking far too much to expect that any single approach would satisfy all the requirements or to be appropriate for all conceivable settings and circumstances. Rather, one hopes that specific instances of performance assessment, such as studies or methods to study organization effectiveness, might be contrasted with the broader range of possibilities to get a better sense of their particular strengths, weaknesses, and overall contribution. We next turn attention to such a comparison using each of the six approaches presented earlier in the chapter.

REACTIONS TO THE SIX CONTRIBUTIONS

The most striking reaction one has in reading this volume's six contributions is frustration. Each author is, in varying ways, frustrated with the lack of progress, the confusion, and the impotence discovered in one specialty field after another. In turn, each contributor summarizes and then rejects theories, methods, and applied studies of organization effectiveness stemming from the representative disciplinary perspectives. But though differences in degree are evident, nearly all then proceed to recommend—in essence—some version of "more of the same" as a corrective.

Frustration extends to the reader of the collective effort, too. At best, and only occasionally, are passing efforts made to define fundamental terms, such as *effectiveness, complexity,* and the like. This is not to say that definitions have not been proposed by others: Many other scholarly works are duly referenced and then quickly passed by in the six contributions. It is to say that it is extraordinarily difficult, if not impossible, to assess each of these contributions in its own terms or to make clear comparisons among them. There is little underlying basis for doing either.

Having denied the possibility for meaningful comparison or separate appraisal, one must consider the following summary with some trepidation, at least equal to that affecting me in carrying it out.

Schneider

An orientation toward process types of assessment incorporating qualitative determinants of organizational outcomes characterizes this contribution from the "interactionist perspective." The main focus for study should, from this viewpoint, be individuals within organizations—particularly the means by which they are hired, retained, and placed within the institution. Additionally, one interested in effectiveness needs to pay attention to attrition's consequences for the hardening of perspective and reductions in organizational resiliency they engender.

Unabashedly normative, the interactionist model barely considers what an organization is doing and whether its effects on the surrounding environment are positive, desirable, and the like. Nor are the many possible purposes for doing effectiveness assessments addressed. As a result, the main purpose emphasized here seems to be continuance of business as usual, albeit with happier workers. If an orienting objective is discernible, it would be toward the enhancement of existing control, where the researcher becomes a willing, if somewhat unwitting, accomplice. A conclusion is thus that organizational effectiveness studies ought to be a main means to secure the willing acquiescence of one's employees.

Seashore

This contribution's primary assumption is that simple explanatory models are needed to underpin organization effectiveness studies. Three classes of existing models are selectively characterized—psychological, goals-oriented, and information theories—and an appeal is made to integrate them for purposes of intellectual enrichment. A bow is made toward operational needs: "We still need to understand the bases for such assessments and to form ideas about how assessments can be made that better fit the action choice requirements of the several classes of constituents." But the overwhelming objective of improving theoretical bases of this understanding runs throughout the chapter. Not nearly so pronounced are an appreciation for the different types and purposes of assessment, a concern for differences between outcomes and effects, or guidance about how one might adapt and apply the proposed "integrated model of organizational effectiveness" to any realistic setting. As is common, definitions of organizational effectiveness are treated by assumption, they are not carefully specified. And, to the extent that this occurs, one deduces that scholarly needs and preferences will dominate specific applications of the proposed model.

Weick and Daft

Based on principles derived from cognitive psychology, this contribution joins substance even less than the previous, sociologically based, example. Underlying the work is an undefined, but very strong, presumption about the complexity generally confronting one in organizations: The world is a complex place and no two individuals will perceive selected aspects of this complexity in equivalent ways; consequently, one needs to be sensitive to the problems various interpretations of reality create for organizations. The scheme is, in the authors' own terms, so difficult as to present "enormous methodological problems," so far removed from concrete circumstances that the set of possible interpretations may be open-ended: "Organizations vary from one another in ways that may influence interpretation processes," and so tenuous that "we hope exploratory research is undertaken . . . any insight, however meager, will enhance our understanding of organizations." In other words, the needs of cognitive psychologists and their theories are best served by the approach and recommendations it contains, not the needs for improved organization effectiveness.

With respect to various elements contained in Table 9.1, it is extremely difficult to make any statements about what the approach is, emphasizes, or does. Measurement and data strategies are only vaguely presented; the type and emphasis of the assessment could be just about anything; and a variety of purposes one might have in mind for such work is not treated at all—except by inference, and here the needs of cognitive psychology seem to prevail.

Nord

This selection pays particular attention to the contextual arrangements that exist to condition organizational life, and comes closest to the spirit of the "basic premises" sketched out in the opening section of this chapter. An internal or process perspective on organizational effectiveness is inadequate. Organizations are constrained and respond to their environments; they affect and are affected by the flow of events. Furthermore, multiple objectives are sought through organizational means, and studies of organizational effectiveness that pursue one or a select few performance criteria usually fail to acknowledge this and thus misrepresent reality and bias our understanding. And some concern is voiced for differences between outcomes and effects.

Despite these notable, positive aspects of the work, one is provided little assistance with problems of measurement strategy or data acquisition and treatment. The concepts presented are appealing, but one simply does not know what to do with them. Likewise, few distinctions are made between assessment's various stated and unstated purposes.

Starbuck and Nystrom

The process and outcome, quantitative, direct measurement biases of operations research and systems engineering are displayed and called to task in this selection. Indeed, specific violations of the old modeler's dictum to "Model simple, think complex" are continually cited (the final prescriptions contained in "Reaping Benefits from Ambiguities" can be summarized by reciting the dictum).

At the most general level, one comes away from this selection with the feeling that the analysts' preferences must prevail over all others and that these are mainly determined by the rigid and simple forms the available tools allow. Thoughtless rationalization of the *status quo,* ignorance of various perspectives and interpretations of the context, and heightened attention to the maximization of a small and arbitrary set of artificial goals or objectives all figure prominently in the approach. Furthermore, a strong orientation to near-term and proximate outcomes shows throughout the various representative examples cited; virtually no appreciation of either the response or impact types of assessment is evident, nor is there much sensitivity shown for differences between outcomes and effects. Indeed, in order to gain analytic tractability, the possibility of effects occurring outside the tight boundaries of overly simple models is overlooked, if not discounted substantially.

Other specific biases and characteristics are also noted. Qualitative elements are eschewed, but if treated at all, these are imposed on the analyses (e.g., by numeric specification of a decision-maker's "judgment" or "preferences"). Time is not directly or unambiguously treated either. The usual form of maximizing or optimizing with respect to certain constraints presupposes that an equilibrium condition is both desirable and attainable. How long it may take to reach this state of grace is not usually directly considered—a matter of some consequence given the many well-known problems of implementation. Assessment purposes are usually not explicitly considered, rather objectives of efficiency or optimality are treated as self-evident and given. Various other possibilities for assessment sketched out earlier here are simply irrelevant or nonexistent for this approach.

Much to their credit, Starbuck and Nystrom report most of these limitations of the operations research approach for studies of organization effectiveness. One must, however, take pause with their general prescription to invent "simple, approximate solutions to complex problems," especially as a means to facilitate mathematical representation. The point here is that much of what one wishes to accomplish by studying effectiveness may simply not be amenable to mathematical specification—and then what?

Goodman, Atkin, and Schoorman

Based on a general disciplinary background of applied microeconomics, this contribution goes beyond the standard, textbook approach one might expect and includes consideration of the process by which organization effectiveness is carried out. As expected, a large number of studies and approaches to the subject are noted and dismissed. The means used here are five "basic theses," stressing, respectively, the following ideas:

- No single model or theory exists for organizational effectiveness.
- Without theory, the usual experience has been ad hoc and noncumulative.
- Theoretical convergence has not occurred because the studies represent analysts' value preferences that are so disparate as to prevent it.
- In-depth, microstudies of organizational outcomes are needed to correct these deficiencies.
- And, there should be a general moratorium on "overall" studies of organizational effectiveness.

Despite an initial claim to avoid disciplinary bias in their perusal of the field, an economic predisposition and value bias intrude throughout. One broad class of outcomes studies of organizational effectiveness is faulted for its seeming exclusion of "constraints or functional form . . . (and) tradeoffs. . ."; for its inability to account for "market penetration"; and for its casual treatment of other economic concepts such as "cost of production," "adaptability," and "resource exploitation." Another class of studies (related to determination of organizational effectiveness indicators) is likewise discounted along standard economic theoretical lines: aggregation problems among different production units having different production functions, relationships between resource availability and personnel characteristics, and so forth.

The corrective proposed is based on explicit consideration of microeconomic concepts and theories, initial disclaimer notwithstanding. The "fine-grained" analyses used to illustrate the authors' preferred course are little more than applied economic analyses of highly selective aspects of a hospital and a coal mine, respectively. And, in the terms of my Table 9.1, their proposal can be summarized as follows:

- Measurement strategy: quantitative, direct, and absolute
- Data type and treatment: systematic, careful specification, cross-sectional (marginal or incremental time)
- Type and emphasis of assessment: process, total emphasis on outcomes
- Purposes: mainly those of the responsible analysts represented and served, and these are primarily economic and theoretical in nature

The demand to impose a moratorium on organizational effectiveness studies is disingenuous and easily read as a move to impede work that does not conform to the limited perception presented in the "fine-grained" analysis paradigm. And though this paradigm is itself unobjectionable, there is little reason to believe, nor is a convincing argument presented, that its known limitations will be outweighed by its supposed benefits. Finally, no operational definition of organizational effectiveness is offered—even for the recommended paradigm. One surmises, however, that efficiency and productivity goals dominate and with them a reaffirmation and justification of the *status quo*.

All the contributions pay scant attention to distortions that occur in organizational effectiveness studies as a consequence of funding and sponsorship. But, "He who pays the piper calls the tune." Most presume that time and resources for studies of organizational effectiveness do not matter or are ample. Neither condition usually holds, and both have implications for the resulting work. None considers the consequence of having different personal, professional, or institutional configurations involved in organizational effectiveness studies: One does not expect a plumber to be able to repair a leaky heart valve as well as a leaky pipe; nor does one "succeed" in the assessment business by "biting the hand that feeds" nearly so much as by "going along with the program," especially if the evaluation faults one's superiors.

Other general implications are also suggested.

IMPLICATIONS

The contributions to this volume, and the many efforts summarized and cited in them, demonstrate in varying degrees the extraordinary difficulties involved in trying to assess the outcomes and effects of human behavior—whether called program evaluation, policy appraisal, organizational effectiveness, or anything else. Considerable energy has been spent in trying to devise simple and abstract theories and explanations of phenomena both more complex and interesting than the theories would allow. However, what seems to have happened in the face of these shortcomings is an irrational drive to try harder—with the same inadequate approaches. Notably absent is much concern for the reasons contributing to the chronic lack of success.

Foremost among other reasons is a failure to locate assessment with respect to specific, concrete circumstances, no two of which will ever be precisely equivalent. Doing so calls attention to the incredible variety of perceptual and interpretive possibilities inherent as different individuals orient themselves to specific times, places, and circumstances. Illustrative questions suggested here include: Efficient for whom? Under what circumstances? As compared with what? One person's efficiency is quite often another's misery. Effective for whom? At what costs? Over what domain? One organization's effectiveness may well be another's demise, or society's burden. Certainly there will never be a general purpose or universal approach capable of answering all such questions. A more modest and utilitarian aim is required—one that strives for partial illumination more than scientific precision, one that remains mindful of the aggregate consequences of purposive human acts.

As there are numerous real and imagined circumstances attending performance assessment, so too are there diverse purposes for undertaking them. It is simply insufficient to "do an effectiveness study." One must be conscious of why the study is being done, for whom, for what kinds of resources, and what its various consequences might be. Insufficient time and attention have been devoted to these matters; the puny results of hundreds of assessments bear witness here.

But do past failures justify a moratorium on assessments? Hardly. Rather, one hopes that intellectual energies will be attuned to a more responsible accounting of human fulfillment and away from institutional or organizational abstractions. Human fulfillment, in this view, "sees the person as a whole, in all his aspects, not as the embodiment of this or that limited set of needs or interests [Lasswell & Kaplan, 1950, p. xxiv]." And its accounting through scientific endeavors, "prizes not the glory of a depersonalized state or the efficiency of a social mechanism [e.g., an organization], but human dignity and the realization of human capacities [p. xxiv]." Human dignity includes freedom, the sharing of power among the many rather than the few, as well as widespread participation in all value processes. The task confronting us is to specify and respecify means by which human dignity can be achieved and to do so in concrete circumstances, so that whatever potential for progress exists can be realized. Assessing outcomes and effects is an essential means to this end.

REFERENCES

Archibald, R. W., & Newhouse, J. P. *Social experimentation: Some whys and hows.* Santa Monica, Calif.: The Rand Corporation (R-2479-HEW), 1979.

Berk, R. A. Performance measures: Half full or half empty? *Social Science Quarterly,* 1974, 54 (March), 762–764.

Boulding, K. E. *The image.* Ann Arbor, Mich.: Ann Arbor Paperbacks, 1961.

Brewer, G. D. Experimentation and the policy process. *Twenty-fifth annual report of the Rand Corporation.* Santa Monica, Calif.: The Rand Corporation, 1973. Pp. 151–165. (a)

Brewer, G. D. Professionalism: The need for standards. *Interfaces,* 1973, 4(November):1, 20–27. (b)

Brewer, G. D. On duplicity. *Simulation,* 1980, 34 (April), 140–143. (a)

Brewer, G. D. On the theory and practice of innovation. *Technology in Society,* 1980, 2(Fall):3, 337–363. (b)

Brewer, G. D., & deLeon, P. *The foundations of policy analysis.* Homewood, Ill.: Dorsey Press, 1982.

Butler, S., *Erewhon.* New York: E. P. Dutton, 1873. (Shrewsbury edit.)

Campbell, D. T., & Erlebacher, E. How regression artifacts in quasi-experimental evaluations can mistakenly make compensatory education look harmful, in J. Helmuth (Ed.), *Compensatory education* (Vol III). New York: Brunner/Mazel, 1970. Pp. 185–210.

Carley, M. *Social measurement and social indicators.* London: George Allen & Unwin, 1981.

Child, J. What determines organizational performance. *Organizational Dynamics,* 1974, 3 (March), 2–14.

Clark, R. F. Program evaluation and the commissioning entity. *Policy Sciences,* 1975, 7(March):1, 11–16.

Coleman, J. S. *Policy issues and research design.* Chicago: National Opinion Research Center, 1979.

Cronbach, L. J. & Associates. *Toward reform of program evaluation.* San Francisco: Jossey-Bass, 1980.

de Neufville, J. I. *Social indicators and public policy.* New York: Elsevier, 1975.

Etheredge, L. S. Government learning: An overview. In S. L. Long (Ed.), *The handbook of political behavior* (Vol. 2). New York: Plenum, 1981. Pp. 73–161.

Floden, R. E., & Weiner, S. S. Rationality to ritual: The multiple roles of evaluation in governmental process. *Policy Sciences,* 1978, 9(February):1, 9–18.

Greenbaum, W., Garet, M., & Solomon, E. *Measuring educational progress* New York: McGraw-Hill, 1977.

Hatry, H. P. Measuring the effectiveness of nondefense public programs. *Operations Research,* 1970, 18 (September), 772–784.

Kaplan, A. *American ethics and public policy.* New York: Oxford University Press, 1963.

Keeney, R. L., & Raiffa, H. *Decisions with multiple objectives: Preferences and value trade-offs.* New York: Wiley, 1976.

Lasswell, H. D., & Kaplan, A. *Power and society.* New Haven, Conn.: Yale University Press, 1950.

Lerner, D., & Lasswell, H. D. (Eds.). *The policy sciences.* Stanford, Calif.: Stanford University Press, 1951.

Mantel, S. J., *et al.* A social service measurement model. *Operations Research,* 1975, 23 (March), 218–239.

Means, R. L. *The ethical imperative.* New York: Doubleday, 1969.

Moynihan, D. P. Policy vs. program in the '70s. *The Public Interest,* 1970, 20 (Spring), 90–100.

Newhouse, J. P. *Issues in the analysis and design of the experimental portion of the health insurance study.* Santa Monica, Calif.: The Rand Corporation (R-1484-OEO), 1974.

Orlans, H. The political uses of social research. *Annals of the American Academy of Political and Social Science,* 1971, 394, 28–35.

Orlans, H. Neutrality and advocacy in policy research. *Policy Sciences,* 1975, 6(June):2, 107–119.

Ostrom, E. Exclusion, choice, and divisability. *Social Science Quarterly,* 1974, 54 (March), 691–699.

Poland, O. Program evaluation and administrative theory. *Public Administration Review,* 1974, 34 (July), 222–228.

Provus, M. M. *Discrepancy evaluation.* Berkeley, Calif.: McCutchan, 1971.

Quade, E. S. *Analysis for public decisions.* New York: Elsevier, 1975.

Ramsay, P., & Outka, G. H. *Norm and context in christian social ethics.* New York: Scribner, 1968.

Rein, M. *Social science and public policy.* New York: Penguin, 1976.

Riecken, H. W., & Boruch, R. F. *Social experimentation.* New York: Academic Press, 1974.

Rivlin, A. M. *Systematic thinking for social action.* Washington, D.C.: The Brookings Institution, 1971.

Said, K. E. A policy-selection/goal formulation model for public systems. *Policy Sciences,* 1974, 5(March):1, 89–100.

Shubik, M. On concepts of efficiency. *Policy Sciences,* 1978, 9(April):2, 121–126.

Smith, N. M. Jr. A calculus for ethics: A theory of the structure of value. *Behavioral Science,* 1956, 1 (April), 110–118.

U.S. General Accounting Office. *Assessing social program impact evaluations.* Washington, D.C.: U.S. Government Printing Office, 1978.

Webb, E. J., Campbell, D. T., Schwartz, R. D., & Sechrest, L. *Unobtrusive measures.* Chicago: Rand McNally, 1966.

Weiss, C. H. *Evaluation research: Methods of assessing program effectiveness.* Englewood Cliffs, N.J.: Prentice-Hall, 1972.

Williams, W., & Evans, J. The politics of evaluation. *Annals of the American Academy of Political and Social Science,* 1969, 385, 118–132.

Winter, G. *Elements for a social ethic.* New York: Macmillan, 1966.

LAWRENCE B. MOHR

The Implications of Effectiveness Theory for Managerial Practice in the Public Sector

Both organization theorists and public-sector managers shop around for useful commodities among the results of conceptual and empirical research on organizational effectiveness. This chapter will argue that, to a great extent, their needs are different. Furthermore, it appears that the needs of the managers for research results can be much more satisfactorily supplied. This means that effectiveness theorists are quite limited in what they can do with academic research, that managers are quite limited in what they can gain from theory, and that the most fruitful connection in the triad will probably be the direct link between good research and good management.

The initial sections of the chapter will elaborate on the troublesome point that effectiveness models—managerial and theoretical—are difficult to construct because, conceptually, the content of the organizational goal is infinite. It must therefore be arbitrarily circumscribed. That problem is perhaps not categorically obstructive to managers, but it is devastating to theorists. Subsequent sections will deal with a way out that has been sought for theorists: Goal content must evidently be determined arbitrarily, and that is unsatisfactory, but the day may perhaps be saved by developing effectiveness theories in relation to limited organizational goals once the latter have been arbitrarily selected. That avenue, however, is also apparently closed; we shall see that effectiveness theories have been sought in two forms, goal specific and goal free, but theories of effectiveness are not likely to be attained in either form.

ORGANIZATIONAL EFFECTIVENESS
A Comparison of Multiple Models

On the other hand, the kinds of empirical research that have been conducted for the sake of theory can, with some redefinition of purpose and modest attendant modifications in procedure, be extremely useful to managers.

THE INFINITY PROBLEM

One of the most important results of the recent flurry of inquiry into organizational effectiveness theory is broad agreement on the impossibility, in principle, of specifying "the organizational goal." That concept has been found to be an intractable one, at least from the standpoint of effectiveness theory: The content of the goal is arbitrary, depending on one's perspective, and too vast and complex in its nature to allow exact specification (Hannan & Freeman, 1977; Mohr, 1982, pp. 179–210; see also Goodman, Chapter 7, this volume). To the public-sector manager who might have expected guidance from organization theory, this would appear to be bad news; it suggests that one cannot inform one's planning of organizational structure and effort by an objectively derived statement of what is to be accomplished, and also that one cannot objectively judge the efficacy of organizational activity because the proper criteria of achievement are too slippery.

If one thought it still possible somehow to get around this apparent limitation of organizational theory, Chapter 5 in this volume effectively dashes one's hopes. Nord's discussion in that chapter makes one realize that the problem is insurmountable because the content of "the organizational goal" from the standpoint of effectiveness theory is not only arbitrary and complex, but logically infinite.

It is not Nord's explicit intention to present an argument on this issue; the argument emerges, rather, by implication and extension from the theme of the chapter. What Nord does is merely to suggest and summarize certain criteria of organizational effectiveness that are rarely considered (e.g., the effect of organizational choices on such outcomes as consumer sovereignty, the efficiency of social resource allocation, warranted and unwarranted organizational failures, the scope and nature of the role of government in the economy, the vitality and independence of the worker, the democratic nature of political institutions, the ability of the citizen to be an effective consumer, the availability of employment for various types of people, stress and health in the society, and the quality of family life). The list is a most stimulating one for two reasons. Primarily, it suggests that fascinating information may be obtained from research on the concrete connections between organizational choice on one hand, and conditions in this list on the other. Secondarily, and more to the point here, the list is a peremptory reminder that the content of the organizational goal is even more vast than has been thought; the kind of concerns emphasized by Nord have typically not been included in it at all, but they should be.

It may well be that these criteria should mean little to the individual public-sector manager. For one reason, it is unlikely that the individual manager through his or her own organizational choices can have anything but a negligible impact on most of these conditions. Nord is correct, in other words, to think of the criteria he emphasizes as being especially appropriate when one considers a *population* of organizations rather than an individual organization or unit. Many of these issues may indeed be of critical relevance for public-sector managers, but more in their role as advisers to chief executives and legislators, shapers of general social policy, and caretakers of the public interest, than as managers of their own shops. Nevertheless, and this is the crux of the theoretical implication, these impacts are indeed impacts. If the organization is conscious of its impact on such conditions and steers itself to some extent by a concern for them, the status of each condition functions as a *constraint* on mainline organizational activity. Pollution and other environmental impacts are constraints of this nature that already occupy much of the attention of managers in both the public and private sectors. Nord's list could conceivably become similarly salient. If, on the other hand, the organization is not yet particularly conscious of the same impacts, or if it is aware of them but does not incorporate them as criteria in its decision making, they are generally called *side-effects*.

It is, perhaps, most of all through the study of public program evaluation that one develops a heightened sensitivity to the theoretical role of constraints and side-effects. From the perspective of the evaluation of program or policy effectiveness, these kinds of impact are inescapably part of "the organizational goal." Consider the possibility of a negative income tax, for example. Most would agree that the central goal-set of that policy would have to do with the quality of life of the poor—that sort of impact is the true *raison d'être* of the policy. Nevertheless, there have been several experiments to evaluate the policy (e.g., Burtless & Hausman, 1978; Rees, 1974; Tuma & Robins, 1980), and all have essentially ignored this obviously crucial goal, perhaps taking an impact for granted, to concentrate nearly exclusive attention on a side-effect or constraint—the impact of a negative income tax on work incentives.

Many similar examples could be cited. What bothers the evaluator about this is not the inclusion of specific side-effects in a research project but rather the problem of *finding* the side-effects to include. They are potentially infinite, and there is always the danger—and no small or merely academic danger, either—that the worth of an evaluation will be seriously undermined by its failure to consider impacts that suddenly emerge as important (e.g., the potential impact of school integration, not on educational opportunity, as in the original Coleman report—Coleman, Campbell, Hobson, McPartland, Mood, Weinfeld, &

York, 1966—but on the phenomenon of "white flight" from central cities to suburbs—Coleman, 1975).

There can be no question that impacts in the nature of constraints and side-effects are part of organizational effectiveness because a program simply cannot be considered "effective" in any inclusive sense if it is having ruinous, even though unintended, consequences. The infinity problem therefore is bothersome to the evaluator, the manager, and the theoretician alike. The first of these, the evaluator, has just been treated. For the last, the theoretician, the problem forecloses absolutely any hope of constructing a logically sound, objectively determined criterion for determining organizational effectiveness. And for the manager, it means that not only must one be concerned about impacts desired and urged by a great variety of already-interested parties, but also about those totally obscure impacts that may, if they are found to come about, become the concern of parties not yet heard from in any form.

THE NECESSITY OF ARBITRARY CIRCUMSCRIPTION

What, then, is the public-sector manager to do? How is he or she to accomplish so much that is so vague and potentially so inconsistent? Some would say that the manager in the private sector can fall back on a summary notion such as "profit." That is, as long as the company is turning a healthy profit, it must be meeting all relevant goals. This is a false view; the issue is not resolved nearly so simply (see Chapter 7, this volume). But even if it were true, or to the extent that it might help to have such summary concepts, they are not available either for theoretical or practical use in the public arena. One cannot suggest that effectiveness is proven by continued appropriations or mere survival; those outcomes depend too much on political inertia. Moreover, one wishes to discriminate *degrees* of effectiveness among those agencies or programs that have equally survived.

Several analyses have now converged on a response to this problem at the theoretical level: Organizational effectiveness must be determined only in terms of selected goals or criteria, and not in terms of the whole idea of "the organizational goal" (Kahn, 1977, pp. 237–238; Mohr, 1982; see also Goodman, Chapter 7, this volume). Viewing this from the manager's perspective, one would say in the terms of Seashore's analysis (Chapter 3, this volume) that there are a variety of "goals for" the organization held by different organizational constituencies, and that the public-sector manager must pick and choose among them in allocating effort. Thus, the literature on organizational effectiveness indicates that the appraisal function is best seen as a two-step and not a one-step procedure. It consists not only in determining how well the public-sector manager does, but in appraising first what he or she has chosen to do well on. This then is a proper and even a necessary form of critique of the public manager, from the lower levels to the highest. One must recognize first, as specifically as one can, the great range of impacts that the program might reasonably have selected to try to attain. One would then try to determine (not always an easy task) which of these the program's management has sought to pursue, and *critique that choice* from the perspective of one's own or any interesting valuational perspective. Lastly, and this aspect can be almost disconnected from the former one, one would try to determine by the normal methods of program evaluation what impact the program has had, not necessarily on management's goals alone, or even at all, but on any in the infinite set of outcomes that are of interest and value to investigate.

It follows, of course, that not everyone who appraises the effectiveness of an organization or who pays for a program evaluation will reach the same or even a comparable conclusion. Effective to some may be ineffective to others, not so much because of possible differences in measurement or data analysis at the scientific evaluation stage, but because of differences in judgment at the first stage—judgment regarding the most important objectives, constraints, and side-effects to be concerned about. This is as it should be in the public sector, for the arbiter of such differences is most properly the political process, not organizational theory or program evaluation. Theory establishes the necessity of the two-stage nature of the appraisal function. The political process decides whether the organization is emphasizing the right outcomes, perhaps on the basis of creative data collection by evaluators or other social researchers. Lastly, standard evaluation research and statistical decision criteria demonstrate the organization's impact on certain selected conditions, leaving others to more impressionistic analysis.

Another lesson from program evaluation, however, is that the public-sector manager's choice of goals and constraints is not so arbitrary as an analysis conducted purely on the basis of effectiveness theory might make it seem—and this is quite apart from the caveat that the manager's hand might be forced by the power balance of participants. A review of experience suggests that, for no analytic reason that has yet been successfully defended but rather simply for common practical reasons, one sort of goal stands out among all the rest. Not always, to be sure, but certainly quite often there is a major effectiveness criterion. It is the particular kind and set of outcomes that are commonly thought of as "the" program goal, or the primary mission—the one that in ordinary language is often used to refer to or title the program.

Goal theory and effectiveness theory long ago established that primary missions have no more claim on inclusion in the goal concept than do other outcomes of concern. It has been shown that many public organizations are indeed not guided by their primary missions (see Etzioni, 1960). But logical and theoretical claims are one thing and practical demands are another. In practice, there is a tendency in the effectiveness-appraisal function to consider performance on such measures quite seriously: A malaria eradication program is supposed to control malaria, a Head Start program should give the children a head start, a Scared Straight program is expected to result in reduced criminal recidivism, a stroke rehabilitation program should enable people to reclaim the use of the limbs, a highway department should be able to show a well-placed and good quality road system, the local CETA office is expected to increase employment among the poor, and so forth. It is true that in many cases and for a variety of reasons this rule does not apply. It is difficult, for example, to pick out the basic aim of Federal housing policy (Downs, 1974) or the National Park system. The official mission is sometimes vague, or characterized by multiple salient functions that are not authoritatively ordered in importance and are perhaps not even consistent with one another. In cases other than these, however, the rule does tend to apply. If one peruses the public-program evaluation literature, for example, one finds very few instances in which a primary mission, constraint, or side-effect does not have a major part in the evaluation performed (e.g., see the collection of reports in the volumes of the *Evaluation Studies Review Annual* issued by Sage Publications).

In short, if a close look at program effectiveness is taken in the public sector, it is highly likely to be directed in large part toward a primary mission or similar major concern, and not exclusively toward minor ones. It therefore behooves the manager to have a care for his or her record on these concerns. Neglect of the record can mean vulnerability to budget cuts, media criticism, and so forth. A demonstrably good record with respect to the primary mission, on the other hand, is a fortress of strength against attacks oriented around any of a host of alternative concerns, despite the fact that they may properly be considered coequal components of the goal by organization theorists. In practice, circumscription of the goal is mandatory, and circumscribing around the primary mission is known to be generally advisable.

The Failure of Arbitrary Circumscription to Rescue Theory

The theoreticians have recognized the futility of attempting to conceptualize "the organizational goal" as a basis for the assessment of effectiveness. They properly emphasize that effectiveness can only be measured against a standard of certain particular goals or criteria, and that the choice of criteria is a matter of interest and values, not theoretical necessity (Mohr, 1982; Scott, 1977; see also Nord, Chapter 5, and Goodman, Chapter 7, this volume). It is too optimistic a leap, however, to conclude that researchers should seek theories of effectiveness with respect to particular, circumscribed outcomes and that such theories are attainable (Goodman, Chapter 7, this volume). They are not attainable—not, at least, in the strong sense of the term *theory* as generally used in science. Thus, arbitrarily circumscribing the goal is a solution of sorts for managers and evaluators, but not for theorists.

In order to elaborate on this important and controversial issue, let us note that there are two basic approaches to theories of program effectiveness with respect to particular, circumscribed objectives—a goal-specific approach and a goal-free approach. The theoretical content of the former would apply only to means toward the attainment of explicitly named objectives, such as in the program of Scott, Forrest, and Brown (1976) to understand variance in the effectiveness of surgical units in hospitals on a standard of patient mortality. The goal-free approach names no objectives; it takes on the imposing task of specifying a single mechanism for achieving effectiveness no matter what the objectives.

The Goal-Specific Approach

As Hannan and Freeman argue (1977), the goal-specific approach actually deals with design (as in engineering) rather than theory (as in physics): "The pure scientist seeks to formulate abstract and timeless theories that explain properties of nature. The engineer seeks to use science to modify nature. . . . Our point here is there is ample practical experience implying that both science and engineering benefit when the division of labor is explicit and different standards are used to evaluate the two kinds of work [p. 108]." This distinction need not be a deterrent from the perspective of the manager, because a reliable *design* to ensure the effectiveness of a given surgical unit, for example, is precisely what the manager of such a unit seeks to discover. In the theorist's perspective, however, designs do not begin to satisfy the requirements; they are poor specimens of scientific theories or laws under common definitions of those terms. They tend to lack necessity, universality, and durability, and the hope of goal-specific theories of effectiveness as suggested by Goodman is dimmed by these shortcomings. Regarding necessity, one might exterminate yellow fever, for example, by a design emphasizing the draining of swamps, and one might achieve the same end by spraying with DDT. Neither can be considered a theory of effectiveness, let alone *the* theory, but rather only one of many possible techniques—in principle one of infinitely many—that will achieve the same end. Regarding universality, one encounters the vast complexity represented by the possible contexts in which a design must be applied. No design is likely to work in all of them, or even nearly all. Certainly, no design will do equally well in all of them. No matter how much data might be collected on the correlates of patient mortality in surgical units, for example, and no matter how the whole might be modeled mathematically, the explanation is highly likely to be inadequate when applied to some present or future hospitals. Furthermore, the conditions under which such designs would and would not apply, or would apply better or worse, are unlikely to be specifiable with accuracy. Regarding durability, a design to accomplish a specific recurring task can be perfectly adequate for the moment. It can hardly be considered a theory of effectiveness, however, because one knows that an augmentation of the design that will accomplish the same end *more* effectively is always possible and is often imminent. It is philosophically weak to consider something a theory that, in principle, is permanently temporary. In short, one might arbitrarily define the term *theory* so as to include goal-specific designs, but these are quite sadly lacking in the qualifications generally considered to be desirable from the scientific standpoint.

Consider managers in the public sector as executives operating on the basis of their current designs for effectiveness in achieving a circumscribed set of aims. Their mode of procedure over time is to improve their designs when they can on the basis of input from their own experience and from communication with colleagues facing similar challenges. This process has always existed. Unfortunately, goal-specific "theories" of effectiveness cannot help definitively; they are simply different designs, subject to the same process. What can help are potentially constructive insights gained through the systematic approach to the problem area employed by researchers armed with the scientific method—strong program structures and ideas that managers may well find expedient to apply to their own situations in whole or in part. In this valuable role of communicating discoveries based on systematic as opposed to impressionistic or experiential observation, the researcher and author of academic articles is truly functioning more in the capacity of consultant than theorist.

The Goal-Free Approach

The alternative approach to theories of effectiveness is the goal-free approach. The idea is to present a mode of attaining effectiveness (or at least greater effectiveness than would otherwise be the case, *ceteris paribus*) that will work in any organization, no matter what its products. In this case the intractability of the goal concept might be considered *not* to be an obstruction to theories of effectiveness. Specification of the organizational goal would not be needed in order to know how to achieve effectiveness because the answer would be explicitly given a priori and would be always the same. However, escape is not so easy because a goal or other standard would still unavoidably be needed for the *testing* function; one must know what is to be accomplished in order to demonstrate whether the method proposed is effective in accomplishing it. Because an idea such as "the organizational goal" is too indefinite and unwieldy for this purpose, one must again fall back on a circumscribed criterion that is arbitrarily selected. Thus, if a technique or structure is truly a goal-free avenue to effectiveness, it is essentially proposed as a channel to effectiveness on *any specific set* of circumscribed goals that the users of the technique might adopt. If any mechanism actually satisfied this requirement, it would be a powerful instrument indeed.

The most prominent mechanisms offered in the past have been structural. They include the Weberian hypothesis that the bureaucratic form is the most effective for modern (in his day) complex organizations, the "human relations" hypothesis that supportiveness and participation in decision making produce favorable outcomes, and what has been called the "consonance hypothesis," namely, that effectiveness depends on the fit between structure on one side and technology, size, and the environment on the other. These goal-free theories have been found both empirically and analytically to be inadequate. The full analysis is presented elsewhere (Mohr, 1982), but its highlight is certainly the problem of complexity. There are too many organizational contexts that are too radically and subtly different from one another for any one nostrum to be successful in all of them. Clearly, these techniques must have greater or less success depending on context, and that observation is a strong hint that, by extension, they would sometimes have no success at all or even do more harm than good. That is precisely what has been found in research. A categorical, logical demonstration that goal-free theories are invariably inadequate cannot be given, but the nature of the research results on those goal-free remedies that have been offered strongly suggests the extreme unlikelihood that any one technique will work all the time. The uniqueness and complexity of the individual organizational context means that many organizations will undoubtedly be "exceptions" to any structural rule for effectiveness. What has in fact been found is that a large proportion always do seem to be exceptions (Mohr, 1982).

In the present volume, several additional proposals in the goal-free category are suggested—by Seashore, Daft and Weick, Starbuck and Nystrom, and Schneider. Before reviewing them briefly, two caveats must be entered that are equally applicable to all goal-free models suggested. The first is that although one is free to *evaluate* against any goals, one cannot expect attention by organizational actors to structural adaptation, human relations, or some newer theory to result in organizational effectiveness on criteria that just any random interested party may happen to have in mind. The organizational actors may not even know about these criteria. If such goals are therefore not attained, one cannot blame the theory. One can only expect a goal-free theory to work in pursuit of the goals of those organizational members who are implementing the idea. In most cases, this is management; thus, one is usually talking about what management can do to achieve its own goals—adopted as well as self-generated. There is no reason to expect the theory to render the organization effective in the pursuit of other people's goals, such as those of workers or clients, unless they are shared by managers—the theory's implementers. I am not, of course, implying that organizations pursue the goals of management exclusively, but only that no one else's private goals are relevant to a critique of an instrumental mechanism that is being implemented by management alone.

The second caveat is the following: Sometimes in the organizational effectiveness literature, and it has always been so, it is difficult to tell whether a goal-free proposal is a particular *definition* of effectiveness or a means of attaining it. The kinds of offering that are ambiguous on this point tend to be put, not literally but nevertheless essentially, in such terms as "Doing X is critical for effectiveness." Or "This model of effectiveness emphasizes X." Each of these statements can be taken in two ways. Are they definitions or methods? Statements about effectiveness that define the meaning of the term, thus imposing criteria of appraisal on the organization, are of limited value in the struggle for theory. Each one merely constitutes a suggested circumscription of the concept of organizational goal from one academician's perspective: If the organization does not do "X," it is by definition ineffective. It seems more appropriate to consider such proposals as hypotheses about how effectiveness is attained and to examine their validity purely in light of circumscriptions of the goal that are generated by others, such as the managers of the evaluated organization itself.

Seashore's proposal is classically in the category of goal-free theory. The goals themselves, or whatever one would call the criteria of appraisal, may come from any interested party and are conceptualized as that party's "goals for" the organization. The model offered emphasizes a certain triangular equilibrium. It suggests that a proper balance among system concerns, goal concerns, and information-processing concerns will enhance the achievement of whatever criteria are selected. It is beyond the scope of this chapter to comment on the basic substance of the proposal either positively or negatively. Attention must rather be directed toward the question of the implications of this and other goal free theories, *qua* theory, for managers in the public sector. The major point to be made is therefore that the model may undoubtedly be extremely helpful as a guide to some managers in some situations, but probably not to all. That is, just as certain human relations techniques or bureaucratic structures have been shown to fail to get better results in many instances than alternative behaviors and structures, so one must expect that a good triangular balance of attention, concretely defined in advance, will fail at times to produce better results on the output goals of management than "unbalanced" attention.

Weick and Daft emphasize managerial attention to the interpretation system (making it clear that this is not an approach to effectiveness in all organizations, but only those of a certain type and level of complexity). They also, by the bye, provide the rudiments of a design for attaining the *specific* goal of an effective interpretation system. The hypothesis that such a design is a theory of effectiveness is subject to the analysis just offered of goal-specific approaches. The good interpretation system itself as a general, goal-free approach to effectiveness may be seen in the same light as the Seashore model. It would undoubtedly be well for public-sector managers to think about their interpretation systems, to have a care for the adequate and proper functioning of those systems. Nevertheless, on the basis of past research experience, one must expect that, frequently, managers with the better interpretation systems will be no more effective in attaining their own goals, however framed, than those with the poorer interpretation systems will be in attaining theirs, in a different context, whether the various goal-sets concerned be radically different, similar, or identical.

Schneider, in Chapter 2 in this volume, emphasizes recruitment as a goal-free approach. He implicitly defines effectiveness in terms of adapting to a changing environment. The organization that recruits new executives who are very much the same as the old ones will stultify, whereas the organization that recruits executives who are different by being in tune with the changing environment will be effective, or at least more effective. There is a hint of tautology here in the terms "effective" and "in tune" to which we shall return momentarily. For the moment, one must re-emphasize the observation made in connection with the previous authors. It seems highly likely that this sort of attention to recruitment would pay handsome dividends for many organizations, but not all, and perhaps not even nearly all. Once a precise definition is given of what it means to recruit managers who are "different" or who are "in tune with the new environment," it is highly likely that some organizations who do recruit in these terms will be no more effective in achieving their circumscribed goal than others who do not. Not only may managers who are different fail to enchance effectiveness for technical or personal reasons, but the differences themselves can create offsetting problems in terms of erosion of trust and of coordination, virtues that, as Barnard (1938) has stressed, can be heavily dependent on similarity of outlook.

Last, Starbuck and Nystrom point out that organizational effectiveness is generally ambiguously defined (and this would apply even to what we have been calling arbitrarily circumscribed goal-sets) and that it is therefore impossible to rationalize all organizational effort toward goal achievement. These authors do, however, go on the premise that one can tell when an organization has been effective. To get there, they suggest that instead of denying the ambiguity, managers and operations researchers should accept it, live with it, game it, take advantage of its undeniable strengths, and that these goals and subgoals may be accomplished by such techniques as decomposition, optimizing suboptimally, and incremental development or evolution. Again, once these various techniques are nailed down with greater conceptual specificity, so that one can tell whether an organization has or has not implemented them (or to what extent it has), and, once effectiveness is defined, despite the ambiguity of goals, it remains very much an open question whether the one will be powerfully related to the other. The ideas make excellent sense; they comport well with the important new wave of research and advice to managers based on ideas such as loosely coupled systems (Weick, 1976) and goal inconsistency and ambiguity (March, 1978); they must undoubtedly be welcome and helpful in many quarters. Nevertheless, they must also, in all probability, frequently fail. Otherwise, and this is true for all of the goal-free techniques, it is certain that nearly all organizations of the future will be effective ones because nearly all can implement the techniques and would undoubtedly do so, the stakes being so high and the odds ostensibly so good.

It must begin to be clear from this brief review of suggested goal-free theories that vagueness creates a certain problem of exaggerated expectations. In the rather vague terms that are almost always used to introduce such proposals, they tend to appear highly plausible and convincing. When, however, the empirical researcher gets down to specifying conceptually just what is meant by a proper balance, a good interpretation system, an executive who is different, or a suboptimal optimizing, and also specifies what is meant by effectiveness, it begins to be clear that the correlation between the two across many organizations is not going to be as high as one would have hoped. Yet, one might well be left with the nagging feeling that the original idea was a good one, if only it could be properly applied. This scenario surely describes much of the history and fate of human-relations research. How can it not be profitable to treat people well, so as to win their cooperation, good will, and ideas? The rub comes in the need to specify precisely what one means by treating people well, and by profitable or effective, and then to apply such a hypothesis universally. At bottom, it seems that a tautology underlies the goal-free approach to theory, so that the theories are too good to be true simply because they are too true to be good. The tautology says that X will produce greater organizational effectiveness when effectiveness is suffering because of inadequate X. In objective empirical research, the goal-free hypothesis is exploded. It tends to produce unexciting results when suffering and X are independently defined beforehand. Once that is done, it always turns out that some organizations are suffering for other reasons, so that a high X makes little difference, and some are not suffering very much at all, despite poor human-relations practices, the absence of managers who are "different," and so forth. If one were to apply the goal-free remedy only when it was needed, it would get good results, but that by no means assures good correlations in a random population. It is not the equivalent of valid theory.

This same vagueness in the general terms and scope of application of goal-free hypotheses, however, is not nearly so bothersome to the manager as it is to the theorist. The manager can tolerate such vagueness quite well, at least for a time. What he or she does is to think about his or her *own shop* alone in connection with these ideas and remedies. The manager may, in some instances, be uninspired by the ideas because they can do him or her no good, but the ideas might, on the other hand, produce a powerful insight that turns out to be highly constructive in this manager's operational context. In this light, the ideas from earlier chapters just reviewed all have the earmarks of being excellent ones and truly valuable. That should not be surprising because they come from organizations scholars with a great deal of experience and data, who have devoted much energy to the issues they discuss. The ideas have the ring of a certain palpable, if nonuniversal, soundness. One further conclusion may, perhaps, therefore be drawn. It is that further development of the ideas by students of organizational behavior might most profitably be oriented around the aim of being of assistance to managers in certain types of situations rather than the aim of developing theory. I am not arguing for a program of case-oriented, problem-oriented research, but rather in favor of a systematic search for limited generalizations together with guides, even though not infallible ones, to the conditions under which those generalizations are applicable. Such an orientation would appear to be not only possible but promising. Further study to perfect goal-free theories of effectiveness, however, is unlikely to bear fruit.

RETAINING AMBIGUITY AND
MITIGATING CROSS-PURPOSES

It has been shown elsewhere (Mohr, 1982) that the older goal-free theories of organizational effectiveness—Taylorism, the principles of management, bureaucratic theory, human-relations theory, and structural-consonance theory—would operate largely through a common intervening mechanism. That mechanism is mitigation of the extent to which organizational effort is directed at cross-purposes, or divergent purposes. Most of these ideas are quite different from one another in content, but they share a common orientation toward achieving effectiveness and efficiency through the rationalization of organizational activity. Organizations in all of these views need to be harmonious, predictable, and coordinated. Seashore's model in Chapter 3 continues in this tradition with its emphasis on systems theory and attaining a balance between three different groups of salient organizational objectives.

The chapter by Starbuck and Nystrom, however, juxtaposes to this tradition a newer perspective. In this perspective, not only is it not possible to mitigate divergent purposes, it is not even desirable. The organizational goal-set is inherently inconsistent and ambiguous and will always be so. Furthermore, there are many solid advantages to keeping it so in terms of conflict reduction, creativity, flexibility, and other desiderata (see also March, 1978). Schneider makes a similar kind of point in Chapter 2 when he stresses the need for new executives whose orientations are different from and not easily harmonized with those of the older executives.

This newer approach to organizational effectiveness is radically different in emphasis from the older one and may even be seen as logically contradictory. It would seem that the manager would have to choose either to try to clarify goals and bring them into harmony or seek to profit skillfully from their perpetual ambiguity and mutual inconsistency. It is difficult to believe, however, that this is a stark dilemma that truly and commonly exists. It must rather be true, on one hand, that goals cannot and should not be thoroughly harmonized nor effort thoroughly rationalized. But on the other hand, it is unlikely that inconsistency and ambiguity can be allowed to run wild in organizations without producing serious inefficiency and debility.

To the manager in the public sector, and the private sector is probably no different, the true need is to walk a tightrope successfully between these two orientations without overemphasizing either one. Although the orientation emphasized by Starbuck and Nystrom is relatively new, it is probable that managers· have in some sense been practicing it since the genesis of organizations. Until recently, however, only the older view was tolerated or even contemplated by academics, with a few iconoclastic exceptions from such scholars as Mary Parker Follett (Metcalf & Urwick, 1941). In other words, the managers have in the past gotten very little help from the effectiveness theorists in walking this particular tightrope. Now, the new view is emphasized as though it would supplant the old altogether, or at least with little attention to how the two might peaceably co-exist. This is a bit unrealistic and not optimally constructive. The theorist finds it strongly advantageous to make *ceteris paribus* assumptions and explore cause and effect in isolated systems, but the manager does not operate in a *ceteris paribus* world. The apparent need for coordination arises in one organizational locus just as the apparent desirability of divergent purposes surfaces in a neighboring one, or perhaps both arise at the same time and in the same place.

What is needed is precisely the same kind of thought and research that has always been needed in effectiveness theory (Simon, 1976, pp. 20–36). The question is not what will make organizations effective, for that question is unanswerable with any substantial degree of generality. Rather, it is one of how to learn approximately *when* an apparently valuable approach to effectiveness will work. In this new antinomy between the mitigation of cross-purposes and the tolerance of ambiguity and inconsistency, it will be most helpful to the practitioner when researchers produce some insights into the questions of when and why each is efficacious. This is relatively uncharted research territory at the moment. For the present, managers must muddle through, as they always have, on the basis of their own private and unarticulated effectiveness theories of the proper balance between the rational and the nonrational in organizational behavior.

REFERENCES

Barnard, C. I. *The functions of the executive.* Cambridge: Harvard University Press, 1938.

Burtless, G., & Hausman, J. A. The effect of taxation on labor supply: Evaluating the gary negative income tax experiment. *Journal of Political Economy,* 1978, 86(6), 1103–1130.

Coleman, J. S. Recent trends in school integration. *Educational Researcher,* 1975, 4(7), 3–12.

Coleman, J. S., Campbell, E. Q., Hobson, C. J., McPartland, J., Mood, A. M., Weinfield, F. D., & York, R. L. *Equality of education opportunity.* Washington, D.C., U.S. Department of Health, Education and Welfare, Office of Education, 1966.

Downs, A. The successes and failures of federal housing policy. *The Public Interest,* 1974, 34, 124–145.

Etzioni, A. Two approaches to organizational analysis: A critique and a suggestion. *Administrative Science Quarterly,* 1960, 5, 257–278.

Hannan, M. T., & Freeman, J. Obstacles to comparative studies. In P. S. Goodman & J. M. Pennings (Eds.), *New perspectives on organizational effectiveness.* San Francisco: Jossey-Bass, 1977.

Kahn, R. L. Organizational effectiveness: An overview. In P. S. Goodman & J. M. Pennings (Eds.), *New perspectives on organizational effectiveness.* San Francisco: Jossey-Bass, 1977.

March, J. G. Bounded rationality, ambiguity, and the engineering of choice. *Bell Journal of Economics,* 1978, 9(2), 587–608.

Metcalf, H. C., & Urwick, L. (Eds.), *Dynamic administration: The collected papers of Mary Parker Follett.* London: Management Publications Trust, 1941.

Mohr, L. B. *Explaining organizational behavior: The limits and possibilities of theory and research.* San Francisco: Jossey-Bass, 1982.

Rees, A. An overview of the labor-supply results. *Journal of Human Resources,* 1974, 9(4), 446–459.

Scott, W. R. Effectiveness of organizational effectiveness studies. In P. S. Goodman & J. M. Pennings (Eds.), *New perspectives on organizational effectiveness.* San Francisco: Jossey-Bass, 1977.

Scott, W. R., Forrest, W. H., Jr., & Brown, R. W., Jr. Hospital structure and post-operative mortality and morbidity. In S. M. Shortell & M. Brown (Eds.), *Organizational research in hospitals.* Chicago: Inquiry Book, Blue Cross Association, 1976.

Simon, H. A. *Administrative behavior* (3rd ed.). New York: The Free Press, 1976. (Originally published, 1947.)

Tuma, N. B., & Robins, P. K. A dynamic model of employment behavior: An application to the Seattle and Denver income maintenance experiments. *Econometrica,* 1980, 48(4), 1031–1052.

Weick, K. E. Educational organizations as loosely coupled systems. *Administrative Science Quarterly,* 1976, 21(1), 1–19.

CAROL T. SCHREIBER

Organizational Effectiveness:
Implications for the Practice of Management

Among the general managers I talk with, the book most frequently mentioned is Peter Drucker's *Managing in Turbulent Times* (1980). In that work, Drucker issues a warning to contemporary management based on his observations of current and impending change in the international political, social, demographic, economic, and technological environment.

Drucker spells out his warning and a prescription for survival in today's dramatically changing times. He points to "the need for the decision-maker in the individual enterprise to face up to reality and to resist the temptation of what "everybody knows," the temptation of the certainties of yesterday, which are about to become the deleterious superstitions of tomorrow [p. 5]."

Drucker identifies a critical capacity for the contemporary practice of management as the ability to move beyond conventional wisdom to an accurate perception and assessment of the changing environment. Thus, for Drucker, management's ability to read and address changing realities is a critical determinant of an organization's effectiveness.

Not coincidentally, I have found similar themes in the six chapters on organizational effectiveness addressed in my review. The commonalities between Drucker, these academic writings, and current practitioner interest will be explored and exploited as a feature of my task for this volume: that of translating academic discussions into implications for the practice of management. With an eye to their practical implications then, the themes I have

ORGANIZATIONAL EFFECTIVENESS
A Comparison of Multiple Models

chosen to extrapolate from this collection of papers are those that emphasize an organization's need to obtain and use information about its environment, procedures to optimize that capacity, and, in this light, the fundamental role of "question raising" as an approach to obtaining realistic information about an organization's internal and external environment.

Predictably perhaps, because of the nature of the work we do and our assignment for this volume, my academic colleagues have a different emphasis than I. Each of the previous authors has spent time developing the conceptual argument for his piece, carefully honing supporting logic from the traditions of his discipline, and constructing his contribution to current thinking about organizational effectiveness. Thus, each of the first chapters is based on certain assumptions arising from a particular disciplinary perspective. That is, Seashore's model is grounded in sociology and general systems theory; Weick's and Daft's in cognitive psychology; Schneider's in industrial–organizational psychology; Starbuck's and Nystrom's in operations research; Goodman's in a modeling (economic) framework; and Nord's in political–economic theory. Each of these disciplinary perspectives offers a different vision of an organization—makes different assumptions about how to look at organizations, about what is worth looking at in organizations. The disciplinary differences between the authors are clear in their orientations, their emphases, and their idioms. Less apparent, and far more interesting to me, are the common themes woven through these chapters. Despite the different perspectives, different language, and different theoretical underpinnings, the areas of shared interest have profound implications for the practice of management in today's world.

Though intrigued with the areas of shared interest in these chapters, I am also troubled by a generic deficiency in the collection, a deficiency created by single-minded attention to rational processes. On the whole, these chapters neglect the affective facets of organizational and personal life. By ignoring whole classes of phenomena ranging from organizational politics and intergroup conflict to personal anxiety and concerns with self-esteem, the authors omit consideration of important determinants of organizational effectiveness. In the current discussion, for example, affective processes often offer potent resistance to the effective implementation of the rational systems described and recommended by the authors.

To do justice to the authors' shared arguments and my own areas of agreement and disagreement, I shall begin this discussion with a review of each author's contribution to the question-raising theme. With these reviews, I shall add examples from practice to illustrate the authors' points. Following the individual reviews, I shall accumulate the pieces of shared themes and point out major gaps in the conceptual framework proposed by the cumulative work. Then, I shall suggest ways in which organizations can use some of the authors' suggestions to optimize their effectiveness, considering as well some practical, often nonobservable, impediments to implementation.

FIRST RESPONSES: FROM NORD TO SCHNEIDER

As Nord himself has commented, at first glance there appears little immediate reason for today's practicing manager to shift from a microquality perspective to Nord's macroquality approach. After all, it is hard enough to keep intraorganizational goals in mind while managing. It would be well-nigh impossible to sustain a perspective encompassing effectiveness criteria for multiple constituencies. Just pursuing the economic mission of an organization is full-time work. Still, Nord argued that contemporary management will be forced by adversaries and circumstances to question assumptions about the single-minded pursuit of economic goals in a competitive economy.

Nord proposes that critical theory supports the first step toward organizational flexibility—a questioning of assumptions, belief systems, and practices on which an organization bases its operation. Once management can adopt a critical posture toward an organization's shared assumptions and definitions, that management has enhanced potential comprehension of the contemporary environment, and, in turn, enhanced the organization's capacity for a flexible response.

Critical theory takes no assumption as ineluctable and considers beliefs and practices as features of a historical, social, and political context, relevant to a particular time and place, perhaps less useful in another time and place. For example, all organizations have developed assumptions, traditions, and practices at different times in their histories. These traditions often reach the contemporary manager as gospel. Positions and practices are often viewed as the glue that has kept an organization together. They are seen as central to continued smooth operation, rather than accommodation to time-limited political exigencies. Practices and assumptions that have gained such status handicap us in a number of ways. First, by not questioning their contemporary applicability, we direct our attention away from the current environment. Second, if an assumption is not up for question, then we do not focus on it and its utility, and we continue to believe in its relevance. In not questioning, we divert attention from the assumption, from the current environment, and from the *match* between the assumption and from the current environment.

As a specific example, many contemporary U.S. employment policies were based on assumptions about workforce demographic composition, well founded until the late 1970s. Prior to that time, it was realistic to assume that the modal employee in the U.S. workforce was a married, white male, functioning as the sole supporter for his nonworking wife and 2.1 children. Yet, as of 1977, Department of Labor statistics showed that only *14%* of the U.S. domestic labor force participants represented this type of employee; 63% were from multi-earner domestic situations. Acknowledging this change in workforce composition means re-examining assumptions for practices such as benefits.

Does today's male or female member of a multi-earner family unit still need or value two separate company-supported medical insurance policies? How realistic is it to assume that today's employees' insurance and pension needs are the same as they were in the 1950s and 1960s. If employees no longer value what the organization views as appropriate, motivating, or equitable, then the question of organizational effectiveness is salient here. How does a different assessment of benefits' value affect employee motivation to stay with a company? When that employee's scarce skills are in demand, and the organization has a high stake in attracting and retaining that employee, the question pertains to organizational effectiveness. Such is the case with electronics engineers in the increasingly competitive employment of high technology companies.

Questioning assumptions about the interests of a changing work force does not mean in itself that assumptions or corresponding practices will change. It does mean, though, reconsideration of policies intended to accomplish a particular organizational objective, with some potential consequences for change. As another example, many large U.S. companies are now questioning the assumption that geographic mobility is necessary for the development of corporate general managers. Today, ease of geographic mobility is constrained by the cost of moving, interest rates on new homes, by dual-career considerations, and by the correlated reluctance of managers to move as frequently as had their predecessors.

Such resistance to previously accepted practices of large organizational life contributes to re-examination of those practices. Is it essential to skill development that managers make frequent geographic moves? Are there alternative approaches to the provision of developmental experience for general managers? How do alternatives compare to the traditional approaches? At what times can alternative developmental experiences be substituted for geographic mobility in a manager's career? These questions can be addressed empirically, once they are raised.

The geographic mobility assumption has been a basis for "the way we do things"—supporting norms and expectations for general management development, until lack of fit with contemporary circumstances forced review of the assumption and its supporting policies and practices. From this review emerge more realistic employment practices and new definitions of the way we do things.

Another of Nord's central contentions is *his* question of the assumption that organizational effectiveness can be defined solely in terms of what is effective for a particular focal organization. Under certain conditions this perspective can assume central importance to the practice of management, though perhaps not to the individual manager. These conditions occur, as Pfeffer and Salancik (1978) have noted, when one organization slips in its capacity to provide resources necessary to another. If no other organizations in a population can produce the necessary resources, then the dependent organization may assume new responsibilities to fill its own needs. Thus, there may come a time when current exigencies force organizations to take on functions never previously considered. For example, responsibility for basic education has not been undertaken by private industry at any time in U.S. history. Yet, a current shift in the capabilities of public education, resulting in declining literacy skills, could readily pressure the private sector to assume some basic educational responsibilities to ensure the availability of a minimally-skilled entry-level labor force.

To anticipate a new set of educational demands on industry means that organizational antennae are directed toward the collective behavior of a population or organizations (e.g., traditional education institutions); that this population is seen as changeable and changing; that indicators of change are noted; and that moves are made to discern possible outcomes from early subtle indicators. From this anticipation, actions can be undertaken to modify the direction of a trend, or to prepare an organization for an inevitable outcome over which it has no control. In this education example, that preparation could lead to a number of different kinds of actions including efforts to "beef up" public education or the development of internal literacy-skill training programs for entry-level employees.

WEICK AND DAFT

From a conceptual orientation different from Nord's, Weick and Daft also highlight the value of raising questions. In their explication of interpretation systems, the process of question raising is directly linked with clear vision and organizational effectiveness. Weick and Daft refine the concept of interpretation and the process of question-raising systems, enabling us to assess such systems against their criteria. They suggest that the closer an interpretation system comes to their criteria, the more effective it is. The more effective (realistic) is an interpretation system, the more effective the organization—or the more available is the organization for effectiveness.

For these authors, question raising is a central feature of organizational effectiveness. From their perspective, one task of an organization is making sense of the swarm of apparently random events that compose that organization's environment. Thus, interpretation systems are processes by which organizations unrandomize an array of random environmental events to make sense, leading thus to more sensible actions. Basic approaches to sense-making involve test-making or test-avoiding behavior, both of which provide environmental information.

The test-making approach is more characteristic of younger, new organizations (or individuals), who break through traditional presumptions about environmental interpretation, and are thus able to bring vision different from the ordinary, to use this extraordinary vision to acquire and interpret data differently from others. Test avoiders, on the other hand, interpret via perceived rules and traditional presumptions, and acquire and transmit interpretations consistent with those typically accepted by the organization. These interpretations are more familiar, though perhaps less currently realistic, than those of the test makers. Here, the test-avoiding posture of an older organization (and long-term organizational members) could present an impediment to realistic interpretation. Clearly, the authors value the less constrained, more active posture and vision of the test maker, and highlight its interpretative capacities.

The test-avoiding posture has important and problematic sequellae for an organization. Here, assumptions are made about limitations to action, assumptions that themselves prevent the action necessary to test hypotheses derived from that assumption. Without the test, the organization receives no data about the environment, and is left only with historical interpretations, those which contain the assumptions of limitation. Based on these assumptions of limitation, the organization limits options for action, creating a limited array of behavioral choices and, ultimately, crippling action. Such a posture leads to what Weick has called "stunted enactments," actions limited by the actor's perceptions of environmental constraints, which probably do not exist. Such actions represent dwarfed or underdeveloped versions of the actions that *could* take place were a test-making posture adopted. The test-avoiding system is crippled in two ways: first, by the limited array of action alternatives available due to perceived constraints in the environment. Second, those options that *are* available to the test avoiders are based on incomplete, perhaps misleading, interpretations of the organization's environment. When actions are taken based on these interpretations, they could be misinformed and off-target.

This contention leads to questions about changing the test-avoiding organization. Is it possible to transplant the test-making capacity into an older organization? As in medicine, if aged, defective organs can be replaced by younger, more effective versions, can we replace the sensors of an older organization with more alert, younger sensors? Assuming that such sensor transplants would be valuable to an organization, how can we ensure that new organs are not rejected by the host organization, which has some stake in homeostasis, some stake in the continuation of its own historical perceptions? Can the new sensors themselves propel the organization toward the enactment style valued by the authors? Must we introduce additional resources to ensure that the introduction of new sensors does move an organization from the more passive test-avoiding posture to a more active posture? What remains unclear for practice are possibilities for revitalizing an older organization's interpretation systems. From these authors' vantage points, this effort is necessary for organizational survival in today's unpredictable and unfamiliar environment. How to implement such a revitalization is the practical question, a question to be considered later in the discussion.

To review then, Weick and Daft have concurred with Nord about the necessity of questioning traditional assumptions, especially assumptions about what is possible and not possible in an organization's current environment. Both critical theory and the emphasis on interpretation systems appreciate the historical, time-bound rootedness of organizations' assumptions about the internal and external environment. Both theories would emphasize the active posture of question and experimentation.

Among the other authors, two have emphasized similar themes to these; others have chosen different emphases. Starbuck and Nystrom have analyzed the effectiveness question via the discipline of operations research, reaching observations similar to those of the first three authors. Schneider emphasizes the same theme, with much attention to the practical organizational implications. Goodman and Seashore, though referring to question raising, have emphasized different themes not to be considered here.

STARBUCK AND NYSTROM

Starbuck and Nystrom delineate their argument within an operations research paradigm, communicating in that idiom. From my perspective, their observations and recommendations are quite similar to those of Nord, Weick and Daft, and Schneider and Drucker, as well. Essentially, Starbuck and Nystrom warn against a deductive approach, against the reliance on prior belief as a source of information. They suggest that organizational policies and structures be viewed and handled as sequences of experiments. We are warned not to define situations before entering them; to use techniques within the organization's decision-making process that permit dissent; to support tolerance of ambiguity, discussion, risk-taking, and experimentation; and to question whether espoused constraints are real. In addition, they recommend that sequences of experiments be planned and that organizations move forward via a planned series of experimental steps. These authors concur with Weick and Daft in their emphasis on the importance of improved knowledge, and the appreciation of information acquired via actions, even actions that are suboptimally effective (failures?). They suggest that the results of all actions are sources of enriched information, and enriched information contributes to an organization's effectiveness. They do emphasize, as did the others, that organizational effectiveness is more a developmental process than a static condition to be achieved.

GOODMAN

Goodman, who has frequently considered the question of organizational effectiveness, takes on a challenge different from the others. He focuses on the task of formulating a researchable approach to the topic of organizational effectiveness. In this respect, he moves from the more generic assertions of his colleagues to the specification of measurable, observable variable relationships that can be empirically documented. In deriving his implications for the practice of management, Goodman emphasizes the need to measure effectiveness by linking outcomes with variables over which a manager has some measure of control. According to Goodman, it does not make sense to measure managerial effectiveness in a situation where the manager has no control over the variables with most impact on the outcome. Yet, it seems to me that organizational effectiveness may be inextricably linked with those such variables.

Perhaps we should find ways to measure managerial effectiveness in terms of the manager's ability to gain *some* control over the uncontrollables. To this point, in order to know which variables are within a management's control, we cannot rely on traditional assumptions about constraints on control, but instead need to raise questions about which features of the environment are actually beyond control. Weick and Daft would have the practicing manager undertake an experiment to text the assumption of presumed constraints or limitations. By testing these assumptions, those environmental features presumed to be beyond control might be found to be more amenable to influence than anticipated. From my perspective, Goodman's linkage of environmental variables and outcomes must take into account the view that even current definitions of what is controllable or uncontrollable cannot be taken for granted. Though this suggestion might obscure Goodman's prospects for clearer empirical work, the perspective becomes necessary for practice, and for realistic research as well.

SEASHORE

Seashore also approaches the issue of effectiveness from an angle different from the others, although he does touch on the themes emphasized thus far. He considers the varieties of organizational constituencies—both internal and external. In addition, he proposes that organizations need to monitor effectiveness in relation to multiple constituencies, and need to keep in touch with various constituencies to assess effectiveness regularly. Seashore recommends a data-oriented monitoring mechanism for effective tracking, again, a rational system for obtaining and processing information about a salient piece of the organization's environment. Seashore shares the others' concern with question of traditional assumptions about constituencies, as he clearly recommends that new environmental information be monitored on a regular basis. In this respect, he too moves from reliance on traditional assumptions about constituencies to the questioning posture emphasized through the other chapters. Among the three perspectives on organizational effectiveness he cites, he suggests that the capacity for obtaining and using diverse informational resources enhances an organization's effectiveness in regard to problem solving.

SCHNEIDER

With his emphasis on the question of traditional assumption, Schneider joins others in selecting this key characteristic for an effective organization. He asserts that a major challenge for any organization is the comprehension of present and future realities. Yet, as he points out, organizations seem to attend to and use those processes that worked in past realities.

In this respect, organizations select members who are similar to those already there, and in this way, act to reproduce those who have been running the system, the right-types. Right-types reflect a model of what worked well in the past, but may not exemplify the skills demanded by the changing course of an enterprise in a changing world. Here then, the right-types end up being the wrong-types to ensure organizational flexibility, vitality, and perhaps survival, in a changing world. The author argues that organizations need people with comprehension competencies, the capacity to make sense out of external realities, to move beyond a conventional, internally focused orientation to acquire information and understanding critical to the organization's function. Ideally, Schneider recommends that this comprehension competency be included in the skill repertoire of the general manager. Without an ideal situation, though, Schneider proposes that organizations begin to attract, select, and retain non-right-types who will question conventional wisdom, monitor and sense the environment, and keep in touch with current demands and future probabilities.

SIX AUTHORS: COMMON THEMES

In reviewing these six authors, I have emphasized themes that cluster around the recommendation to raise questions. Though each author brings other perspectives to bear on this theme, and does introduce additional contributions to thinking about organizational effectiveness, the emphasis on question raising is apparent. Each author suggests the active question of historical assumption, enhanced receptivity to contemporary environmental data, the capacity for informed experimentation, and the use of data from that experimentation to inform and reform assumptions about an organization's internal and external environments.

AFFECTIVE CONSIDERATIONS

Despite their collective commitment to the question-raising posture and their thoughtful considerations of the value of that posture, this group generally ignores those features of organizational life that impede, constrain, or inhibit the effective implementation of question raising. Here, my criticism of this group of authors is of practice and perspective as well. In my view, the collective limitation of these chapters is their failure to take into account the effects of the affective side of personal and organizational life on procedures they recommend to enhance organizational effectiveness.

Often, the effectiveness of individuals, groups, and organizations is determined by unarticulated, perhaps unconscious, unexamined processes which pervade and invade our thinking with remarkable subtlety, and which are visible neither to other actors nor observers. Examples of these processes range from such diverse phenomena as organizational politics, the effect of organizational conflict on the sharing of information, and the individual need for stability and the protection of self-esteem.

Political Processes

Any questioning–monitoring system is affected by the formal and informal distribution of power in an organization; by the politics of organizational vision, decisions, and practices; and by alignments and coalitions. These phenomena affect what kinds of questions *can* be raised and heard in organizations, who can raise them, and how the information generated can make a contribution to organizational effectiveness. Withholding or sharing information represents a major source of political leverage in organizations. Similarly, power struggles can determine who asks what questions to whom and who provides what information to whom. In these ways, information control can be a power strategy. When information control is or becomes a power strategy, the kind and quality of information available for decision making must be affected. Clearly, both the provision and use of information can be influenced by political relationships. Additionally, the most adept intelligence-gathering units can be rendered less effective by the political context in which they operate.

Psychological Processes

Another affective impediment to the efficacy of the recommended question-raising posture lies in the potency of individual emotional "needs." One such need especially pertinent to this discussion seems to be a pervasive, positive attachment to the familiar, to tradition. Though organizational scholars have extensively appreciated the dysfunctional aspects of tradition and unquestioned assumption, we may have underestimated the importance of tradition to the sense of stability and continuity of individuals, groups, and organizations. Tradition as psychological ballast may fulfill individual need for support, especially during times of change and ambiguity.

On a similar theme, Janis proposes (1972) that under situations of duress, when individual self-esteem is at stake, group and organizational members will be more likely to seek solace and comfort in the experience of a cohesive group decision. The protection of self-esteem may be such a dominant motive for individuals that they opt for solace rather than accuracy of information or clear perspective. Here again, though organizations may be equipped with the best possible information-gathering resources, their use and application can vary significantly for reasons not apparent to actor or observer. I shall elaborate on Janis's observations later.

Some additional examples of psychological impediments to the rational processes recommended by this present collection of authors include the effects of trust and mistrust, the pressures toward shared vision that emanate from organizational socialization processes, and individual fear—fear based on such personal concerns as job security, promotion, or loss of position. Some of these affective considerations will be discussed in terms of their impact on implementation strategies.

CONTRIBUTIONS TO THE PRACTICE
OF MANAGEMENT

Though it is possible to offer more examples of affective dimensions that constrain the impact of the authors' recommendations, I share with the other authors the contention that question raising and the realistic interpretation of environmental information make an important contribution to organizational effectiveness. Acknowledging the utility of this orientation leads to consideration of implementation strategies. Are there methods to ensure that questions be raised, that realistic environmental information be acquired and used in the management of organizations? What are some of the problems attached to the practical recommendations made here? To what kinds of organizational conditions should we attend to ensure effective implementation of recommended methods, systems, and programs? I shall conclude my discussion with a consideration of these questions.

Of all these authors, Schneider has elaborated most thoroughly on practical approaches to the infusion of question asking into organizations. He contends that the effective organization is one that attracts, selects, and retains people who continually question assumptions generated in the past, whose questions move the organization toward the future. He characterizes these people as nonright-types who act as boundary spanners, accepting positions between different facets of an organization and its environment. Schneider contends that the addition of these nonright-types to an organization would enhance that organization's sensor capacities, question-raising abilities, and overall flexibility. Though I generally agree with Schneider and endorse his prescriptions, I doubt that these prescriptions alone will assure the efficacy of question raising. I have observed that even the best reasoned programs are limited by unanticipated affective processes. To illustrate this contention, I shall describe the potential impact of unforeseen affective processes on specific suggestions made by the authors.

Schneider has considered some of the difficulties in the attraction and support of nonright-types for an organization. He refers to Janis's work in *Groupthink* to illustrate how groups tend to discount information that contradicts shared conventional wisdom, especially if it comes from nonright-types, those who are different from the mainstream. Thus, contradictory or counterintuitive information about the environment can easily be ignored or resisted if it comes from a nonright-type.

Ironically, a review of Janis's work itself reveals that it is not just nonright-types whose information capacities can be ignored. Janis describes the role of the CIA's intelligence in the Cuban missile situation:

> The intelligence branch . . . had not been asked to estimate the chances of an invasion's being supported. . . . Nor were any of the experts on the Cuban desk of the State Department . . . asked for their judgments. Most of the participants in the White House meetings did not know this and simply assumed that the estimates mentioned by Dulles and Bissell had the full authority of the government's intelligence agency behind them.
>
> Had the policy advisers asked more penetrating questions, some of the excluded experts might have been consulted. . . .
>
> Even a few skeptical questions put to Dulles or Bissell might have corrected gross misconceptions [1972, p. 25].

Clearly, in the U.S. government at this time, processes were working to prevent the asking of information-oriented questions of the information-gathering body. Janis explains the paradoxical nonuse of information and information resources via the "groupthink" hypothesis—that pressures toward group cohesiveness blot out the expression of difference, of question, and shape cognitive processes toward shared vision, diminishing the potential for acquiring data to contradict this shared vision.

Janis's explanation of the *why* behind groupthink suggests why he offers numerous organizational mechanisms to counteract the process. He contends that in situations of most personal threat to self-esteem, decision-makers are least likely to pursue a rational course, least likely to ask the full range of questions of experts, least likely to *want* alternative definitions of threatening situations (1972, pp. 202–203).

In the most difficult times, then, when more information could enhance the practice of management, perhaps ensuring organizational survival, such information may not be sought. Janis identifies some situations that foster the tendency to groupthink, including situations where an individual "is faced with a perplexing choice that he considers beyond his level of competence or that forces him to become keenly aware of his personal inadequacies [p. 203]." Such situations would be different for different individuals, and some individuals might find fewer situations where such threats appear. Still, history is rife with examples of situations where more accurate information could have informed decisions and modified an unsuccessful outcome. How often has the need to protect self-esteem prevented question raising and the acquisition of critical environmental information?

There are other limitations to effective question raising linked more specifically to the use of nonright-types as sources of new insight or information. Even in a situation where information is requested from the nonright-type in a boundary-spanning role, there is a danger that such information will be uncomfortable, or perhaps undermining to conventional wisdom. In such situations, if the information is too uncomfortable, or the nonright-type is too persistent, an organization or group could respond by "shooting the messenger," eliminating the individual information transmitter rather than hearing the discrepant, undermining transmitted information.

In my own research on men and women in transitional occupations, I studied the experiences of individuals who had moved into jobs typically held by the opposite sex, entering situations where they were in the minority, both in the immediate present and in the context of history (Schreiber, 1979). These individuals were thus nonright-types, people who were different from those around them in their gender.

As they joined their work groups, "newtype" (my label) newcomers were greeted with more suspicion and mistrust than "sametypes," those who resembled the group they were entering. The question of group membership, of belonging, was raised frequently in advance of the newtype's arrival, and the newtypes took longer to feel they fit into their work groups. For the newtype newcomers, the universal question about group inclusion was more acute than for others because they were, by definition and appearance, different from other members of the group. For members of the group they joined, their membership raised questions about who was an acceptable group member. These questions raised other members' anxiety about belonging, accompanied by their mistrust of the unfamiliar newcomer.

Though the mistrust of the newtype newcomer did fade over time, it took a longer period of time for work groups to trust the newtype group member. To extend this observation to an organizational context, it would probably take longer for organization members to trust the veracity, validity, and value of information purveyed by newtypes who were different than others. Realistically, I would expect that the perspective and information they communicated would be greeted with (implicit) mistrust and disbelief, especially when that perspective and information ran counter to the organization's conventional wisdom. From this perspective, the efficacy of nonright newcomers as sources of environmental information or as question-raisers about organizational assumptions may be compromised by their differentness.

It takes time to develop trust between different newcomers and long-term members of an organization. During this time, other pressures, including organizational socialization processes, affect the newcomer's orientation and behavior. Socialization processes have a powerful impact on new organizational members, perhaps even more on those selected for their difference. The new nonright-types may, in fact, receive a far more profound set of socialization messages than the right-types, those who appear to fit in from the start. There is a dilemma here because the nonright-type is expected by the formal organization to make a contribution through his/her difference—in perception, information, and comprehension. At the same time, though that difference and its results are formally sanctioned, the nonright-type is informally bombarded with socialization pressures, pressures to conform to organizational norms, to become more like the right-types in carriage, demeanor, language, and perhaps in perception. Thus, the person hired for sensitivity to the external environment and the ability to question tradition is pummelled by demands for responsiveness to the traditional assumptions shared in the internal environment.

Van Maanen and Schein (1979) have described the impact of organizational socialization. They have also acknowledged the interchange between the newcomer and the tradition of the organization, asserting that though newcomers bring with them the potential for change, for question of current practice, they are a source of threat to the current workings of the system, bringing impertinent questions to the historical workings of the system. In this role, newcomers elicit responses from old hands, responses intended to shape, to educate the new people, to inform their view of the world in terms consonant with the prevailing views already in the system.

If organizational socialization processes are considered then as a real factor in the lives of organizational members, the role of nonright-type newcomers as purveyors of new information and perspective is jeopardized even further. As they are performing their role as question-raisers, they elicit those responses of long-time members intended to perpetuate the knowledge and orientation already present in the system, often sustaining those procedures and practices under question by the nonright-type newcomers.

Socialization processes can conflict with position and function for the nonright-type newcomer. Though such conflict need not cancel out the contribution of the nonright-type, it may create stresses for the position and mitigate the effectiveness of the person-in-role as a source of question of organizational assumptions.

Additionally, the boundary-spanner position itself is fraught with difficulties well documented in empirical studies. My own research concurs with Schneider's observation that these positions are characterized by conflict, suspicion, strain, and ambiguity. The position of the boundary spanner is a challenge to stability, a signal for change, a focus of resistance. The person in this position acquires meaning far beyond title and job description, and takes on demands far beyond the capacity and awareness of the individual. The boundary spanner is subject then to different kinds of pressures than are other people.

Miles (1980) has discussed the array of positive and negative features of organizational boundary roles. Clearly, though the roles bring valuable and varied sources of intelligence to organizations, they also bring difficulty for persons in these positions. Miles's research found that occupants of these positions, in general, were more subject than others to symptoms of work-related stress, with psychological and health-related problems as concomitants. Still, Miles acknowledges the necessity and value attached to these roles and suggests approaches to counteract problems inherent in these positions. Such approaches range from the specification of individual selection criteria (skills, experience) to the modification of organizational structure to provide support and protection for persons in boundary-spanner roles.

On at least two counts the nonright-type in the boundary-spanner position, bumps into organizational processes that create pressures beyond the job itself. First, by representing forces of change to a stable system, this person elicits immediate distrust of the information purveyed. Next, in selecting the nonright-type, the organization is probably encouraging a more powerful socialization effort than usual. Both of these processes make the work of the nonright-type and the organization more difficult. These pressures make retention of these people in role more questionable. The very position and role demands create a personally stressful and vulnerable situation.

Differences in individual-coping capacities suggest a need for organizational support for the nonright-types. Such supports would allow these members to sustain their perspective and perceptions for contribution to the system and to feel assured of their value despite their different, nontraditional roles. They would be rewarded for performances on bases different from others who maintain a system and positioned so that the value of the nontraditional contribution is recognized. Without these supports, the constant discomfort of the role and pressures toward right-type perceptions and behavior could drive nonright-types away from their competence, out of the job, or out of the organization. In this situation, Schneider is wise to raise the practical issue of cost in attracting and retaining these types. Every time one is lost, also lost are dollars, progress, and credibility.

PRACTICAL ALTERNATIVES

The dilemmas raised by these recommendations become real dilemmas for individuals in organizations, and, in turn, for the practice of management. There are, though, alternative approaches to enhance, support, or complement the role of the boundary spanner. Though ideally both Schneider and Drucker would agree that management leadership, such as the chief executive office, be equipped with the vision and perspective to raise questions, procure information, and generate novel interpretations to guide the organization, this recommendation ignores the obvious limitation of any one individual's perspective.

One alternative to this suggestion would be to equip the chief executive office of an organization with additional sources of question and interpretation, through peer, staff, or advisory positions. Clearly this approach is not novel and has been amply tested throughout history, both in the governmental and commercial sectors, with varying success in different circumstances. The most obvious threat to the efficacy of this approach is the human propensity toward groupthink described by Janis, a propensity enhanced by the effects of hierarchy, which can also limit the expression of diversity and difference.

As mentioned earlier, Janis does propose a variety of mechanisms to protect against groupthink, most of which involve the use of organizational structure and group-process mechanisms to counteract insulation and collusion around illusion of group members. Additionally, Janis suggests that organizations and policymaking bodies work closely with externally based behavioral scientists as sources of perspective and information. Clearly, Janis developed his recommendation based on the assumption that affective processes *will* have an impact on rational decision making, and that his recommended mechanisms will provide some limits to the deleterious effect of affective processes on important decisions. Still, even the best constructed organizational–group process mechanisms can be undermined by human foible, by the pursuit of self-interest, and the small wars of competing political personalities and factions.

For these reasons, a more comprehensive network of resources located throughout an organization may offer the best combination of visions and questions necessary for organizational reality testing. In many respects, today's large, diversified, multifunctional corporation already has in place the sources necessary to implement the information-gathering function recommended by these authors. To make the information-gathering, question-raising function work requires a deliberate, sustained commitment to design organizational components, to create processes that link these components to their environments and to decision-makers, and finally, to protect their intelligence-gathering and communication capacities from the undermining processes previously described.

As part of this larger network of intelligence-gathering capabilities, the boundary-spanning person and organization have an important function to fulfill. By definition, those groups that are charged with the responsibility to gather outside intelligence will occupy boundary-spanning positions in relation to the larger organization. If their function is clearly delineated, if the staff is rotated through the boundary-spanning organization so that no one individual becomes identified with externally-related information, it is more likely that information generated by these organizations will elicit more organizational credibility than a system permanently staffed by outside-oriented staff.

Though the boundary-spanning activity could be enhanced by the presence of some nonright-type organizational newcomers, such people must be connected to longer-term members to be effective. A more effective, though modified, use of the nonright-type could build on the organizational practice of assigning general managers from operations to staff positions with which they have limited prior experience. By assigning a nonright internal person to a new situation, useful questions about organizational policy and practice can be raised. In this situation, or a comparable one, where managers are newcomers to an organizational component, or business or staff function, they can raise questions about what others in those situations take for granted.

Because internal managers have presumably already been socialized in the larger organization, the organizational socialization pressures should be less demanding than for real outsiders; their local newcomer status less vulnerable to others' influence; and their question-asking capacity most effective. Such assignments would work optimally in situations where there is a strong management capability already in place, so that day-to-day operations could continue without interruption while the new manager is asking questions of assumption and policy. Thus, the disruption of operations would be minimal, until such time as the questions raised do affect decisions about policy and practice.

Many organizations have stumbled into this mixed assignment recommendation, while many have undertaken it deliberately (usually for development purposes for the manager). I have not seen this approach mentioned as one *intended* to serve an organization's need to be questioned in a systematic way, though I have observed that outcome occur as the result of these "inside-outsider" assignments. Inside-outsiders combine the credibility of organizational work history with their specific perspective of a newcomer. Most of their impertinent questions cannot be dismissed as "naive" and do require serious attention from old hands (usually their subordinates). From this serious attention can come thoughtful review of assumption, practice, and program.

Actually, none of these approaches individually will serve to keep an organization under self-scrutiny, to keep sensitive antennae regularly trained on the environment, to keep realistic perceptions informing an organization's flexibility and capacity to respond to internal and external change. The combination of question-raising–information-gathering sources planted throughout an enterprise, coordinated and managed by design and organizational structure, can have some impact on top management decisions only when management *uses* available resources and available perspectives.

CONCLUSIONS

Today's management leadership is mandated by circumstances to introduce new vision. As the demands of today's internationally competitive world become ever more pressing, as the assumptions behind our production systems are revolutionized by technology, as our workforces are reshaped by demographics, educational trends, and family economic structures, those who manage an enterprise are faced with rapid change in the internal and external environments. Keeping up with this rapid change is a requirement for survival.

As I noted earlier, today's top managers seem to be aware of the need to keep up with change, to direct their organizations toward the demands of the contemporary environment. Still, despite the heightened awareness of the need for adaptation, old pulls toward past belief and practice will continue to counteract forces for change. Most people and organizations that are made up of people have some ambivalence about change. Organizations do not welcome change because it threatens comfort and familiarity and makes the immediate daily environment seem less predictable and appear less manageable.

This general ambivalence about change creates a subtle climate of constant tension for organizations, a tension between those forces that promote change and those that resist. This tension between progress and resistance marks the human condition. In this respect, the tension is a predictable challenge for the practice of management, especially during times which demand fast-paced change. At the time when environmental fluctuations require more organizational agility, internal resistance may slow down an organization. When the environment becomes more ambiguous, and more accurate sensors are needed, uncertainty and anxiety may diminish sensitivity and vision, rendering a system *less* capable of functioning realistically. Again, we, managers and thinkers alike, are confronted with the potentially disabling impact of affective processes. Again, we are faced with a challenge to our most rational, ordered approaches by disabling forces extant within our own systems, within ourselves.

Acknowledging then that all these recommended efforts will be accompanied by unforeseen, unrecognized, and unappreciated nonrational processes leads to the caveat that the most carefully designed system can be impeded in its mission by internal affective forces. Still, the effect of these forces can be constrained by the construction of systems and organizational structures that recognize and accommodate the powerful effect of affective processes. For optimal effectiveness, the most thoughtful organizational design will place information-gathering people and resources in protected places throughout a system in a network of question-asking–information-gathering nodes. These nodal organizations can be connected to their specific function and connected as well with other organizations with similar capacities. Formal connections between these nodes allow for cross-fertilization of ideas, for checking out the reliability of information obtained from internal and external sources, and for combined activities that extend beyond one function.

In the end, there is great value for management in the recommendations for organizational effectiveness developed in these authors' chapters, and in the current, more popular management literature as well. It is striking that the topics of question raising, assumption challenging, and evidence gathering emerge as recommended practice by such different authors, from such different disciplines and perspectives. In the fact of their convergence, a compelling case is made for the development of organizational sensors. This case is enhanced by consideration of those affective issues that could impede the development and effectiveness of such sensors. With both rational and affective considerations in mind, the useful application of these contributions to organizational effectiveness is an imminent possibility.

REFERENCES

Drucker, P. *Managing in turbulent times*. New York: Harper & Row, 1980.

Janis, I. *Groupthink*. Boston: Houghton Mifflin, 1972.

Miles, R. Organization boundary roles. In C. Cooper & R. Payne (Eds.), *Current concerns in occupational stress*. London: Wiley, 1980. Pp. 61–96.

Pfeffer, J., & Salancik, G. *The external control of organizations: A resource dependent perspective*. New York: Harper & Row, 1978.

Schreiber, C. T. *Changing places: Men and women in transitional occupations*. Cambridge, Mass.: MIT Press, 1979.

Van Maanen, J., & Schein, E. H. Toward a theory of organizational socialization. In B. Staw (Ed.), *Research in organizational behavior* Greenwich, Conn.: JAI Press, 1979.

KIM S. CAMERON
DAVID A. WHETTEN

12

Some Conclusions about Organizational Effectiveness

This book began with a review of reasons why there is a state of confusion surrounding the literature on organizational effectiveness. We proposed in Chapter 1 that this confusion has resulted from particular characteristics of the construct of organizational effectiveness, and that there has existed in the literature an inattention to mapping its construct space. Though there has been no dearth of writing about effectiveness, that writing largely has been aimed at replacing previous perspectives on effectiveness rather than adding to them. Past authors have pointed out a plethora of problems, but answers and specific guidelines have been scarce.

To illustrate, Pennings's (1978) review of Steers's (1977) book on organizational effectiveness stated:

> This book is rather vague and clearly unable to bring order to the examples of organizational effectiveness literature that Steers selected . . . there is no clear line of thinking going through these sequentially arranged reviews and prescriptions.
>
> Altogether, it is evident that this book cannot justify the claim on its cover. We still have to wait for some gifted theorist who can develop a paradigm that can unify the present accomplishments and provide theoretical guidance for those who like to tackle this construct [pp. 539–540].

Steers (1978) reviewed books on effectiveness by Spray (1976) and by Goodman and Pennings (1977) and pointed out a similar weakness in their volumes:

261

ORGANIZATIONAL EFFECTIVENESS
A Comparison of Multiple Models

> Both books lack integration. In particular, one must lament the fact that, after repeated references by Goodman and Pennings to the lack of integration on earlier works on effectiveness, their book suffers from the same deficiency. They have few answers, and we already know the problems. Both books could have been improved significantly if a more careful attempt had been made to summarize and integrate the many useful ideas presented. One could even hope that someone might have taken the trouble to suggest what all this means to the poor beleaguered manager but, alas, this is not to be found [pp. 514–515].

Authors in this volume, likewise, have espoused their own particular viewpoints on effectiveness, each from a different disciplinary base. But their approaches have differed from previous books on effectiveness. Each author in Chapters 2–7 addressed a common set of questions regarding issues of management practice, research, and theory. The point was to compare directly the models of effectiveness in terms of their relative contributions to theory, empirical assessment, and management application. Trade-offs inherent in each of the models have thereby been exposed.

Authors of the last four chapters (Chapters 8–11) each directly compared the previous six perspectives on effectiveness from the standpoint of a specific role: theorist, researcher, or manager. These authors pointed out both strengths and weaknesses of the different disciplinary perspectives, and they made their own suggestions for improving clarity of the effectiveness construct.

In this chapter we seek to tie together the problems of effectiveness pointed out in the first chapter with the contributions of the authors in Chapters 2–11. That is, the purpose of this chapter is to draw some conclusions and to offer some guidelines for future work on organizational effectiveness. The conclusions we draw are not, of course, a complete summary of all the major points made in the previous chapters. Our intent in this book is to clarify the nature of organizational effectiveness and to steer researchers in new directions. The conclusions and guidelines proposed in this chapter reflect that intent.

In the section immediately following, we specify two main conclusions that summarize what we know about the nature of organizational effectiveness. In the section entitled "Guidelines for Assessing Organizational Effectiveness," we propose seven prescriptive guidelines for defining and assessing the construct in research, managerial practice, and theoretical development.

CONCLUSIONS ABOUT
ORGANIZATIONAL EFFECTIVENESS

Conclusion 1: There Cannot Be One Universal Model of Organizational Effectiveness

As pointed out in the first chapter, all general theories of organizations have built into them implied criteria for measuring effectiveness. If one conceives of organizations as deliberate, rational, goal-seeking activity systems, then it is natural to argue that successful goal accomplishment is an appropriate measure of effectiveness (Perrow, 1970). Similarly, if one views organizations as political arenas wherein competing interest groups vie for control over resources, then it logically follows that effectiveness should reflect the extent to which critical constituencies are satisfied with their involvement in the resource allocation process (Pfeffer, 1978).

The conclusion that multiple models of organizational effectiveness are required, then, follows because there is no universal theory of organizations. The ongoing debates in the literature regarding the utility of competing models of effectiveness are fundamentally debates between advocates of competing theories of organizations. This conclusion is supported by three themes in the contributed chapters.

DIVERSITY IN THE USE OF EFFECTIVENESS

First, several of the authors argue that inasmuch as the construct or organizational effectiveness is a product of personal values and preferences, there always will be great variety and divergence in its meaning and use among researchers and practitioners alike. As Starbuck and Nystrom point out, "Judgments about organizational effectiveness generally tell one more about the judges' implicit theories than about the organization being judged [p. 152]."

Organizational effectiveness, like most terms in the English language, is dependent on usage for its meaning. As Bishop (1971) noted, definitions may be classified as standard or nonstandard, formal or informal, but not right or wrong. "Definition describes usage, it piously avoids prescribing it [p. xxiii]." In this sense, definitions of organizational effectiveness that appear in the literature are historical recordings, not prescriptions. Several authors have pointed out that usage has been so diverse, and the indicators so various, that a single, clear definition is neither possible nor desirable. Consensus in the usage of organizational effectiveness among theorists, researchers, and practitioners would have to precede the emergence of a single definition or a single model. But, as pointed out by Goodman, Atkin, and Schoorman (Chapter 7), Brewer (Chapter 9), and Mohr (Chapter 10), such a consensus is highly unlikely. The needs of theorists, researchers, and managers differ substantially relative to organizational effectiveness. Managers use judgments of organizational effectiveness to justify what they already do well, to manage conflict, to motivate social change, to stimulate examinations of assumptions, to contribute to an image, to displace or assign responsibility, and so on (Cameron 1980; Chapter 9, pp. 211–214, in this volume). Researchers are more apt to focus on circumscribing effectiveness so that measurable indicators can be identified and reliable judgments made (Chapter 7 and 10). Theorists prefer not to circumscribe effectiveness but to develop propositions and relationships that have generalized applicability in organizations (Chapters 4 and 8). This divergence of usage of the construct serves to inhibit a single model of effectiveness from emerging. But it is precisely this divergence that has given organizational effectiveness its utility (see Chapter 1).

EXPANSION OF CRITERIA OF EFFECTIVENESS

Second, several authors in this volume advocate expanding the relevant indicators of organizational effectiveness to include more than the relatively narrow and largely goal-oriented indicators used so prevalently up to now. (See Campbell, Brownas, Peterson, and Dunnette [1974] and Steers [1975] for a review of the most used indicators of effectiveness.) Expanding the criteria of effectiveness, however, implies that other conceptions of organizations should be used in addition to the ones that dominate current effectiveness research (i.e., open systems models, rational goal models, economic models). Finding new ways to think about organizations helps generate new and potentially useful criteria of organizational effectiveness.

Several of the authors in this volume propose new criteria, for example, that derive from their unique perspectives. Specifically, Schneider (Chapter 2) suggests assessing the presence of "nonright-types" among organizational employees; Seashore (Chapter 3) suggests assessing "triangulation," or the integration of goals, decision processes, and maintenance systems; Weick and Daft (Chapter 4) discuss the importance of organizational interpretation systems as a criterion of effectiveness; Nord (Chapter 5) enumerates several macroquality criteria of effectiveness that have not been included heretofore in research on effectiveness (e.g., consumer sovereignty, suitable workforce, alternatives for employment). He also points out that Hage's (1978) 28 indicators of the quality of societies, which also have been ignored in effectiveness research, should be relevant indicators. Starbuck and Nystrom (Chapter 6) suggest analyzing the experimental behavior of organizations; Cummings (Chapter 8) suggests analyzing the growth opportunities provided to individuals by the organization; and Brewer (Chapter 9) suggests analyzing the perpetuation of human dignity as a necessary condition of effectiveness. Brewer also makes a case for analyzing the *effects* of organizational performance more than the *outcomes* of organizational performance as criteria of organizational effectiveness. Yet, when effects are taken into account, the possible indicators and definitions of effectiveness become almost innumerable. The effects of a single organizational action, for example, are so far-reaching and wide-ranging that it is impossible to identify all of them. Some effects are latent, some occur only when coupled with other factors, some emerge incrementally, some occur suddenly and then dissolve, and some have influence on factors that are unmeasurable.

Nord, Brewer, and Mohr (Chapter 10) also each imply that evaluations of organizational effectiveness not only should focus on the outcomes and effects that organizations *do* produce, but consideration of what they *could* produce also should be included as criteria. This idea that effectiveness should be evaluated on organizational potential in addition to organizational behavior suggests that organizations may do things right (traditional efficiency models), and they may even do the right things (traditional effectiveness models), but when the question is asked, "What else *could* the organization do?" additional preferences become exposed, and the criteria of effectiveness are greatly expanded. For example, could a corporation such as General Electric produce an electric light bulb that would never wear out? Could they improve the quality of life among the poor in southern Connecticut? Could their employee morale be substantially increased? Could they improve the general level of corporate management effectiveness in this country? Some "could" questions simply extend current organizational emphases; others introduce entirely new activities. Moreover, constituency preferences and expectations often are changed when new organizational potentials are suggested, so that pressure from these interest groups helps motivate the organization to reach potentials that previously would not have been considered.

The impossibility of circumscribing a single set of criteria of organizational effectiveness, as pointed out by these authors, prohibits a single model of effectiveness from being developed. The construct space is so broad, and it accommodates so many indicators, that there would be little utility in any model that tried to encompass them all.

DIVERSITY IN DISCIPLINARY FRAMEWORKS

Third, the models of effectiveness discussed in this volume illustrate that when different disciplinary frames are imposed, the organizational processes and attributes that receive attention are substantially different. Cummings (Chapter 8), for example, points out the differences in the models of effectiveness presented in Chapters 2–7 in their emphases on rational versus nonrational processes and micro versus macro levels of analysis. Dubin (1976) claimed that models of effectiveness necessarily differ in their internal (phenomena within the organization) versus external (phenomena outside the organization) orientation. Campbell (1977) and Scott (1977) differentiated models based on their focus on means versus ends. And Brewer (Chapter 9) differentiates between models emphasizing outcomes (short term) versus effects (long term). Other distinctions also are used in the literature, but these five are sufficient to make the point.

Table 12.1 locates each of the six models relative to these distinctions. The table points out that each model is unique in its emphasis, and it illustrates how difficult it would be for one model of effectiveness to consider each of these orientations adequately. The challenge, however, is not to formulate one model that attempts to account for all possible emphases and all possible indicators. Such a model is hardly possible or useful. Rather, the challenge is to develop

TABLE 12.1
The Major Emphases of the Models of Organizational Effectiveness Discussed in This Volume

Authors	Disciplinary base	Rational versus nonrational	Internal versus external	Micro versus macro	Means versus ends	Outcomes versus effects
Schneider	Industrial–organizational psychology	Rational	Internal	Micro	Means	Outcomes
Seashore	Sociology and systems theory	Rational	Internal	Macro	Ends	Outcomes
Weick and Daft	Cognitive and social psychology	Nonrational	Internal	Micro	Ends	Outcomes
Nord	Macroeconomic and critical theory	Rational	External	Macro	Ends	Effects
Starbuck and Nystrom	Operations research	Rational and nonrational	Internal	Macro	Means	Outcomes
Goodman, Atkin, and Schoorman	Microeconomics and positivistic philosophy	Rational	Internal	Micro	Ends	Outcomes

models that are comparable, even cumulative, and that account for many of the indicators neglected up to now.

This impossibility of developing a single, all-encompassing model leads to a second conclusion about organizational effectiveness.

Conclusion 2: It Is More Worthwhile to Develop Frameworks for Assessing Effectiveness Than to Try to Develop Theories of Effectiveness

Generally, the authors in this book argue that selecting appropriate criteria of organizational effectiveness is the major challenge facing researchers and managers. Though it is true, as discussed in Chapter 1, that the best criteria of effectiveness cannot be determined, these authors point out that *appropriate* criteria that are consistent with particular viewpoints can be. Consequently, the engineering of effectiveness is a more productive activity than is theorizing about effectiveness.

ASSESSMENT PRECEDES UNDERSTANDING

As stated in Chapter 6, "Organizational effectiveness affords another instance of the general proposition that prescription has to come before understanding (Starbuck and Nystrom, 1981). The notion that one should understand organizations before one tries to improve them is backward . . . [p. 155]." In investigating organizational effectiveness, making choices to limit the construct space so as to focus on a limited set of criteria is the only way to come to grips with definitional and assessment problems. That is, measuring constructs generally leads to an improved understanding of constructs.

In this regard, organizational effectiveness is no different from other complex constructs in the social sciences. Constructs such as intelligence, motivation, or leadership—whose construct space, by definition, also is not bounded—have been better understood as limited aspects of their total meaning have been measured. For example, a variety of approaches to motivation have been developed, each limited to a specific domain of the construct. Approaches relating to the satisfaction of needs (Alderfer, 1972; McClelland, Atkinson, Clark, & Lowell, 1953; Maslow, 1954), to increasing expectancies (Porter & Lawler, 1968; Vroom, 1964), to reinforcements (Lawler, 1971; Skinner, 1948), to goal setting (Locke, 1968), to task design (Hackman & Lawler, 1971), and so on, have each been pursued in research. These different approaches are not designed to replace one another, but to augment one another, and by pursuing these multiple models of motivation the construct is understood to a greater degree.

In assessing organizational effectiveness, a similar attack seems appropriate, that is, to concentrate on measuring limited domains of the construct. This requires making informed choices about what criteria to include and what aspect of the organizational effectiveness construct space to focus on. The next section of this chapter points out specific guidelines for making those informed choices. Here we simply want to make clear the crucial nature of those choices.

PRINCIPLES OF ASSESSMENT

Zammuto (1982) pointed out that organizational effectiveness has characteristics of a "wicked problem" (Rittel & Weber, 1973). That is, the major challenge in considering wicked problems is to *formulate* the problem. Specifying the boundaries of the problem, or delimiting possible alternatives, defines the solution. "The formulation of wicked problems is the problem! The process of formulating the problem and of conceiving a solution are identical . . . [Rittel & Weber, 1973, p. 161]." In examining organizational effectiveness, therefore, formulating what to measure, how to measure, when to measure, and other practical (or engineering) concerns should receive first priority. These formulations should not be done haphazardly or thoughtlessly, however. Certain principles should be kept in mind.

For example, the construct cannot be so narrowly defined in an investigation as to make it useless in a practical sense. From the point of view of managers, it is precisely the complex and contradictory nature of organizational effectiveness that provides its utility. A wide variety of behaviors, preferences, and performance standards, for example, can be accommodated under the single rubric of effectiveness. Therefore, the more researchers delimit the construct to satisfy a need for precision, the more they destroy the essential value of the term for managers. Because of the complexity of effectiveness, it is inappropriate to rely on univariate measures and singular ratings. Following the axiom that a measuring device must be as complex as the phenomenon it is measuring, multiple indicators of effectiveness are essential.

This point of view is contrary to the point of view of those who advocate limiting research to the building of theories of single variables that may compose effectiveness, such as turnover, productivity, satisfaction, etc. Instead, it acknowledges the utility of the complexity of the construct, and it advocates the inclusion of complexity in assessments.

Another principle to keep in mind, on the other hand, is that though assessments of effectiveness must be multivariate, selecting indicators of organizational effectiveness randomly just to make the assessment broader or to increase complexity does not serve a good purpose. The criteria to be included should be those that match the organizational setting in which they are applied. In loosely coupled systems (Weick, 1976), for example, criteria relating to goal accomplishment and goal clarity are not appropriate. In those types of organizations, goals are purposely absent or are kept ambiguous. Similarly, including macroquality criteria may be appropriate when investigating effectiveness in an organization such as Sears (where environmental impact and wide-ranging influence on consumerism is central), but inappropriate in assessing effectiveness in a neighborhood hardware store (where these criteria are not relevant).

Criteria also must be central to the interests of some important constituency. That is, organizational effectiveness differs from many other constructs in the social sciences by being based on the preferences and values of individuals. Therefore, the criteria included in assessments must be important to someone. This suggests that assessing effectiveness is at least partly a political endeavor. Because various constituencies engage in bargaining behavior and power trade-offs in an attempt to have their interests met by organizations, selecting criteria of effectiveness that are compatible with one group's interests and incompatible with another group's interests helps give visibility (if not credence) to those interests. An interest group's power or bargaining can be enhanced by the selection of their criteria. Kanter and Brinkerhoff (1981) underscore this point:

> Classic definitions of organizational effectiveness and models of measurement often favored, implicitly if not explicitly, some constituencies over others. Certainly profit (through supposedly an objective market measure of effectiveness, based on the efficiency with which input could be transformed into output) makes paramount the interest of owners. Those analysts who define effectiveness as the ability of an organization to adapt to, manipulate, or fulfill expectations of the external environment use the "super-system" as the judge, and thus make paramount the interests of supporters, sponsors, clients, regulators, etc. Those who consider as the central criterion the satisfaction of customers or participants similarly choose one set of interests over others, at least implicitly [p. 324].

Investigators of organizational effectiveness, therefore, frequently are immersed in political activity in their assessments, and their criteria selections should be made with this fact in mind.

What these two conclusions point out is simply that effectiveness cannot be assessed nor fully understood by using only one model or one point of view. A single, comprehensive theory of effectiveness is neither likely nor useful. On the other hand, assessments of effectiveness using multiple models should continue to be pursued because it is primarily in that way—not in debating which model is the correct one—that progress is made in understanding and mapping the construct space. In the next section of this chapter we present major decision guides for helping to frame assessments of effectiveness.

GUIDELINES FOR ASSESSING ORGANIZATIONAL EFFECTIVENESS

Seven major decision guides are presented in what follows (see Cameron [1980], Goodman & Pennings [1980], and Steers, [1975], for an elaboration).

They are framed in the form of questions that should be answered in every assessment of organizational effectiveness, in every formulation of a definition of organizational effectiveness, and in every project designed to improve organizational effectiveness. The purpose is to provide an itinerary for mapping the construct space of effectiveness and for helping to make studies of effectiveness comparable. If widely used, these guides can help develop a cumulative literature in organizational effectiveness by providing a general framework against which research can be compared. The seven decision guides are highly interrelated, so that making appropriate choices about one will depend on the choices made about others. No one choice is inherently right for any of the decision guides, but some choices are more appropriate than others when answers to each of the seven questions are considered in concert.

Guide 1: From Whose Perspective Is Effectiveness Being Judged?

Effectiveness must be defined and assessed from someone's viewpoint, and it is important that the viewpoint be made explicit. Chapter 1 in this volume suggests that one reason there are no best criteria for effectiveness is because there is no best constituency to define effectiveness. The criteria used by different constituencies to define effectiveness often differ markedly, and spirited debates about which constituency's criteria are most valuable continue in the literature. Some have advocated using a dominant coalition as the source of criteria (Cameron, 1978), others have argued for top managers (Scott, 1977), external resource providers (Miles, 1980), organizational members (Van de Ven & Ferry, 1980), and so on. No agreed upon decision rule is available to identify one constituency's criteria as being more important than another constituency's criteria because it partly depends on the other decision guides (to be discussed) and partly on the personal biases of the evaluator. Nevertheless, organizations never satisfy all their constituencies, and what appears to be high effectiveness from one point of view may be interpreted as being mediocre or low effectiveness from another point of view. The specific point of view being accepted, therefore, must be made explicit.

Guide 2: On What Domain of Activity Is the Judgment Focused?

Organizational domains are circumscribed by the constituencies served, the technologies employed, and the services or outputs produced (Meyer, 1975). Domains arise from the activities or primary tasks that are emphasized in the organization, from the competencies of the organization, and from the demands placed upon the organization by external forces (Cameron, 1981; Miles, 1980).

A variety of domains can be identified for almost all organizations, but no organization is maximally effective in all its domains. In a study of the domains in which colleges and universities are effective, for example, no institution was highly effective in more than two of the four major domains identified (Cameron, 1981). Quinn and Cameron (1982) found, in fact, that achieving effectiveness in one domain in a public service agency mitigated against achieving effectiveness in another domain. In another study of production organizations, Cameron and Whetten (1981) observed that the major domains of activity changed over organizational life cycles, and that to have assessed effectiveness in the wrong domain would have been misleading. When analyzing organizational effectiveness, therefore, it is important that the domain(s) being assessed are clearly specified. Not being clear about the differences in the effectiveness of organizational domains may lead to confusing or contradictory research results, as well as to inaccurate judgments of effectiveness.

Guide 3: What Level of Analysis Is Being Used?

Judgments of effectiveness can be made at the individual level of analysis (e.g., Is the human dignity of the individual being preserved?), at the subunit level (e.g., Is the work group cohesive?), at the organization level (e.g., Does the organization acquire needed resources?), at the population or industry level (e.g., Does the primary function of this population of organizations have legitimacy?), or at the societal level (e.g., What is the effect of the organization on society?). Although effectiveness on each of these different levels of analysis may be compatible, often it is not, and effectiveness on one level may mitigate against effectiveness on another level. Freeman (1980) argued that selecting the appropriate level of analysis is critical because data on effectiveness at one level are often nonsensical when viewed from another level. Without attention being paid to which level of analysis is most appropriate, meaningful effectiveness judgments cannot even be made. The appropriateness of the level depends on the constituency being used, the domain being focused on, the purpose of the evaluation, and so on. The choice, in other words, must be made in the context of other decision guides.

Guide 4: What Is the Purpose for Judging Effectiveness?

The purpose(s) for judging effectiveness almost always affects the judgment itself. For example, Brewer (Chapter 9) discussed some of the purposes for evaluating effectiveness that were enumerated by Floden and Weiner (1978). He pointed out that changing the purposes of the evaluation creates different consequences both for the evaluator and for the unit being evaluated. Different data will be made available, different sources will be appropriate, different amounts of cooperation or resistance will be encountered, and different types of assessment strategies will be required all as a result of differences in purpose (also see Argyris, 1970). (Consider the differences that would arise, for example, when evaluating effectiveness to determine which department to eliminate in a university versus evaluating effectiveness as a part of building an organizational theory.) The purposes of the evaluation also help determine appropriate constituencies, domains, levels of analysis, and so on, hence they must be clearly identified. Sometimes the evaluator can determine his or her own purposes, but frequently the purposes for judging effectiveness are prescribed a priori by the client, the participants in the evaluation, or the external environment. Whatever the case, a clear conception of purpose is important in judging effectiveness.

Guide 5: What Time Frame Is Being Employed?

Selecting an appropriate time frame is important because long-term effectiveness may be incompatible with short-term effectiveness. For example, in a study of the U.S. tobacco industry, Miles and Cameron (1982) found that one company was the least effective of the six tobacco firms when short-term criteria were applied, but it jumped to second most effective when long-term criteria were applied. Another firm was the most effective firm in the short term, but it dropped to fifth in the long term. Some organizations, moreover, may sacrifice short-term effectiveness in order to obtain long-term effectiveness, or vice versa, so that not being clear about what time frame is being employed would severely handicap an assessment. Also, as was noted earlier, effects and outcomes sometimes cannot be detected if the wrong time frame is selected because they may occur incrementally over a long period of time, or they may occur suddenly in the short term. Judgments of effectiveness are always made with some time frame in mind, so it is important that the time frame be made explicit.

Guide 6: What Type of Data Are Being Used for Judgments of Effectiveness?

This is a choice between using information collected by the organization itself and stored in official documents, or relying on perceptions obtained from members of various constituencies. The choice is between objective data (organizational records) or subjective, perceptual data (interviews or questionnaire responses). Objective data have the advantage of being quantifiable, potentially less biased than individual perceptions, and representative of the official organizational position. However, objective data frequently are gathered only on "official" effectiveness criteria or on criteria that are used only for public image purposes. The official focus may make the data rather narrow in scope. In addition, official data often relate to criteria of organizational effectiveness that do not have readily apparent connections to the organization's primary task (Cameron, 1978).

The advantage of subjective or perceptual data is that a broader set of criteria of effectiveness can be assessed from a wider variety of perspectives. In addition, operative criteria or theories-in-use (Argyris & Schon, 1978) can more easily be tapped. The disadvantages, however, are that bias, dishonesty, or lack of information on the part of the respondents may hinder the reliability and validity of the data. The selection of data by which to judge effectiveness is important because an organization may be judged effective on the basis of subjective perceptions while objective data may indicate that the organization is ineffective. Or, contrarily, objective data may indicate organizational effectiveness while constituencies may rate the organization as being ineffective (Hall & Clark, 1980).

Guide 7: What Is the Referent against Which Effectiveness Is Judged?

There are a variety of referents or standards against which organizational effectiveness can be judged. For example, one alternative is to compare the performance of two different organizations against the same set of indicators (comparative judgment). The question is "Are we more effective than our competitor?" A second alternative is to select a standard or an ideal performance level (e.g., Likert's [1967] "System 4" characteristics), and then compare the organization's performance against the standard (normative judgment). Here the question is "How are we doing relative to a theoretical ideal?" A third alternative is to compare organizational performance on the indicators against the stated goals of the organization (goal-centered judgment). "Did we reach our stated goals?" A fourth alternative is to compare an organization's performance on the indicators against its own past performance on the same indicators (improvement judgment). "Have we improved over the past year?" A fifth alternative is to evaluate an organization on the basis of the static characteristics it possesses, independent of its performance on certain indicators (trait judgment). In this approach, desirable organizational characteristics are identified, and the judgment reflects the extent to which the organization possesses those characteristics. Because judgments of effectiveness can differ markedly depending on which referent is used (e.g., an organization may be effective in accomplishing its stated goals but be ineffective relative to the competition), it is important to be clear about the referent that serves as the basis for those judgments.

The advantage of these seven decision guides is that they help to circumscribe the construct boundaries of effectiveness as well as to identify explicitly the indicators of effectiveness that are being considered. Using these guides makes it clear that the definition of effectiveness being used in an evaluation is just one of several possibilities. But it also provides a basis for comparing one definition (based on a certain set of choices about the decision guides) with other definitions. The construct space of effectiveness can then begin to be mapped.

CONCLUSION

The history of organizational theory is commonly divided into several periods, or eras, whose names (e.g., human relations, open systems, resource dependence) identify the emergence of a new model highlighting organizational phenomena previously overlooked (Perrow, 1972). As these models or organizations have been added to the existing conceptualizations over the years, a more complex (meaning composite) understanding of organizations has resulted. Much of the confusion in the organizational effectiveness literature today, however, stems from the fact that the measurement of effectiveness has generally been viewed as an occasion to espouse one of these particular models of organizations. Because this practice ignores the fact that no single theory represents a complete model of organizations, it quite predictably has led to severe, but justified, criticism that the literature on organizational effectiveness is fragmented, noncumulative, and confusing. Some writers have clamored loudly for one particular model of effectiveness. Others have let convenience or accessibility of data guide their definition and assessments of the construct. Still others have taken a position on effectiveness similar to the one taken by Justice Potter Stewart on pornography: "I can't define it, but I know it when I see it."

The resulting confusion has led some to propose that we abandon the construct totally, and focus our attention on less global, univariate measures of outcomes. In contrast, we have argued that this confusion can be rectified through systematic comparisons of multiple models, and it should not be viewed as grounds for abandoning an extremely valuable concept. Those interested in organizational effectiveness must recognize that its construct space accommodates a wide variety of criteria, all of which cannot be assessed in any single study. Moreover, there is no algorithm to identify one criterion as being inherently better than another. The value of criteria lie in the perceptions and preferences of individuals. Consequently, multiple viewpoints all may be equally legitimate, but under different circumstances and with different types of organizations. To map the entire construct space of effectiveness, multiple theories of organizations that generate multiple criteria are needed. Univariate indicators of effectiveness or single theories of organizations that generate criteria are not likely to be helpful. Once we break out of the "one best model" framework and, instead, work to design studies that recognize the composite nature of the construct, we can begin to develop a more cumulative body of knowledge.

The challenge, however, is to avoid a continuation of the fragmented, isomorphic approaches to effectiveness typical in past literature. Instead, these multiple models of organization with their own espoused criteria of effectiveness need to be systematically compared and integrated with one another. On a theoretical level, this can be done as the authors in this book have done—by addressing common theoretical, empirical, and practical issues in order to highlight trade-offs required by each approach. (For example, Table 12.1 shows what one gets and gives up on some dimensions by selecting one model versus others.) Empirically it can be done by applying the seven decision guides explained in this chapter. Our understanding of organizational effectiveness will likely increase, therefore, as we cease trying to develop universal models of effectiveness, and instead concentrate on specifying clearly the characteristics of our own circumscriptions.

REFERENCES

Alderfer, C. P. *Existence, relatedness, and growth: Human needs in organizational settings.* New York: Free Press, 1972.

Argyris, C. *Intervention theory and method.* Reading, Mass.: Addison-Wesley, 1970.

Argyris, C., & Schon, D. A. *Organizational learning: A theory of action perspective.* Reading, Mass.: Addison-Wesley, 1978.

Bishop, M. Good usage, bad usage, and usage. In Morris, W. (Ed.), *The American heritage dictionary of the English language.* Boston: Houghton Mifflin, 1971.

Cameron, K. Measuring organizational effectiveness in institutions of higher education. *Administrative Science Quarterly,* 1978, 23, 604–632.

Cameron, K. S. Critical questions in assessing organizational effectiveness. *Organizational Dynamics,* 1980, 9, 66–80.

Cameron, K. S. Domains of organizational effectiveness in colleges and universities. *Academy of Management Journal,* 1981, 24, 25–47.

Cameron, K., & Whetten, D. A. Perceptions of organizational effectiveness across organizational life cycles. *Administrative Science Quarterly,* 1981, 26, 525–544.

Campbell, J. P. On the nature of organizational effectiveness. In P. S. Goodman & J. M. Pennings (Eds.), *New perspectives on organizational effectiveness.* San Francisco: Jossey-Bass, 1977.

Campbell, J. P., Brownas, E. A., Peterson, N. G., & Dunnett, M. D. The measurement of organizational effectiveness: A review of relevant research and opinion. Final Report, Navy Personnel Research and Development Center. Minneapolis: Personnel Decisions, 1974.

Dubin, R. Organizational effectiveness: Some dilemmas of perspective. *Organization and Administrative Sciences*, 1976, 7, 7–14.

Floden, R. E., & Weiner, S. S. Rationality to ritual: The multiple roles of evaluation in governmental processes. *Policy Sciences*, 1978, 9, 9–18.

Freeman, J. The unit problem in organizational research. In W. Evan (Ed.), *Frontiers in organization and management*. New York: Praeger, 1980.

Goodman, P. S., & Pennings, J. M. *New perspectives on organizational effectiveness*. San Francisco: Jossey-Bass, 1977.

Goodman, P. S., & Pennings, J. M. Critical issues in assessing organizational effectiveness. In E. E. Lawler, D. A. Nadler, and C. Cammann (Eds.), *Organizational assessment: Perspectives on the measurement of organizational behavior and the quality of work life*. New York: Wiley, 1980.

Hackman, J. R., & Lawler, E. E. Employee reactions to job characteristics. *Journal of Applied Psychology*, 1971, 55, 259–286.

Hage, J. Toward a synthesis of the dialectic between historical-specific and sociological-general models of the environment. In L. Karpik (Ed.), *Organization and environment*. Beverly Hills, Calif.: Sage, 1978.

Hall, R. H., & Clark, J. P. An ineffective effectiveness study and some suggestions for future research. *The Sociological Quarterly*, 1980, 21, 119–134.

Kanter, R. M., & Brinkerhoff, D. Organizational performance: Recent developments in measurement. *Annual Review of Sociology*, 1981, 7, 321–349.

Lawler, E. E. *Pay and organizational effectiveness: A psychological view*. New York: McGraw-Hill, 1971.

Likert, R. *The human organization*. New York: McGraw-Hill, 1967.

Locke, E. A. A theory of task motivation and incentives. *Organizational Behavior and Human Performance*, 1968, 3, 157–189.

McClelland, D. C., Atkinson, J. W., Clark, R. A., & Lowell, E. L. *The achievement motive*. New York: Appleton-Century-Crofts, 1953.

Maslow, H. *Motivation and personality*. New York: Harper, 1954.

Meyer, M. W. Organizational domains. *American Sociological Review*, 1975, 40, 599–615.

Miles, R. H. *Macro-organizational behavior*. Santa Monica, Calif.: Goodyear, 1980.

Miles, R. H., & Cameron, K. S. *Coffin nails and corporate strategies*. Englewood Cliffs, N.J.: Prentice-Hall, 1982.

Pennings, J. M. Review of R. M. Steers, *Organizational effectiveness: A behavioral view*. Santa Monica, Calif.: Goodyear, 1977. In *Administrative Science Quarterly*, 1977, 22, 538–540.

Perrow, C. *Organizational analysis: A sociological view*. Belmont, Calif.: Brooks/Cole, 1970.

Perrow, C. *Complex organizations: A critical essay*. Glenview, Ill.: Scott Foresman, 1972.

Pfeffer, J. *Organizational design*. Arlington Heights, Ill.: AHM Publishing, 1978.

Porter, L. W., & Lawler, E. E. *Managerial attitudes and performance*. Homewood, Ill.: Irwin-Dorsey, 1968.

Quinn, R. E., & Cameron, K. Life cycles and shifting criteria of effectiveness: Some preliminary evidence. *Management Science*, 1982.

Rittel, H. W. J., & Weber, M. M. Dilemmas in a general theory of planning. *Policy Sciences*, 1973, 4, 155–169.

Scott, W. R. Effectiveness of organizational effectiveness studies. In P. S. Goodman, and J. M. Pennings (Eds.), *New perspectives on organizational effectiveness*. San Francisco: Jossey-Bass, 1977.

Skinner, B. F. *Walden two*. New York: Macmillan, 1948.

Spray, S. L. *Organizational effectiveness: Theory, research, and application*. Kent, Ohio: Kent State University Press, 1976.

Steers, R. M. Problems in measuring organizational effectiveness. *Administrative Science Quarterly*, 1975, *10*, 546–558.

Steers, R. M. *Organizational effectiveness: A behavioral view*. Santa Monica, Calif.: Goodyear, 1977.

Steers, R. M. Review of S. L. Spray (Ed.), *Organizational effectiveness: Theory, research, and application*. Kent, Ohio: Kent State University Press, 1976 and P. S. Goodman & J. M. Pennings (Eds.), *New perspectives on organizational effectiveness*. San Francisco: Jossey-Bass, 1977. In *Administrative Science Quarterly*, 1978, 23, 512–515.

Van de Ven, A. H., & Ferry D. *Measuring and assessing organizations*. New York: Wiley, 1980.

Vroom, V. H. *Work and motivation*. New York: Wiley, 1964.

Weick, K. E. Educational organizations as loosely coupled systems. *Administrative Science Quarterly*, 1976, *21*, 1–19.

Zammuto, R. F. *Assessing organizational effectiveness: Systems change, adaptation, and strategy*. Albany, New York: SUNY-Albany Press, 1982.

Author Index

Subject Index

ORGANIZATIONAL AND OCCUPATIONAL PSYCHOLOGY

Series Editor: PETER WARR
MRC Social and Applied Psychology Unit, Department of Psychology,
The University, Sheffield, England

A complete list of titles in this series appears at the end of this volume.

ORGANIZATIONAL AND OCCUPATIONAL PSYCHOLOGY